Decoding the U.S. Healthcare System

Joe Stevens is a leading expert in commercializing pharmaceutical and medical technologies that fill unmet clinical needs and improve patient outcomes. His work focuses on helping companies understand complex market dynamics, develop value strategies, and design commercial models to engage effectively with life sciences' organized customers. Joe is a principal in the ZS San Francisco office and leads the firm's pharmaceutical market trends and policy analysis team.

Anush Khandelwal is a global market access expert who advises pharmaceutical and healthcare organizations on strategies to improve patient access and enhance affordability. His work focuses on payer and provider strategy, managed care and commercial insights, data-driven analytics, and digital transformation to help life sciences companies deliver impact. Anush is a principal in the ZS Pune office and a leader in business-to-business access and value realization practice.

"This book is a practical and timely guide for anyone trying to understand the US healthcare system, including career switchers looking to enter the field, professionals seeking a better understanding of their customers and suppliers, and patients navigating a confusing landscape."

David Ridley, *Faculty Director, Center for Health Sector Management, Duke University's Fuqua School of Business*

"This book provides great insights into current complexity of interactions and likely future developments under influence of cost pressures and AI opportunities. A must read!"

Ed Schoonveld, *Author,* The Price of Global Health

"From negotiating payer contracts to scaling specialty services, this book delivers the contextual intelligence every health executive needs to make informed, strategic decisions—and why alignment matters."

Jorge J. García, *Assistant Vice President, System Oncology Pharmacy Services, Baptist Health South Florida*

"A must-read for anyone involved in healthcare. By illuminating the priorities and pain points of each key player, this book paves the way for meaningful collaboration and better patient outcomes."

Shweta Sahani, *Associate Director, Market Access Analytics, Johnson & Johnson Innovate Medicine*

"The book offers a compelling narrative of how healthcare data has evolved, from paper to digital, from silos to emerging ecosystems, and why we must accelerate integration to realize its full value."

Jennifer Mueller, *Senior Vice President, American Health Information Management Association*

Decoding the U.S. Healthcare System

Navigating the Complex Maze of Payers, Providers, Producers, Physicians, Patients, and More

Edited by
Joe Stevens and
Anush Khandelwal

Routledge
Taylor & Francis Group
LONDON AND NEW YORK

Designed cover image: Suresh Kainthola and Amirkhan Pathan

First published 2026
by Routledge
4 Park Square, Milton Park, Abingdon, Oxon OX14 4RN

and by Routledge
605 Third Avenue, New York, NY 10158

Routledge is an imprint of the Taylor & Francis Group, an informa business

British Library Cataloguing-in-Publication Data
A catalogue record for this book is available from the British Library

ISBN: 978-1-032-99339-3 (hbk)
ISBN: 978-1-032-98211-3 (pbk)
ISBN: 978-1-003-60359-7 (ebk)

DOI: 10.4324/9781003603597

Typeset in Adobe Garamond
by Newgen Publishing UK

Contents

Figures

Tables

About the Editors

Joe Stevens is a leading expert in commercializing pharmaceutical and medical technologies that fill unmet clinical needs and improve patient outcomes. His work focuses on helping life sciences companies understand complex market dynamics, develop value strategies, and design commercial models to engage effectively with life sciences' organized customers. Joe is a principal in the ZS San Francisco office and leads the firm's pharmaceutical market trends and policy analysis team.

Anush Khandelwal is a global market access expert who advises pharmaceutical and healthcare organizations on strategies to improve patient access and enhance affordability. His work focuses on payer and provider strategy, managed care and commercial insights, data-driven analytics, and digital transformation to help life sciences companies deliver impact. Anush is a principal in the ZS Pune office and a leader in B2B Access and Value Realization practice.

Contributors

Howard Deutsch is a leader in Business-to-Business Access and Value Realization Practice, advising life sciences companies on a broad range of topics throughout a product's life cycle, from value proposition development to launch planning to contracting strategy and analytics. With over 20 years of experience, he has worked across a wide array of therapy areas and reimbursement modalities, recently focusing most prominently on obesity treatments. Howard is a recognized author and speaker on the evolving the US healthcare landscape. He is based in the ZS Boston office.

Harshil Gagnani is an expert in the US Healthcare Ecosystem and Market Access space, focused on organized providers, payers, and other evolving customer insights through next-generation customer-centric methodologies. He specializes in using these insights to help clients design and transform their go-to-market strategy to suit the needs of the evolving healthcare landscape. Harshil is a Manager in ZS's India office and a member of the B2B Access and Value Realization Practice.

Komal Gurnani is a leader in the Strategy and Transformation Practice at ZS and brings 15+ years of deep life-sciences expertise across global clinical and commercial strategy development, accelerating asset launches and driving cross-functional alignment across medical, market access, and commercial functions. As the Global Pharma Vertical Lead for Immunology and Cardio-metabolic CoEs,

Komal leads ZS' thinking in these disease areas and brings together industry partnerships to help clients accelerate capabilities. She is based in ZS's Princeton office.

Himanshu Patni is a leading expert on the US healthcare ecosystem, specializing in helping clients navigate the complex dynamics among key stakeholders—including patients, payers, providers, manufacturers, and big tech. As former leader of ZS's Healthcare Ecosystem Insights and Analytics practice, he helped multibillion-dollar companies advance their understanding of the healthcare data ecosystem and capitalize on its ongoing evolution. A recognized industry thought leader, he has shared his expertise at prominent conferences and seminars. He is based in ZS's San Francisco office.

Matt Ruple is a leading expert in commercial strategy, Go-To-Market models, and brand marketing, with nearly 30 years of leadership in life sciences and consulting. He excels at helping companies navigate the evolving healthcare ecosystem, optimize engagement with organized customers, and build winning value propositions. As a principal at ZS's Princeton office and B2B marketing practice leader, Matt empowers clients to achieve commercial excellence and sustainable growth.

Sean Scobell has spent the last 12 years at ZS as a leader in our B2B Access and Value Realization Practice with a concentration on the US market access and affordability. Sean has worked across a broad range of pharmaceutical & biotechnology manufacturers, ranging in both size and therapy area. Sean has had a focus on the US market access strategy, contracting strategy, buy-and-bill economics, policy planning, and patient affordability solutions.

Amudha Sharma is a seasoned expert in the therapy area strategy with 10 + years of experience guiding clients across Immunology, Oncology, Neurology, CVM, Retina, and Vaccines. As a core member of the Immunology Center of Excellence, she brings a unique blend of scientific depth and strategic insight, consistently driving impact through opportunity assessment, competitive intelligence, and go-to-market strategy. Amudha is a manager in ZS' Noida Office and is a leader in our Knowledge Services Group

Asheesh Shukla is a managing principal at ZS, leading the real-world data and patient insights practice, with a focus on patient-led transformation and analytics. He also heads ZS's technology advisory services for pharma CIOs. With deep expertise in strategy execution, digital transformation, and AI-driven innovation, Asheesh helps life sciences clients drive impact across the healthcare value chain. Asheesh is the Principal of the ZS Princeton office.

Jennifer Tedaldi is an expert in market access and the US healthcare ecosystem. Jennifer helps clients optimize clinical development programs, develop marketing strategies, set launch prices, prepare for price negotiations, evaluate business development opportunities, and better integrate market access dynamics into their forecasting processes. Jennifer is a principal in ZS's New York office and is a leader in the B2B Access and Value Realization Practice.

Karishma Trikha is an expert on the US Pharma and Healthcare industry. She has 14+ years of experience working with clients to help inform strategic decisions on innovation, offshoring, and potential partnerships from an ecosystem perspective. She specializes in Commercial strategy and transformation with a focus on Digital customer experience and market access. Karishma is a senior director in ZS' Bangalore Office and is a leader in our Knowledge Services and Competitive Intelligence Group.

Maria Whitman brings passion and 20+ years of deep domain expertise to organizations across healthcare. As managing partner, global commercialization strategy and solutions, Maria oversees the practice areas that guide ZS' clients to modernize their global models and capabilities. She was previously ZS' global pharmaceutical industry lead and, in 2015, was recognized as one of 12 top women consultants globally. Maria hosts ZS's "Transforming Biopharma" podcast. She is based in ZS's Philadelphia office.

Jennifer Wong is an expert in global market access, reimbursement, and pricing. She specializes in helping clients to define their access strategies, craft payer value communications, and develop evidence-based pricing strategies from due diligence and early asset phases through to post-launch and lifecycle management. Jennifer is a Manager in ZS's Boston office and is a member of the B2B Access and Value Realization Practice.

Ricky Yuen is a leading expert in US Market Access, specializing in guiding clients through the complexities of the US market access landscape, including the dynamics of money and product flow across various customer and stakeholder segments. He is an industry thought leader across numerous topics, including the Inflation Reduction Act, 340B program and revenue leakage, gross-to-net (GTN) optimization, digital transformation, and end-to-end contracting. Ricky is a principal in ZS's Princeton office and leads the US Market Access Insights and Analytics space within the B2B Access and Value Realization Practice.

Acknowledgments

This book is the result of many hands, minds, and hearts coming together. What began as a shared desire grew into a journey that was shaped, enriched, and ultimately brought to life by the contributions of countless individuals.

Collaborating with 15 leading experts in their respective areas of expertise has been an extraordinary privilege. Each co-author brought not only deep knowledge but also curiosity, humility, and a spirit of generosity. Their insights sharpened our understanding and often challenged us to look deeper into the layered, complex realities of the US healthcare system. Their names, photographs, and biographies appear in the "Contributors" section—and we are proud to have walked this path with them. All are members of ZS, a global consulting firm whose 10,000+ consultants partner with some of the world's most influential organizations to transform innovation into real-world impact.

Many others at ZS played vital roles behind the scenes. Swati Chandra was the heartbeat of this project—our tireless project manager and editor, who kept us moving forward with grace and precision while offering invaluable editorial guidance. Rohini Jamdade and Sasha Yachu lent their research acumen and enthusiasm at every turn, supporting our authors with thoughtfulness and care. Our creative partners, Suresh Kainthola and Amirkhan Pathan, brought the book to life visually through their cover design and graphic contributions. Many of the initial ideas for how to structure this book and "tell the story" of US healthcare derived from conversations with Nicolle Hamilton. Mike Moorman provided invaluable advice on how to edit a book like this, organize the many authors, and engage effectively with the publisher. Without these contributions, this book couldn't have existed.

We're also grateful to our publishing partner, Routledge. A special thanks to Rebecca Marsh and her exceptional team for their steady guidance and belief in this project. We are also grateful to Angela Hummel of the Alterra Group for her excellent copy editing and feedback that undoubtedly made this book clearer and easier to read.

And finally, to our families: thank you for holding space for us through the chaos—through late-night writing sessions, half-finished dinners, and weekends that quietly disappeared. Whether it was a knowing nod, a quiet room, or a hot cup of tea placed gently beside the laptop, your support was our invisible scaffolding. You gave us the time, the peace, and the grace to create. This book may have our names on it, but it carries your love between the lines.

Looking back, it's humbling to realize just how many people it takes to write a book. And how lucky we are to have had the very best in our corner.

Thank you for being part of this journey.

—Joe Stevens and Anush Khandelwal

Chapter 1

Introduction

Anush Khandelwal and Joe Stevens

The United States is home to some of the world's great research institutions, innovative hospitals, and groundbreaking medical innovations. It is one of the most talked about, complex, and consequential healthcare ecosystems in the world. For decades, it has inspired debate, driven innovation, and experienced policy shifts while continuing to grow in scope and economic importance. Meanwhile, the system often feels impenetrable, confusing, and fragmented—both to those within it and those observing it from afar. For patients, providers, policymakers, and business leaders alike, understanding the country's healthcare system requires navigating a labyrinth of interconnections, trade-offs, and tensions.

Why did we write this book?

This book was born out of countless conversations across time zones, meetings, and years of working in the world of healthcare consulting. We found ourselves returning to the same challenge: explaining the US healthcare system in a way that made sense to people.

Whether it was a curious colleague, a new team member, or a client from within or outside the industry, the questions were always the same—how it all worked, who does what, who pays for it, and why the system is so complicated. As professionals working at the intersection of healthcare, data analytics, and consulting, we realized that even within our own circles, the system often felt opaque. As professionals, we believe that gaining a clearer view of this system is

DOI: 10.4324/9781003603597-1

no longer an academic exercise for policy experts. It's an imperative for anyone directly or indirectly involved in shaping the future of health.

It became clear there was a need—not just for another academic analysis or technical white paper, but for a practical, accessible guide that walks readers through the system step by step. We believed there would be a benefit in a book that helps both insiders and curious newcomers understand the fundamentals, the hidden dynamics, and the evolving trends of US healthcare.

This book is our attempt to create just that.

In our professional careers, this book's authors have worked closely with many of the world's leading life sciences companies. As expert consultants, we routinely help clients navigate market dynamics, pricing strategies, patient access, and innovation adoption. Understanding how all these individual pieces fit into the broader health ecosystem is not always straightforward and requires a lot of details. In this book, we have tried to "tell the story" of each major player in the ecosystem. We start off by talking about what each one does, then share a little bit of history on how they became what they are today, discuss the incentives that drive the decisions of each as a business, and where possible suggest how best to work with each group.

Through the following pages, you will see how the US healthcare system is evolving in response to a variety of structural, technological, and societal changes. Increasing demand, advancement in digital health, shifts in regulation, and the growing emphasis on patient-centric care are all driving innovation in how healthcare is delivered and financed. Additionally, new entrants—from retail organizations to technology platforms to AI-driven startups—are expanding the ecosystem, contributing to a broader redefinition of roles traditionally held by providers, payers, and life sciences companies. Hence, the timing for a comprehensive guide to the US healthcare system couldn't be more relevant.

Who should read this book?

This book is our attempt to piece together this large puzzle. It's written not just for industry leaders, but for anyone who works in or with healthcare companies and wants a clear, structured understanding of the system they're helping shape. This book is also for anyone who is curious about the US healthcare landscape, including life sciences professionals, marketers, strategists, access and policy teams, healthcare innovators, policy thinkers, and experts outside the ecosystem trying to decode and understand the healthcare system.

We believe this book fills a crucial gap: Many discussions on US healthcare tend to be either too technically focused on a narrow topic, too surface-level to really describe what is happening, or too focused on advocating for a particular viewpoint or policy, leading them to cherry-pick facts to suit their narrative. Our goal is to fill that gap by presenting the complexities in a digestible way while retaining the richness needed to support meaningful insights.

Whether you're new to healthcare or looking to sharpen your understanding, this book is for you. It is not focused on evaluating the US healthcare system to decide if it is "good" or "bad," nor is it a policy manifesto. Instead, it's a neutral, structured, and practical lens through which to understand the key actors, forces, and flows that define the landscape, intended to be read by people who want to get things done.

What's inside?

We've structured the book into interconnected chapters, each tackling a foundational aspect of the US healthcare system. While each chapter can stand alone, together they form a holistic picture. Here's a quick look:

1. **Healthcare landscape:** We begin with a broad overview of the US healthcare system—its size, scope, and complexity. This chapter sets the stage by highlighting how healthcare is both a service and a manufacturing industry, driven by medical needs, financial structures, and policy decisions. A multitude of stakeholders are involved in the functioning of the healthcare ecosystem, many of which are not readily visible to the patient interacting with the system and are often unhelpfully named. This chapter introduces the groups that will be the subject of this book, explores the intricate interplay between key stakeholders, and defines various concepts and terminology that will be used throughout the book.
2. **Patient:** At the center of the healthcare system is the patient. This chapter explores the patient experience, from navigating insurance coverage to making care decisions. It also examines how socioeconomic factors, digital access, and consumer expectations are reshaping the patient journey.
3. **Insurance system (payers):** This chapter unpacks the structure and role of payers, including commercial insurers, government programs like Medicare and Medicaid, and employers. It covers the mechanics of reimbursement, alongside the complexities of the insurance system and how insurers' philosophies and payment models have evolved into what we see today.
4. **Providers:** Providers—hospitals, health systems, and clinics—form the backbone of care delivery. This chapter explores how care is organized, financed, and measured, as well as the challenges of scale, coordination, and transitioning to value-based models. We also review how today's provider reimbursement structure incentivizes decisions that don't reward genuine innovation but instead focus primarily on short-term gains and incentives dictated by payers rather than striving for transformative change.
5. **Physicians:** Physicians are key decision-makers in the healthcare process. This chapter discusses how physician roles are evolving due to administrative burden, technological integration, and shifting patient expectations. Multifaceted changes, including shifts in healthcare delivery models and

advances in medical technology, have redefined the physician's role and responsibilities from "god" to "guide."

6. **Pharma and med devices:** Life sciences companies—pharmaceutical and medical device manufacturers—are central to treatment innovation and cost. Though patients are the intended beneficiaries, pharma and med-tech companies must operate within a system shaped by payers and providers, often leading to a disconnect between patient need and what is offered. This chapter covers what makes these companies unique, including their development philosophies, regulatory pathways, pricing strategies, and the growing scrutiny around price and value.
7. **Intermediaries:** A unique feature of the US healthcare system is the number of entities operating between the patient, provider, and payer. This chapter explains the role of intermediaries such as pharmacy benefit managers, group purchasing organizations, and others that influence pricing, access, and supply chains. While intermediaries help streamline healthcare operations, they also introduce complexities that can impact healthcare costs, access, and efficiency. Each intermediary has a reason for existing, but the structure of the insurance system and providers has created great leverage for these entities, which allows them to extract substantial fees from the system while creating significant barriers to positive change.
8. **Data and technology:** In this chapter, we examine the accelerating role of data, analytics, and digital tools. From electronic health records to AI in diagnostics and personalized care, this chapter explores how technology is reshaping healthcare delivery, decision-making, and system efficiency.
9. **Reforms:** Finally, we explore the financial underpinnings of the US healthcare system—who pays, how money moves, and where the incentives lie. From insurance reimbursements to pharmaceutical rebates and government programs, it unpacks the flow of funds that shapes care delivery and business decisions—and all too often makes reform unattainable.

What we hope you will take away from reading

After going through the above-mentioned chapters, readers will develop a clear and comprehensive understanding of the US healthcare ecosystem. In particular, you'll come to understand:

Why the US healthcare system operates the way it does: This book provides an in-depth exploration of various factors that have shaped the US healthcare system. Readers will gain an understanding of why the system functions as it does today—the context that is crucial for professionals looking to understand the system—and insights into the underlying motivations and constraints that drive operations.

Past and present efforts to innovate or reform and their (often counter-intuitive) results: With detailed case studies and examples, the book analyzes past and ongoing efforts to reform the healthcare system and highlights how and why certain initiatives didn't work as expected. Readers will benefit from understanding these pitfalls, allowing them to devise more effective strategies for future reforms and innovations.

Practical guidance to navigate the system for businesspeople: For seasoned practitioners and newcomers alike, navigating the US healthcare system can be daunting. The book offers practical guidance and actionable strategies to help readers effectively engage with key players, such as payers, providers, and pharmaceutical companies. It discusses what each of these key players cares about in their own businesses, and includes frameworks for building partnerships, overcoming barriers to innovation, and adapting to policy changes. The book enables readers to operate more effectively within the system and to drive meaningful changes in their respective roles.

As professionals committed to shaping the future of health, understanding the system in which we work is our responsibility. We hope this book helps illuminate the path forward.

Chapter 2

The Healthcare Landscape

Komal Gurnani, Anush Khandelwal, and Joe Stevens

The modern healthcare ecosystem in the United States is, by necessity, a highly complex construct. Gone are the days of a visiting physician carrying everything they might need in a single medical bag. Today's system is designed to deliver a wide array of sophisticated clinical interventions requiring specialized skills, precise execution, and careful and continuous monitoring as and when needed across a variety of settings.

In this chapter, we explore the key stakeholders in the US healthcare landscape and how they navigate complex coordination challenges to ensure effective care delivery. We'll help readers understand:

- Stakeholder roles: The function and influence of each major group, including providers, payers, manufacturers, regulators, and, of course, patients
- The influence of healthcare resource utilization (HRU) and competition: How these forces shape the priorities and behaviors of various stakeholders
- Evolving disease states and market archetypes: How shifts in disease patterns influence the structure and focus of healthcare delivery systems

 DOI: 10.4324/9781003603597-2

We'll also provide high-level insights into the overall healthcare landscape before we dive deeper into each major stakeholder type in subsequent chapters.

The complexity of the ecosystem demands the involvement of numerous specialized professionals and groups coordinating efforts to ensure effective care delivery. Figure 2.1 illustrates the many different stakeholders involved in the US healthcare ecosystem.

Who shapes what

The most recognizable stakeholder is the **healthcare provider**, a person or a group responsible for delivering direct medical care to a patient. Hospitals are the most common type, providing mostly acute care to patients requiring immediate medical intervention, followed by clinics providing chronic care and addressing less urgent subacute medical issues. Other specialized medical facilities—such as nursing homes, long-term care facilities, ambulatory surgery centers, and dialysis centers—are also part of the provider landscape, each focusing on providing care for a narrower set of conditions than most hospitals and clinics, which allows them to specialize in their specific function.

Providers employ doctors, nurses, and a wide range of medical professionals to care for patients. Enabling this workforce to deliver timely and efficient care requires enormous amounts of supplies and equipment, which come from thousands of pharmaceutical companies manufacturing drugs, medical devices, information systems, and a variety of healthcare devices. Most of these pharmaceutical **manufacturers** are connected to a wide network of distributors, wholesalers, and pharmacies to bring their products to the market. Intermediaries such as group purchasing organizations are also involved in facilitating the administrative aspects of purchasing, price negotiation, etc.

Providers and manufacturers need to be paid for these drugs, devices, medical supplies, and healthcare provider salaries. The groups paying for these items are **funders**, with the largest single funder in the US being the government. Employers providing a health insurance benefit to employees are the second largest category of funders. Funding also comes from individuals who purchase their own insurance or have a co-pay when their insurance doesn't cover the full cost of care, as well as various charitable foundations supporting care for patients in need.

What's common among all funders is that they typically rely on intermediaries to handle the administrative responsibilities of paying for care—and in many cases to control costs by determining whether specific drugs or procedures are medically necessary and therefore eligible for coverage. We collectively refer to this group as **payers**. The US government operates its own set of payers with the Centers for Medicare & Medicaid Services and Veterans Affairs healthcare programs. Employers and individuals, on the other hand, usually purchase insurance through large commercial payers. At the time of this book's publication, the largest of these—often called mega payers—include United Healthcare, Aetna,

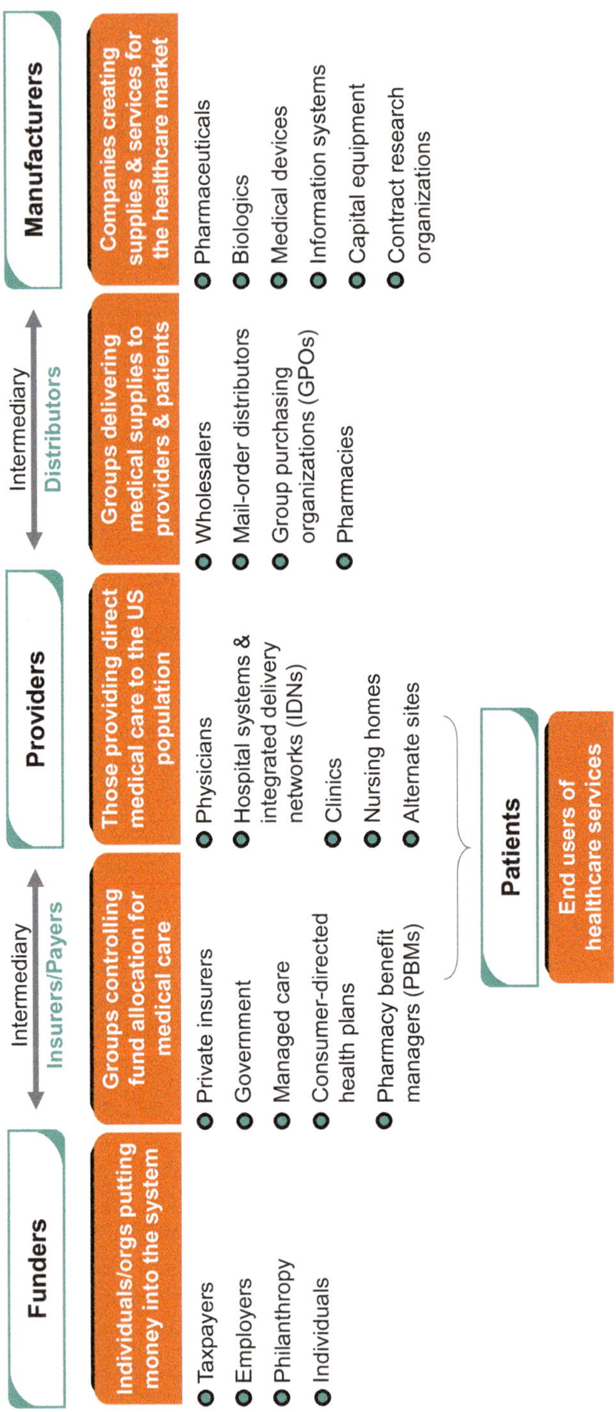

Figure 2.1 Stakeholders in the healthcare ecosystem

Humana, and Cigna. Notably, the government also engages with payers to administer certain government programs, such as Medicare Advantage (MA, Part C) and the Prescription Drug Plans (PDP, Part D). In addition, pharmacy benefit managers (PBMs) serve as specialized intermediaries, often working on behalf of other payers to manage prescription drug benefits and reimburse pharmacies.

Finally, the most important stakeholder for whose benefit all the other pieces of the healthcare ecosystem exist is the **patient**. Patients are far from just passive recipients of care. Their engagement with treatment—that is, the effort they spend on following healthcare providers' advice, taking prescribed medication, and coming for follow-up visits—has a huge effect on the health outcomes they achieve. Additionally, with more health-related information available more easily today than ever before, patients are increasingly taking charge of how they interact with each of the other ecosystem stakeholders to ensure they receive care that meets their needs.

How these stakeholders work together to treat diseases

The way these stakeholders come together to deliver patient care across various therapy areas can differ substantially depending on the situation. Two dominant factors tend to be good predictors of how a particular disease/indication is addressed:

1. **HRU (per patient)**: The intensity and cost of medical resources required to manage a disease.
   HRU refers to the direct consumption of medical resources, including hospitalizations, specialist visits, diagnostic tests, and drug therapies. It serves as a key measure in healthcare because it translates unmet medical needs into tangible economic and clinical considerations for providers and payers. While unmet need is often discussed in a broad sense and from the vantage point of different stakeholders (patients, caregivers, physicians, etc.), HRU offers a practical gauge of where intervention is most intense.
2. **Availability of different options:** The availability of treatment options and the competitive landscape among healthcare stakeholders.

Availability of competing treatments is another crucial driver in healthcare dynamics. The level of competition varies across treatment options and care delivery models:

Competitiveness across treatment options:

- **"Red ocean" markets**: Characterized by intense competition, often seen in drug classes and device markets with multiple and often undifferentiated

therapeutic options. This creates a situation where providers usually can choose between several different viable options for any given patient. In these markets, payers aggressively negotiate prices, and may seek to limit which products can be used to ensure lower-cost options are tried before more expensive ones (e.g., stents, oral anti-diabetics).
- **"Blue ocean" markets**: Defined as new or uncontested markets where minimal or suboptimal competition exists (think calm waters), often seen in novel or highly specialized treatment areas where providers and payers have fewer alternatives. In these markets, depending on the size of the market, providers probably don't have much choice for how to treat a given patient, and thus payers may or may not try to manage advancement to novel therapeutic options (e.g., rare diseases).

Competitiveness across sites of care:

- In the care delivery domain, competition is fiercer and constrained—providers and payers tend to limit partnerships for integrating workflows to a few select partners that offer tangible improvements in quality, cost, and outcomes. However, when competitiveness across sites of care is low (i.e., when only one or two facilities in a geography treat a particular disease), providers are more cooperative and willing to facilitate integrated workflows. They also tend to be measured less closely.

These two dimensions—HRU and competition—provide insights into what the various stakeholders in the ecosystem will prioritize in different cases. In *high-HRU situations*, we mostly observe that payer, provider, and pharma incentives are often aligned around addressing the most pressing clinical and economic challenges. Hence, all stakeholders are motivated to adopt high-cost innovative therapies to reduce overall HRU and optimize care delivery. As competition elevates in these disease states, we see payers and providers focused on different objectives: Providers may want to adopt innovative therapies even sooner in the patient journey, and payers may fear the burgeoning costs and try to put measures in place to contain them.

In *low-HRU situations*, we see stark divergence of priorities across payers, providers, and pharma manufacturers. While providers and pharma manufacturers continue to focus on unmet needs and seek innovative, differentiated therapies, payers emphasize cost containment and access control to prioritize their budgets for other high resource utilization disease states. Providers, in turn, when faced with significant access hurdles for both therapeutics as well as services reimbursement, may prioritize workflow efficiency and optimization to reduce practice time spent on low-HRU disease states.

Competition can further influence physician priorities and partnership dynamics. In high-competition settings, we observe significant market growth in total patients serviced; further, providers can improve clinical outcomes by leveraging multiple treatment options and focusing on clinical quality and patient satisfaction where possible. In low-competition settings, we observe a tough clinical innovation landscape, with suboptimal options leveraged for most patient types and decision-making limited to a few available alternatives.

Based on the interplay of these two forces, four unique combinations of care delivery models emerge in the market archetype grid:

- **Academic/centers of excellence (CoE)-led:** Large medical centers and CoEs managing complex conditions with high resource needs and often with very limited therapeutic options. Providers and payers are often aligned around accelerating the use of advanced therapies.
- **Specialist-led:** Diverse care settings where specialists service patients, including integrated delivery networks of varied types (academic and financially motivated care sites). In this care setting, given the range of therapeutic options available, we see a balancing act between improving clinical outcomes and containing costs through provider-payer collaboration.
- **Consumerism-led:** Community-based care sites, often under the management of private equity-backed groups, servicing high patient demand with limited specialist capacity and a large number of support roles to extend the impact of each physician (e.g., nurse practitioners and physician assistants). With extensive therapeutic options, payers actively drive cost-based treatment sequencing, often forcing physicians to prioritize other disease states given the overall low HRU.
- **Uncharted:** Either specialist- or primary care physician-driven settings for niche diseases with little to no clinical innovation, minimal practice team mindshare, and low competition. These models often have poor outcomes for the patient. Depending on the disease incidence/prevalence, payers may drive high involvement to contain budgetary risks.

The market archetype grid shown in Figure 2.2 reveals that while diseases and therapeutic areas span all quadrants, the largest ones tend to cluster on the right side of the 2 × 2 grid. This indicates a shift toward greater standardization, payer influence, and consumer-driven care as treatments mature and market forces evolve.

Evolution of disease states across healthcare market archetypes

With therapeutic and care delivery innovations, evolving guidelines, and shifting payer strategies, disease states evolve from one archetype to another. This categorization of diseases is not static and can be predicted based on the upcoming evolutionary steps (see Figure 2.2). Several trends are common as a shift occurs from one archetype to another:

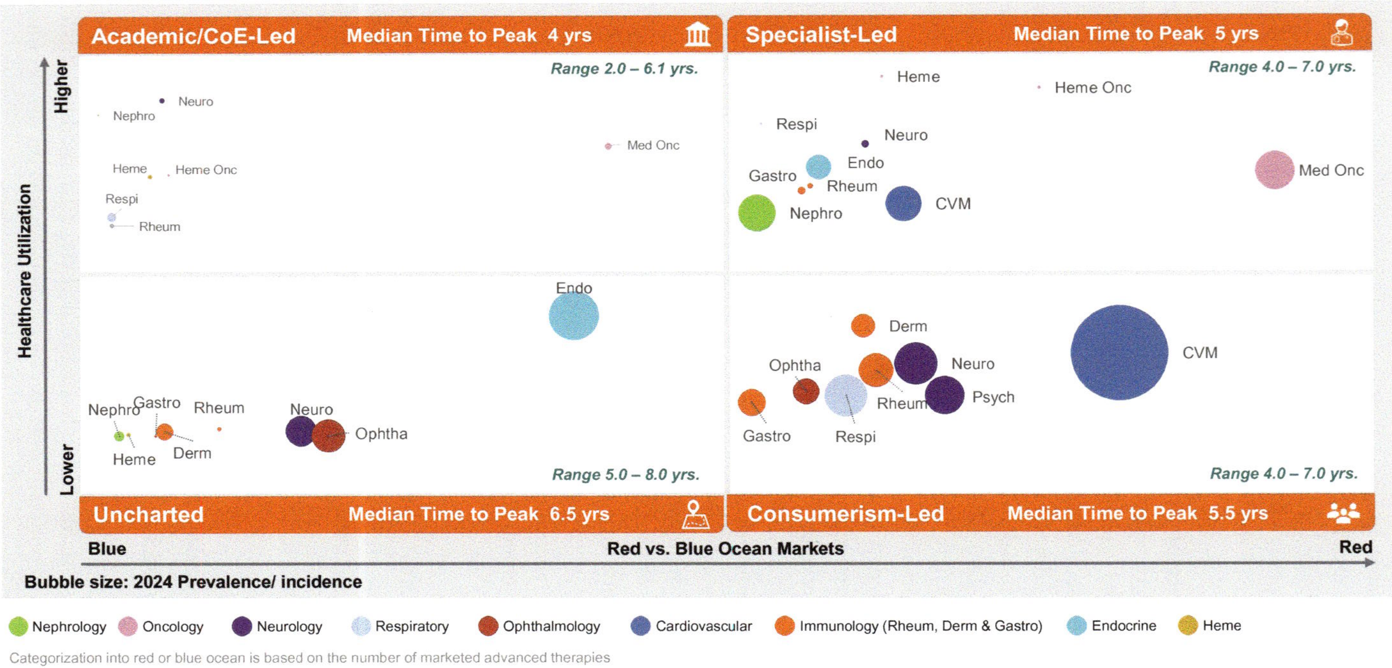

Figure 2.2 Disease states across healthcare market archetypes

***Note*: Categorization into red or blue ocean is based on the number of marketed advanced therapies**

Source: Evaluate Pharma & ZS Analysis

- **Shift from uncharted to academic/CoE-led:** Diseases start with limited understanding, suboptimal to no options, and are often mischaracterized as having a low HRU. Breakthroughs like clinical innovation in the form of novel therapies can shift these disease states to academic/CoE-led as these sites have been leading clinical trials with distinguished scientific faculty pushing the boundary of outcomes for these patients.
- **Shift from academic/CoE-led to specialist-led:** As many innovative therapeutics come to the market, clinical evidence, care quality, and guidelines evolve, leading to care delivery beyond CoEs into a range of specialist networks/settings. This broader adoption and treatment standardization significantly expands the addressable patient population.
- **Shift from specialist-led to consumerism-led:** With enhanced disease state understanding and an improved range of therapeutic options, more sections of the patient journey can be managed in the community-oriented setting. Improved quality of outcomes and efficiency drive payer-led cost control, shifting care focus to accessibility and affordability.

This evolution also shifts who holds the most influence in the different quadrants over available treatment choices, drugs, and services reimbursement, and delivering outcomes with appropriate clinical quality and patient satisfaction.

Academic/CoE-led: Power is concentrated with providers/key opinion leaders (KOLs) who shape treatment guidelines, primarily driven by high complexity and the urgency to reduce overall total healthcare cost. KOLs/providers' institutions own the infrastructure and technology that often drives clinical decision-making.

Specialist-led: Influence is split between specialists and payers, balancing cost and access. Channel partners impact market access, drug distribution, and patient outcomes.

Consumerism-led: Patients drive demand through convenience-focused choices. Payers, PBMs, and digital health players take the lead, while physicians often offer multiple viable options versus a single recommendation.

Uncharted: Life sciences research and manufacturers dominate, with specialists and regulators as key players. In some high-prevalence therapy areas, payer influence is rising, especially for high-cost interventions.

The stage is set for deeper exploration

In the US healthcare system, a variety of stakeholders come together to deliver care in different ways depending on the characteristics of the patient's condition they are treating. We have described how each stakeholder in the ecosystem has a logical role to play and how they come together to treat diseases from the best available scientific and clinical knowledge. So why, then, are there still so many problems? We continue to hear about cases where necessary drugs or procedures are inaccessible, where the cost of care is unreasonably high, or where patients spend years going through the system without receiving the care they need. Why can't all these entities work together more effectively to deliver better outcomes?

The answer often lies in the structure of the system itself—and in the incentives this structure creates for each of these entities operating within it. In the remainder of this book, we will explore each stakeholder group, examining how they view their role in the healthcare ecosystem, the decisions they must make to succeed, and the pressures they face from other entities they interact with. Along the way, we will see how structures originally designed to solve one problem often end up creating new ones. Additionally, solutions and policies that once made sense can produce undesirable results as clinical practice causes its market archetype to evolve. For healthcare leaders, life sciences companies, and policymakers, recognizing these archetypes offers a roadmap for navigating the evolving landscape, ensuring innovations reach the right settings with maximum impact.

As we continue our discussion of the different healthcare ecosystem players in this book, we will review how their individual needs and their influence may vary and evolve over time. Only by understanding the healthcare ecosystem's structure and its own ongoing evolution can we find ways to make the system work more effectively: delivering the care patients need while also achieving the goals of the organizations within it. Gaining this understanding with a deep dive into each of these stakeholder types will be the central focus of the remainder of this book.

Chapter 3

Patients

The Humans at the Center of Healthcare

Maria Whitman, Komal Gurnani, Karishma Trikha, and Anush Khandelwal

Any meaningful discussion about healthcare must start with its core purpose and patron—patients. At some moment, all of us have been and will be patients navigating the complexities and experiences—both positive and challenging—of the healthcare system we seek to decode in this book. In this chapter, we will:

- Explore how innovation is reshaping patient outcomes, access, and engagement;
- Examine the realities of the modern patient experience, which is often fragmented and overwhelming
- Understand that healing not only requires clinical care, but also demands empathy, clarity, and connection
- Consider the future where patients drive change through consumerism and informed decision-making

Every stakeholder in this ecosystem focuses on the patient and drives some type of innovation to meet their needs. Despite varied incentives and methods, the ultimate measure of success is how well the system delivers and enhances patient care, making patient outcomes and experience the true benchmark of the system's effectiveness.

DOI: 10.4324/9781003603597-3

Innovation and improvement of outcomes

Over the past few decades, patient outcomes in healthcare have remarkably transformed, driven by significant advancements in medical science and technology. One of the most notable examples is the reduction in cancer mortality rates. According to the American Cancer Society, improvements in early disease detection and advanced treatment modalities reduced the mortality rate among cancer patients in the United States by 34%[1] from 1991 to 2022.

The advances in metabolic care and obesity with novel Glucagon-Like Peptide-1 (GLP-1) medications hold potential to significantly reduce comorbidities and similarly improve long-term health outcomes for patients with cardiometabolic diseases. GLP-1s[2] could cut the risk of Alzheimer's disease and related dementia by nearly half (45%), especially for people with Type 2 diabetes. In addition to improving survival rate and quality of life, advanced modalities like cell and gene therapies offer potential cures for diseases once considered incurable. A prime example is the treatment of a rare genetic neurodegenerative disorder among children, spinal muscular atrophy, where the gene therapy Zolgensma has achieved a 95%[3] survival rate and improved motor functions in 92% of its patients.

Technological advancements have also revolutionized patient experience and outcomes, from early detection and diagnosis to treatment access, adherence, and continuous health monitoring. For instance, an artificial intelligence (AI) model developed by researchers at Harvard Medical School achieved approximately 94% accuracy[4] in cancer diagnosis. Similarly, integration of advanced technologies like AI, machine learning, and data analytics in drug discovery and development is accelerating the availability of new treatments. A drug discovered using generative AI by Insilico Medicine entered phase one of clinical trials in just one-third the usual time.[5]

Beyond AI, the digital transformation catalyzed by the COVID-19 pandemic fueled a telehealth[6] boom that significantly improved care delivery—reducing specialist wait times by 84%, improving treatment adherence rates by 67%, and cutting emergency visits by 72% in cardiology. Remote patient monitoring for chronic disease management also reduced hospital readmission rates by up to 76%.[7] Healthcare stakeholders are increasingly focusing on predicting and preventing noncompliance with prescribed health interventions, while working to eliminate friction that prevents patients from accessing the care they need.

Though these advancements and outcomes are unevenly distributed across geographies and populations, they collectively illustrate profound progress in terms of discovery, development, and delivery in healthcare. The improvements in survival rates and quality of life are empowering patients with more choices of innovative therapies and more timely support and resources, thereby enhancing their overall opportunity to live healthy lives.

More than medicine: The challenged patient experience

The quality of patients' healthcare experience can shape not only how they engage with the system, but also the outcomes they achieve. It influences their trust, willingness to follow treatment plans, and loyalty to providers. In a world where nothing is more personal than health, it's reasonable to expect that patients' experience with the healthcare system should be among the most supportive and empowering in their lives, but all too often this is not the case.

Research consistently shows that patient experience impacts their health outcomes. Satisfied patients are more likely to adhere to treatments, recover better, and report higher well-being. For instance, one study[8] found patients who experienced strong nurse communication were 33% less likely to encounter hospital complications, while those with effective provider communication had a 56% lower risk of readmission. Another study[9] showed better hospital care and discharge experiences were linked to fewer 30-day readmissions for conditions including myocardial infarction, heart failure, and pneumonia. Patient safety is also closely tied to loyalty[10]—patients who feel safe are 2.5 times more likely to recommend a healthcare facility/provider.

While technological advancements have made healthcare more patient-centered and efficient and innovation continues to accelerate at a rapid pace, the gap between the experience patients deserve and what they actually receive has been widening. The 2025 ZS Future of Health study[11] conducted with Harris Poll found only 32% of patients in the United States feel "cared for" after an interaction with the healthcare system—a drop of 10% from 2023. Meanwhile, physicians remain out of sync, with twice as many believing patients feel cared for. Similar disconnects exist in patients' perceptions of feeling "heard" and "empowered."

The real risk of a declining patient experience goes beyond discomfort—it can significantly influence patient behavior. Poor experiences have the potential to lower outcomes if patients pull further away from prevention and relegate their healthcare to "sick care," where they only expend energy on their health after something goes wrong. Unfortunately, some concerning statistics signal a momentum to disengage, rooted in experience:

- American consumers rate hassle and cost as the top challenges in managing their personal health
- About a quarter of US patients do not have a consistent primary care provider, slightly up from 23% in 2023
- 44% of Americans avoid seeking any kind of medical care until they are already sick

As we explore the vantage points, goals, challenges, and progress of the various stakeholders creating the experience and delivery of care, we will see many reasons why experience is lagging and corresponding opportunities for change. A few prominent drivers include:

- **Complex care navigation:** In healthcare, we often think of a care pathway as a linear progression: from awareness (recognizing something is wrong) to diagnosis, treatment, and ideally, cure or long-term management. However, it is rarely this straightforward in a real-world scenario. Patient journeys are shaped by various factors, such as the nature of the illness, living location and conditions, and site of care. Consider some illustrative examples:
  - Ron, a 60-year-old man, had been experiencing fatigue, excessive thirst, and frequent urination for a few weeks. Concerned with the symptoms, he visited his primary care physician (PCP), who, after a few tests, diagnosed him with Type 2 diabetes. He was promptly referred to an endocrinologist, who ran additional tests and prescribed a structured care plan—medication, lifestyle changes, and behavioral therapy—to manage both his diabetes and related risks.

    Meanwhile, his 28-year-old daughter, Lucy, had been dealing with obesity for years, but her journey looked different. Instead of starting with a doctor, she tried apps, diets, and fitness trackers. It wasn't until she hit a plateau—and started feeling frustrated and isolated—that she decided to consult her PCP. Her PCP offered general advice, encouraged lifestyle changes, and a referral to a nutritionist, but no formal diagnosis or pharmacological support. Unlike her father, Lucy's care lacked a coordinated plan, reflecting how obesity is often treated less seriously despite being a chronic condition.
  - Jake, a 39-year-old mechanic from rural Montana, began experiencing muscle weakness and joint pain. With time, the symptoms worsened. He struggled to lift tools, and even walking became painful. Over the next eight years, he saw 10 different doctors, each offering a different diagnosis—none was correct, and Jake's symptoms never improved. Jake had no clear path to expert care. His symptoms were dismissed or misdiagnosed, and local providers lacked the tools to identify his rare autoimmune condition. Only after a chance referral and a long trip out of state did he finally receive an accurate diagnosis of a rare connective tissue disorder—nearly a decade after his first symptoms. But even then, challenges persisted with limited treatment options available locally and insurance hurdles delaying access to specialty medications.
  - Margaret, a woman in her early 70s, moved to New York City five years ago. She lives in a good neighborhood, is relatively healthy, and has basic

Medicare coverage. Yet, without a consistent PCP, she relies on urgent care centers for even minor issues like a cough or cold. Her trust in the healthcare system has been shaken, especially after losing both parents during the COVID-19 pandemic—leading her to often challenge medical advice and fail to comply with treatment plans. This reflects a growing issue among older adults: Even with access and awareness, lack of continuity in care and emotional disconnection from the system can lead to fragmented, reactive healthcare use.

- **Disparities in care:** It is widely established that only 20% of our health is genetic; the remaining 80% can be attributed to behavior and environment. Disparities across factors like race, ethnicity, and socioeconomic status persist across the US healthcare system and adversely affect care access and outcomes. For instance, Black individuals are twice[12] as likely to die from prostate, stomach, and preventable cervical cancer compared with a similar population of White individuals. Despite cancer disproportionately affecting Black adults, they accounted for only 8.5%[13] of participants enrolled in interventional trials from 2010 to 2021.

  In the case of diabetes, American Indian/Alaska Native adults are 1.5 times[14] more likely than non-Hispanic White adults to be diagnosed with diabetes but don't receive the same treatments. A report from the National Academies of Sciences, Engineering, and Medicine highlights significant disparities in access to diabetes treatment and technology among different ethnic groups. According to Eberly et al. (2021),[15] Asian and Black patients are 41% and 19% less likely, respectively, to use newer, higher-cost GLP-1 RA drugs compared with White patients. Furthermore, Agarwal et al.[16] (2021) found that the use of continuous glucose monitoring is lowest among non-Hispanic Black individuals at 28%, compared with 71% among non-Hispanic White individuals. There are vast income-related disparities as well. Adults with lower or average incomes are 1.5 times[17] more likely than higher-income individuals to skip or delay necessary medical care due to cost and 2.5 times more likely to have unmet social needs, such as food, safe housing, and stable employment, which may make navigation and use of health services less likely.
- **Financial burden**: Healthcare expenses are increasingly financially straining American households. According to the ZS Future of Health study, 88% of consumers believe healthcare is becoming more expensive—and they are correct. Over the past decade, annual per capita health spending has grown at a compound annual growth rate of approximately 5%, rising from $9,038 in 2013 to $14,570 in 2023.[18] During the same period, insurance premiums increased by 52%,[19] far outpacing inflation. Additionally, drug prices in the United States remain exceptionally high—averaging 2.78 times[20] those in other high-income countries.

The rising cost of healthcare is leading to significant medical debt for some Americans, even though most have some form of healthcare coverage. According to a Gallup survey,[21] about 31 million Americans sought loans to pay for healthcare in 2024, resulting in $74 billion in debt. Moreover, the lack of transparency in price and insurance coverage terms further exacerbates the financial strain on patients. For instance, despite regulations mandating price transparency, more than 50%[22] of hospitals still do not fully comply with making their standard charges available to consumers. About 30%[23] of consumers in the United States with private insurance reported difficulty understanding what they have to pay out-of-pocket and specific insurance terms.

Where do we go from here? Consumerism and empowerment

The experience of being a patient in the US healthcare system is far from perfect and patients have begun to push back. Today, the patient is no longer a passive recipient of care. Increasingly, individuals are taking on a more proactive role, seeking information, comparing options, and making informed choices about where, how, and from whom they receive care. This shift reflects a deeper transformation in the role of the patient: from a solitary healthcare user to an empowered consumer, and even further, to an active participant in shaping their care and the broader system.

Moreover, patients are making choices about where and how to engage in healthcare. As consumers, sites of care (both in-person and virtual) that are convenient become more prominently used and are driving decisions at large healthcare institutions (as we will discuss in future chapters). Increased adoption of digital tools, AI-enabled health apps, and the rise of social media signal a change in information consumption and empower control of an individual's health destiny. Engagement in more direct-to-patient channels that eliminate the need for in-person visits and get the patient to an answer more quickly is changing how we think about care for a variety of disease states and creating competition for patient attention.

Consumerism and empowerment are also reshaping the healthcare system at large. Research shows a growing willingness among individuals to share their health data in exchange for more personalized and effective care. At the same time, patients and advocacy groups are emerging as influential voices—shaping policy, advancing research, and driving systemic change, particularly in critical areas such as cancer and rare diseases. For all stakeholders, understanding and adapting to these shifts is essential for building a more responsive, equitable, and patient-centered healthcare system. It begins by placing the patient—and their lived experience—at the core of every decision.

Notes

1 *ACS Annual Report: Cancer Mortality Continues to Drop Despite Rising Incidence in Women; Rates of New Diagnoses Under 65 Higher in Women Than Men.* (2025). American Cancer Society.

2 Mathur, B. (2025). Beyond Weight Loss: Can Ozempic Sharpen Your Brain, Cut Dementia Risk? *Business Standard.*

3 Chongmelaxme, B., Yodsurang, V., Vichayachaipat, P., et al. Gene-Based Therapy for the Treatment of Spinal Muscular Atrophy Types 1 and 2: A Systematic Review and Meta-Analysis. *Gene Ther* (2024); Flinn, R. (2024). *For SMA Patients, Zolgensma Outperforms Other Gene Therapies, Review Shows.* Managed Healthcare Executive.

4 Pesheva, E. (2024). New AI Tool Can Diagnose Cancer, Guide Treatment, Predict Patient Survival. The Harvard Gazette.

5 Goldman, S. (2024). Insilico Medicine Unveils First AI-Generated and AI-Discovered Drug in New Paper. VentureBeat.

6 *Telehealth in 2025: Transforming Healthcare Through Innovation and Policy.* CTeL.

7 Samet, A. (2022). The Technology, Devices, and Benefits of Remote Patient Monitoring in the Healthcare Industry. *Business Insider*; Lamboley, L. (2025). 27 remote patient monitoring statistics every practice should know. Prevounce.

8 Oberle, A., Tian, D., Hayes, K., Howard, S., & Moran, V. (2022). Associations between patient experience and clinical outcomes at a level I trauma center: a cross-sectional survey-based study. *Journal of Hospital Management and Health Policy.* 6.

9 Boulding, W., & Glickman, S. (2011). Relationship between patient satisfaction with inpatient care and hospital readmission within 30 days. *The American Journal of Managed Care.* 17(1):41–48.

10 *Patient Experience in 2024.* Press Ganey.

11 ZS Associates. (2025). *2025 ZS Future of Health Survey Report.*

12 *ACS Annual Report: Cancer Mortality Continues to Drop Despite Rising Incidence in Women; Rates of New Diagnoses Under 65 Higher in Women Than Men.* (2025). American Cancer Society.

13 *2022 ASCO Quality Care Symposium.* (2022). American Society of Clinical Oncology.

14 *Diabetes and American Indians/Alaska Natives.* (n.d.). Office of Minority Health, U.S. Department of Health and Human Services.

15 Eberly, L. A., Yang, L., Essien, U. R., Eneanya, N. D., Julien, H. M., Luo, J., Nathan, A. S., Khatana, S. A. M., Dayoub, E. J., Fanaroff, A. C., Giri, J., Groeneveld, P. W., & Adusumalli, S. (2021, December 17). Racial, Ethnic, and Socioeconomic Inequities in Glucagon-Like Peptide-1 Receptor Agonist Use Among Patients With Diabetes in the US. *JAMA Health Forum.* 2(12):e214182. doi: 10.1001/jamahealthforum.2021.4182.

16 Agarwal, S., Schechter, C., Gonzalez, J., & Long, J. A. Racial-Ethnic Disparities in Diabetes Technology Use Among Young Adults with Type 1 Diabetes. (2021 April). *Diabetes Technology & Therapuetics.* 23(4):306–313. doi: 10.1089/dia.2020.0338.

17 Gunja, M. Z., Gumas, E. D., Williams, R. D., II, Doty, M. M., Shah, A., & Fields, K. (2023, November 16). *The Cost of Not Getting Care: Income Disparities in the Affordability of Health Services Across High-Income Countries.* The Commonwealth Fund.

18 McGough, M., Wager, E., Winger, A., Panchal, N., & Cotter, L. (2024). How has U.S. spending on healthcare changed over time? Health System Tracker.

19 *2024 Employer Health Benefits Survey*. (2024). KFF; Aftermath of Crisis Highlights Challenges in Health Insurance Transparency and Access. (2024). ProgramBusiness.

20 Mulcahy, A., Schwam, D., Lovejoy, S. (2024). *International Prescription Drug Price Comparisons*. RAND.

21 Maese, E., & Witters, D. (2025). *Americans Borrow Estimated $74 Billion for Medical Bills in 2024*. Gallup, Washington, DC.

22 *Not All Selected Hospitals Complied With the Hospital Price Transparency Rule* (Report number: A-07-22-06108). (2024). Office of Inspector General (OIG), U.S. Department of Health and Human Services. https://oig.hhs.gov/reports/all/2024/not-all-selected-hospitals-complied-with-the-hospital-price-transparency-rule/

23 Wallace, R., Salaga, M., Long, M., & Pestaina, K. (2025). *Navigating the Maze: A Look at Patient Cost-Sharing Complexities and Consumer Protections*. KFF.

Chapter 4

Payers

Corporate Giants Writing the Rules

Jennifer Tedaldi, Jennifer Wong, Joe Stevens, and Anush Khandelwal

In healthcare, the term "payer" refers to an entity responsible for financing and/or reimbursing the cost of health services. These entities can be private insurance companies, government entities/programs, employer plan sponsors, or other organizations that manage healthcare expenses (which we will explain in sections below). While they typically are not responsible for care delivery, payers have a vital role in shaping how, when, and where patients access medical services—through the policies, coverage rules, and payment models they define.

In this chapter, we will help readers understand:

- Major categories of payers in the US healthcare system and their distinct roles
- How employer-sponsored insurance, commercial insurers, and third-party administrators function
- The current payer landscape: major players, market share, and challenges
- How payer decisions influence clinical behavior, patient access, and care quality
- The various management tools and payment models payers use

At its core, health insurance operates on a model of risk pooling—where individuals and employers pay into insurance plans that, in turn, cover large

DOI: 10.4324/9781003603597-4

and unpredictable healthcare expenses. Unlike other developed nations with centralized or single-payer models, the US landscape evolved into a patchwork of public and private insurance arrangements. Much of the US health insurance system traces back to World War II. When wage controls were introduced in 1942 to combat inflation, employers began offering health insurance as an added benefit to attract and retain workers.[1] However, what began as a workaround soon became widespread. By the end of the war, nearly 23% of the US population had private insurance.[2]

Today, coverage comes through multiple routes, as illustrated in Figure 4.1: employer-sponsored plans, government programs like Medicare and Medicaid, and individual market plans under the Affordable Care Act (ACA). In the United States, while the funder (the person or group paying into the system) may differ, this principle of risk pooling underpins both private and public insurance programs.

Types of payers

The US insurance market is a wide-reaching network of both government-sponsored and private entities, each with varying scopes of coverage and operational models. Public payers like Medicare and Medicaid provide critical coverage to specific segments, such as the elderly, disabled, and low-income populations, through both federal-state partnerships and programs directly administered by the federal government. Private payers, including employer-sponsored plans and individual market insurers, account for the largest share of the insured population, often offering broader benefit packages and provider networks than public plans. Together, these payers shape access to care, set reimbursement standards, influence healthcare pricing, and drive innovation through contracting strategies and performance-based incentives. Their collective reach spans nearly every American household, making them central actors in the functioning and reform of the healthcare delivery system.

Private payers

Private health insurers cover the lion's share of the US population. These companies—UnitedHealthcare, Anthem, Aetna, Cigna, and others—offer plans to employers and individuals, and support government programs (Figure 4.2). They are major participants in Medicare Advantage (MA) (Part C) and Managed Medicaid, effectively serving as intermediaries between the government and patients.

These private payers exercise significant control over care delivery by influencing provider networks, treatment authorizations, and reimbursement rates. They sometimes, but not always, bear financial risk. For example, while it's possible

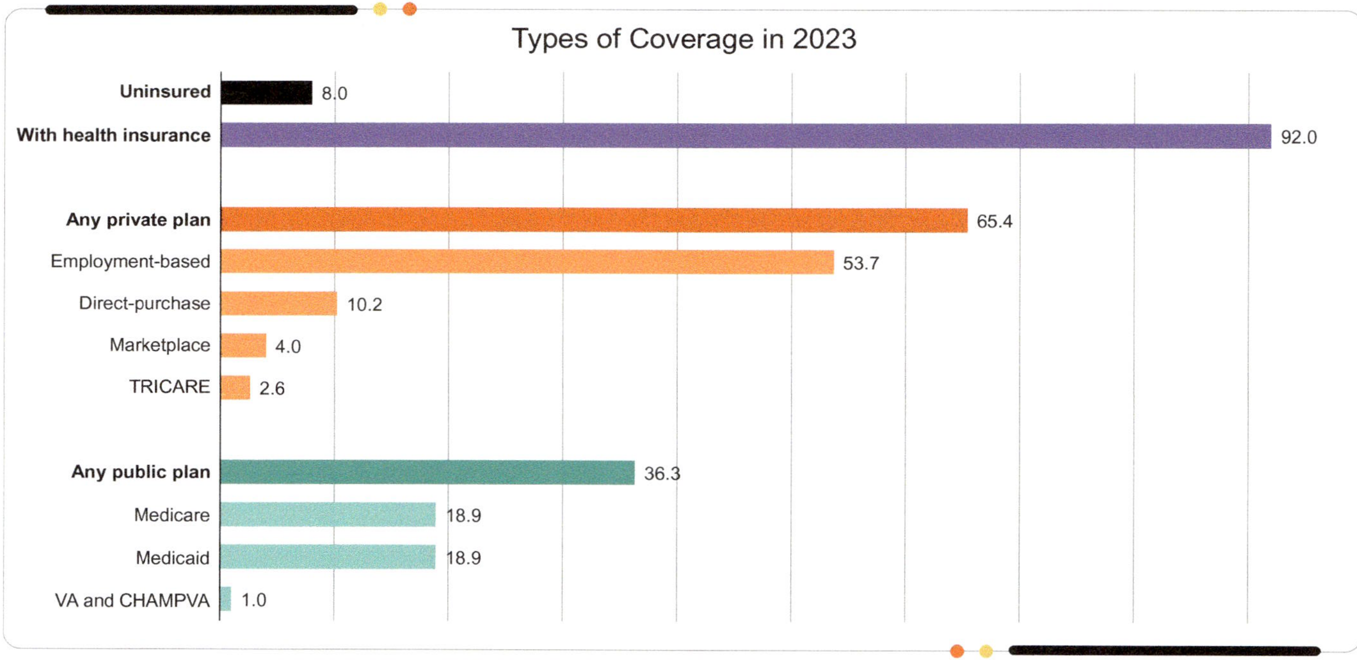

Figure 4.1 Percentage of people covered by different types of health insurance in the US (in thousands)

***Note*: The estimates by type of coverage are not mutually exclusive; people can be covered by more than one type of health insurance during the year.**

***Source*: U.S. Census Bureau, Current Population Survey, 2023 and 2024 Annual Social and Economic Supplements (CPS ASEC).**

in many cases to buy insurance from these companies, in many cases, they may also merely be processing claims for a self-insured employer or sharing risk with another group, such as when cost overruns for Medicare patients are backstopped by the government.

According to the US Census Bureau, as of 2023, private health insurance coverage continued to be more prevalent than public coverage, at 65.4% and 36.3%, respectively (see Figure 4.1).

The United States has more than 1,160 health insurance companies that provide medical coverage,[3] but the industry is dominated by 10 companies that own 60% of the market share (as of 2022). These "mega payers" are no longer just insurers—they own the full value chain of care with integrated healthcare ecosystems that span insurance, care delivery, and pharmacy services, which allows them to manage risk, streamline operations, and influence nearly every touchpoint of the healthcare journey (which we will discuss further in the chapter on intermediaries). Moving beyond the conventional role of claims processing, they have become active participants in clinical decision-making and health outcomes. They have their own networks of physicians, emergency care centers, and virtual health platforms with the aim of improving care coordination while also keeping patients within their ecosystem.

The top three players—UnitedHealth Group, CVS Health (Aetna), and Cigna—cover a significant share of the US population (see Table 4.1). According to recent data, UnitedHealth alone covers more than 50 million people across commercial, MA, and Medicaid plans.

Government-sponsored payers

Medicare and Medicaid represent the largest government-sponsored insurance plans. Medicare covers elderly adults (65+), certain disabled individuals, and patients with specific conditions such as end-stage renal disease or organ transplants. Medicaid is jointly funded by the federal and state governments to cover low-income individuals and families. Beyond Medicare and Medicaid, other government-backed programs address specific populations—for instance, TRICARE and the Veterans Health Administration (VA) provide care to military personnel and veterans, while the Children's Health Insurance Program serves children in families whose incomes are too high to qualify for Medicaid but too low to afford private insurance.

Medicare was enacted initially with two types of benefits:

Medicare Part A: Covering hospital insurance, this component automatically enrolled the country's elderly, ensuring they had access to inpatient care and hospital services without the burden of direct out-of-pocket costs.

Medicare Part B: Covering outpatient and physician services, this component was offered on a voluntary basis. Nearly all eligible individuals opted in,

Table 4.1 Top three mega payers at a glance

Company	*Net Revenue*	*Metrices*
UnitedHealth Group (UHG)	UnitedHealthcare: $222B Optum: $155B	■ 146M unique individuals served globally ■ 12% increase in global revenue from 2020 ■ 60K+ employed physicians
CVS Health Group	$292B	■ 100M+ members with Aetna and CVS Caremark ■ 8.7% increase in global revenue from 2020 ■ 4.5M consumers visit CVS locations daily
Cigna/ESI/ Evernorth	Cigna: $174B Evernorth: $132B	■ 175K+ mental and behavioral health providers ■ 9% increase in global revenue from 2020 ■ 17M medical lives globally

recognizing the value of continued coverage for doctor visits, diagnostics, and outpatient care.

A significant trend reshaping the payer ecosystem is the continued growth and evolution of government-sponsored insurance administered through private plans. Chief among these is the rise of MA (i.e., Medicare Part C) and Prescription Drug Plan (PDP) (i.e., Medicare Part D).

Medicare Part C: Originally called Medicare + Choice and now more commonly referred to as MA. It provides equivalent benefits to Medicare Parts A and B but is administered by a private insurance company under federal oversight. It generally offers additional coverage for items such as dental, vision, and hearing. Medicare Part C enrollees are also generally enrolled in a prescription drug plan, often at no additional cost. Today, MA accounts for over 50% of Medicare enrollees[4] and has become a key growth area for private insurers, which receive capitated (i.e., fixed fee per patient) payments from the government for enrolled patients.

Medicare Part D: Also known as Medicare PDP or MA Prescription Drug coverage. This adds coverage for medication prescribed by a physician and self-administered by the patient (i.e., after picking it up from a pharmacy). More than 80% of Medicare patients have a PDP.

This model of risk-sharing with private insurers has expanded to other government-sponsored programs as well. On the Medicaid front, many states have adopted Managed Medicaid, where private insurers are contracted to deliver care to low-income populations. This shift has enabled more structured care delivery, administrative efficiency, and cost predictability for state governments—particularly states that expanded Medicaid under the ACA.

Where we stand today

The insurance system we have described here is unique among developed nations in its fragmented combination of public and private insurance (see Figure 4.1). Single-payer systems, such as those in Canada, Taiwan, and South Korea, have a public entity that both regulates and funds coverage. Social healthcare models, such as in France, Germany, and the United Kingdom, rely on significant government oversight and involvement and ensure universal access to services but may have a mix of public and private funding and delivery. In all these cases, the government plays a very direct role in setting the price that physicians, healthcare institutions, and drug manufacturers can charge for products and services. In sharp contrast, the United States is an intricate landscape of Medicare, Medicaid, commercial payers, payer intermediaries, providers, and many other stakeholders with their own incentives. Employers must choose an insurance company for their employees, insurance companies must negotiate prices with healthcare providers and pharmaceutical manufacturers, and patients often have multiple options from which they can choose to best fit their needs—but may also impact how much they personally must pay.

At the core of every private insurer's business model lies a balancing act between attracting members and managing costs. Competition among private insurers promotes an ever-increasing focus on how to attract and retain more customers (i.e., individual patients) via more customized offerings, expanding their network of providers, enabling faster access to therapies, and offering ever-increasing options for different plan structures. This competitiveness, among other influences, has also facilitated innovation in medical technology, drug availability, and speed to access many types of specialized care that far surpass the rest of the world.

In the commercial insurance space, success hinges on appealing to employers. These employers evaluate insurers based on plan design, provider networks, administrative simplicity, and ultimately, affordability. For government-sponsored programs like MA and PDPs, insurers compete directly for patients. Their success depends on offering better value than both traditional Medicare and competing MA and PDP plans, which has driven the bundling of additional services such as vision, dental, and wellness benefits, coupled with responsive customer support and simplified access to care. Strong performance in quality ratings (like CMS Star Ratings) also boosts credibility, helping attract and retain enrollees.

Another factor impacting payer decision-making in the US insurance system is the rate of commercial patients switching among employer-based/private insurers

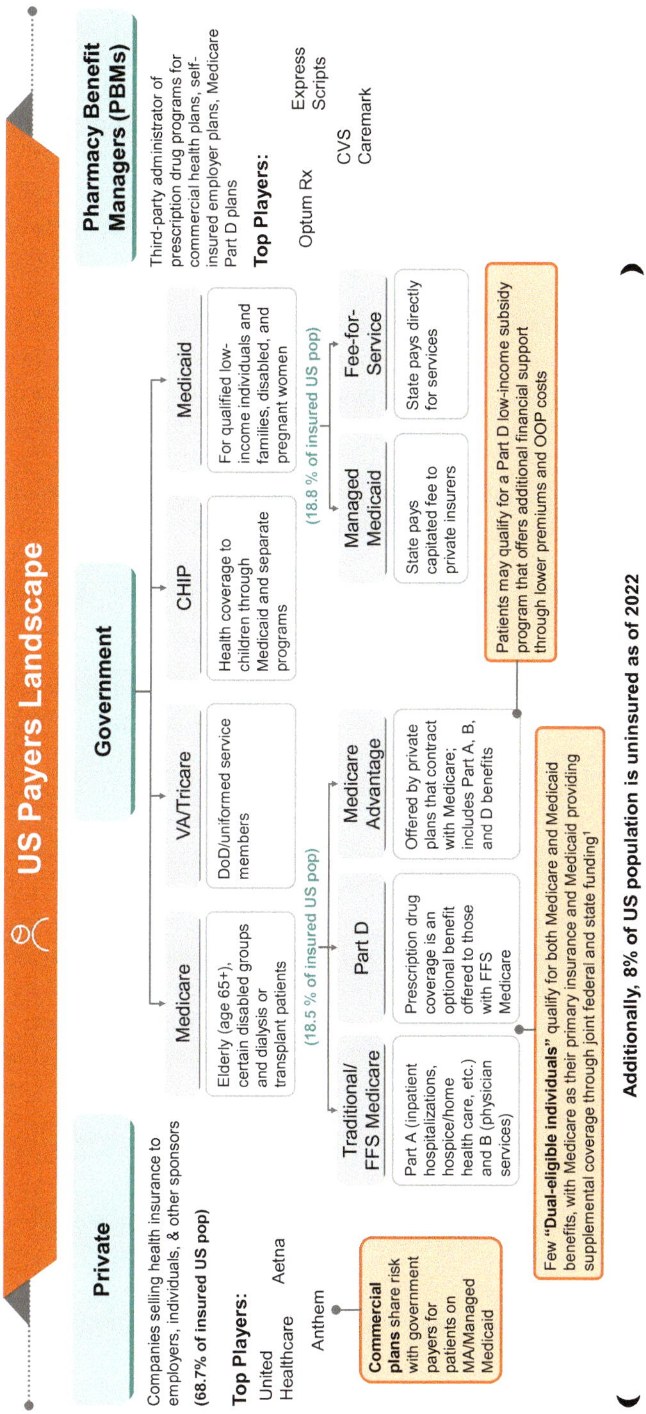

Figure 4.2 US payer landscape

Source: Congressional Research Service; Kaiser Family Foundation.

every few years. The annual turnover or switch rate was assessed as 21.5% in a study spanning 2006–2018.[5] This dynamic often is cited by payers as a reason to focus more on short-term outcomes and costs as opposed to a longer-term view in their formulary policy and management—although interestingly, that same study saw that a third of those patients returned to the original insurer in the following five years.

Insurer incentives ripple across the entire healthcare ecosystem, shaping the behavior of providers, how their services are reimbursed and, through this, how services are priced and delivered. To manage risk and control spending, insurers dictate payment models, set coverage rules, and influence clinical decision-making through tools like prior authorization and utilization reviews. This drives providers to align with insurer priorities—often emphasizing cost-effectiveness, efficiency, and quality metrics. It also impacts how pharmaceuticals are priced and accessed, as insurers and pharmacy benefit managers (PBMs) negotiate drug formularies and rebates. Ultimately, payers wield substantial influence in determining what care gets delivered, how it's delivered, and who can access it—making them central architects of the modern US healthcare experience.

How payers influence healthcare delivery

Of course, payers don't just process claims. They are also responsible for controlling healthcare costs. Healthcare costs in the United States have skyrocketed every year, rising to what once would have been considered an unprecedented level of spending. As of 2022, US healthcare spending soared to $4.5 trillion, translating to an average of $13,493 per person. Further illustrating this exponential growth: the proportion of healthcare spending relative to the size of the economy has surged from 5% of the GDP in 1962 to 17% in 2022.[6]

Various strategies have been attempted to keep escalating healthcare costs under control. Unfortunately, while each of these approaches and strategies tried to solve existing problems, each introduced new shortcomings of its own. Payers have adopted a multi-pronged strategy to manage these costs while simultaneously striving to improve health outcomes. Some of these strategies include:

- **Vertical integration:** Private payers increasingly engage in vertical integration by acquiring or partnering with healthcare providers, PBMs, and care delivery platforms. This integration is designed to increase coordination across the care continuum, support unified patient records, and allow payers to manage cost and quality more directly.
- **Market expansion:** To sustain financial viability and scale, insurers are expanding their enrollment base through more types of employer-sponsored plans, individual market offerings, and public-private collaborations like

MA. This horizontal growth helps distribute risk and improve bargaining power within the healthcare ecosystem.

- **Driving patients to alternative sites of care:** To reduce reliance on high-cost hospital care, private insurers are promoting the use of lower-cost sites such as ambulatory surgical centers, retail clinics, and home-based care. These care settings usually offer comparable clinical outcomes while improving patient accessibility and reducing system-wide expenditures.
- **Member engagement:** Recognizing the critical role of member behavior in health outcomes, payers are investing in digital engagement platforms, personalized wellness programs, and incentive-driven health behavior strategies. These initiatives aim to increase accountability and support preventive care utilization.

All these strategies notwithstanding, the most important tools payers use are utilization management (UM), diagnostic resource group (DRG) payments, and value-based care (VBC).

In the past, most healthcare was paid for under a system called fee-for-service (FFS)—basically, the provider was paid for each service performed, each drug used, etc. Critics have identified FFS, which incentivizes volume over value, as a significant contributor to the rising cost of healthcare. UM aims to prevent providers from delivering care that isn't medically necessary and steer patients toward less expensive care options when available.

UM is imperfect, however. What defines "medical necessity" is often a matter of judgment, and it's possible for reasonable people to disagree on any particular treatment. Additionally, the administrative overhead required to implement a comprehensive system of UM is significant. In response, payers and policymakers are shifting toward cost-containment mechanisms such as DRG payments and VBC. In essence, the goal of these new payment models is to shift the decision on how to control costs onto the provider. With a DRG payment, a provider receives a fixed payment for a particular diagnosis and is then responsible for deciding how that money is allocated to providing care (and keeping any remainder as profit). Usually in VBC, the mechanism compares the cost and outcomes to a reasonable baseline (though there are various ways this baseline can be defined) and then rewards the provider for any cost savings and sometimes penalizes them for cost overruns.

Utilization management: Deciding what is necessity

UM aims to curtail medical services overuse by ensuring patients receive appropriate treatment at the right time and cost. UM tools influence how, when, and what care patients receive to strike a balance between cost control and appropriate care delivery, but they are often debated in terms of transparency, administrative burden, and patient access. Key UM tools (see Figure 4.3) have been described in the following sections.

Major Types of Utilization Management Tools

Tool	Description
Prior Authorization	Requires providers to request approval before a payer will cover medication
Step Therapy	Requires patients to try a lower-cost drug before "stepping up" to a more expensive one
Formulary Exclusion	Not paying for one product to encourage use of other(s)
Tiering	Increases the relative financial burden on patient for less preferred products
Quantity Limits	Control over how often or the amount you can get filled at once
Stop Criteria	Coverage is stopped after specified time if defined response criteria are not met

Figure 4.3 Utilization management tools

Prior authorization
This requires healthcare providers to obtain approval from the insurer before proceeding with specific treatments or medications. This is used to verify medical necessity and prevent misuse or overuse.

Step therapy
This, also called "fail first," requires patients to try more cost-effective treatments before "stepping up" to more expensive or newer medications. The insurer will approve the next level of treatment only if initial therapies fail.

Formulary exclusion
Certain medications may be excluded from a payer's formulary, meaning they are not covered except for rare cases that require special approval. This usually applies to drugs deemed too expensive relative to their clinical value or where alternatives exist.

Tiering
Medications are grouped into cost tiers based on factors such as brand versus generic status, clinical effectiveness, and cost. Lower-tier drugs have lower co-pays, encouraging use of more affordable treatments.

Quantity limits
Payers may impose limits on the amount of medication a patient can receive within a certain time period. This helps prevent overuse, abuse, or unnecessary stockpiling.

Stop criteria
Defined stopping rules are set for certain medications or treatments based on treatment duration or patient response. If specific benchmarks are not met, coverage may be withdrawn.

Each of the tools listed above can be applied during various types of reviews by the payer:

- **Prospective review:** Completed before the treatment, prospective reviews assess the necessity of procedures to prevent duplicate or ineffective treatments. This allows the payer to intervene to prevent delivery of care they do not approve (and thus don't want to pay for).
- **Concurrent review:** Monitors patient treatment in real time to manage resources and track progress, reducing coverage denials. Key aspects of concurrent review include:
  - Care coordination: Ensures the synchronization of a patient's care across multiple providers or specialists.
  - Discharge planning: Identifies the necessary milestones for a patient to be eligible for hospital discharge.

  - Care transition: Facilitates the patient's move from one level of care to another, such as transitioning from short-term to long-term nursing care.
- **Retrospective review:** Conducted after treatment, retrospective reviews evaluate the appropriateness and effectiveness of procedures. This is perceived as crucial for insurance claims, ensuring reimbursement accuracy and addressing denied claims.

For insurers, the primary goal of UM is cost containment by ensuring healthcare services are medically necessary, evidence-based, and appropriately delivered. By minimizing overuse of high-cost or low-value care, UM helps mitigate financial risk and maintain the sustainability of insurance plans. It also enables insurers to analyze utilization patterns, refine benefit designs, and proactively manage high-risk cases through data-driven interventions, as well as support the creation or refinement of future UM policies. UM supports patients by promoting necessary and effective care while helping providers align with standardized, evidence-based guidelines to improve clinical efficiency.

Pitfalls: Prior authorization challenges

Prior authorization processes are perceived as burdensome and tedious. Physicians often face frustrating and time-consuming paperwork when seeking prior authorization for effective treatments. The complexity can significantly impact a doctor's ability to treat more patients effectively. Pharmaceutical companies invest significantly in patient access schemes to mitigate the challenges posed by prior authorization. These streamline the approval process, ensuring timely access to medications. By reducing administrative burdens and enhancing patient support, companies aim to improve treatment adherence and patient outcomes while navigating the complexities of insurance requirements.

- Delays in care linked to prior authorization are reported by **94%** of physicians, according to the latest AMA prior authorization physician survey
- **80%** of physicians indicate that prior authorization occasionally results in treatment abandonment
- **33%** of physicians acknowledge that prior authorization has resulted in a serious adverse event for a patient under their care, with 9% reporting cases leading to permanent bodily harm, disability, or death[7]

DRG: Letting providers decide

The DRG system of payment categorizes inpatient costs based on diagnosis, comorbidities, procedure, and other patient factors. Under this system, each patient is assigned a specific DRG code, which represents a clinically coherent group of diagnoses and procedures that require similar healthcare resources and are used to determine the amount of reimbursement a hospital will receive for treating a particular patient. With the DRG system, hospitals gain an incentive to collectively manage patients' clinical journeys and associated costs within reasonable limits.

Similar to DRGs, bundled payments—also known as episode-of-care payments—extend this concept to outpatient and procedural settings. Under bundled payment models, a single, predetermined payment covers all services related to a specific treatment or condition over a defined period (e.g., joint replacement surgery with 90 days of post-acute care). Like DRGs, it incentivizes providers to coordinate care, avoid unnecessary services, and reduce complications, as financial outcomes are directly tied to the quality and efficiency of care across the entire episode.

The major advantage of DRG payments from the payer perspective is that they provide a strong incentive to deliver care with maximum efficiency. Every dollar spent wastefully is a dollar of lost profit for the provider, putting the financial gain and loss directly on the same group responsible for making the decisions. This is in direct contrast to FFS payments, where the care decision is made by a provider who often stands to make more money if care is provided wastefully (since they are paid regardless).

The disadvantage of DRG payments is that they provide a strong disincentive to innovation. If the standard of care for a given diagnosis is stable, then it makes sense to fully focus on efficiency, and DRG payments work well. What, however, if the standard of care is improving? If a new treatment method offers much faster recovery, far fewer side effects, and/or less risk of complications, one would reasonably expect it to be more expensive than the old treatment. In this case, a provider adopting the new treatment would need to fully absorb the additional cost for the innovation, since the DRG payment is fixed. It should be noted the opposite is also true: If a new technology reduces the cost of delivering the standard of care for a given diagnosis, payers will not quickly reduce their own costs as the provider will capture the savings. Some mechanisms are in place to mitigate this, such as periodically revising DRG payments to account for changing costs. Additionally, mechanisms such as Medicare's new technology add-on payment (NTAP) create additional payments when some innovations are used partially to offset a provider's additional costs. All these methods, however, are imperfect.

For example, inpatient stays involving CAR-T treatment are categorized under MS-DRG 018, with a base reimbursement rate of $247,939. Currently, hospitals receive additional payments for three products with NTAP status due to their high costs: Tecartus, Abecma, and Carvykti—for example, Carvykti launched at a price of $465,000 per patient[8]. However, NTAP coverage is capped at a maximum of 65% of the product cost and varies based on the hospital's case cost relative to the MS-DRG payment. Outlier payments cover exceptionally costly cases, but even with these adjustments, Medicare reimbursement for CAR-T cases often falls short of covering total hospital costs.

As a result, the provider will incur some financial penalty for adopting a more costly innovation, no matter how much better that innovation is for the patient. This creates a large risk of discouraging innovation and is much more serious than the opposite risk to payers of not benefiting from new cost-saving innovations. In the case where a cheaper new technology becomes available, providers will adopt that technology to achieve high profits for a time, then the DRG payment will eventually be revised and profits will return to normal. Alternatively, if adopting a new treatment that creates better outcomes but is more expensive creates a large financial loss for a hospital, there is a significant danger that technology will not be adopted at all.

Moving toward VBC: Fixing the problems of DRG

The VBC model focuses on rewarding healthcare providers for delivering high-quality, coordinated care that improves patient outcomes instead of reimbursing based on the volume of services as in FFS. It is designed to reduce or eliminate the disincentive for innovation created by DRG payments while providing a more flexible framework that can be applied to a wider variety of healthcare interactions (i.e., when the standard of care is not easily defined or when a patient is receiving outpatient or clinic care across multiple diagnoses).

VBC encompasses variations in risk-sharing among payers, providers, and patients, and prioritizes patient-centric care and wellness over quantity of services (see Figure 4.4).

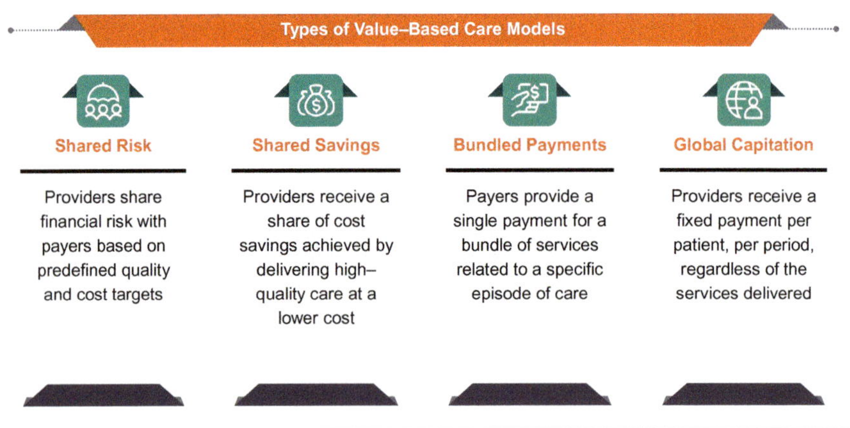

Figure 4.4 Value-based care models

Fast fact

To advance and accelerate value-based payment reform in the US healthcare system, CMS announced its intention to have 100% of original Medicare patients enrolled in accountable care organizations by 2030.[9]

More than 700,000 healthcare providers and organizations will participate in at least one of the three initiatives: the Medicare Shared Savings Program (MSSP) and two CMS Innovation Center accountable care model tests.[10]

By shifting the focus from quantity to quality and outcomes, the model aims to improve overall health outcomes and enhance patient satisfaction by promoting preventive measures and early detection. Effective care coordination is expected to minimize unnecessary hospitalization and resource-intensive interventions, optimizing healthcare resources and reducing overall expenditures. The philosophy behind this is that innovation that leads to better care can reduce costs at the same time.

While the ideas behind VBC are laudable, expert analysis has shown mixed results. A long-term analysis of patients treated in an MSSP (one of the early types of Medicare VBC programs) found a reduction of $234 in annual spend in year three, a $584 reduction in year six, and an overall savings to Medicare of between $4.1 and $8.1 billion.[11] This sounds like a lot of money until you realize overall Medicare spending was $1,029.8 billion in 2023 and growing at 8.1% per year[12]—so all that effort led to less than 1% savings, setting cost growth back by maybe two months (if we are generous). A similar analysis on another Medicare program, the Oncology Care Model, suggested savings varied between $200 and $400 over a course of treatment, depending on cancer type, but noted the cost of administering the program largely consumed these savings.[13]

Notwithstanding the underwhelming impact of VBC on cost control, it has had a huge impact on the operations of healthcare providers in the United States. We will discuss this in greater detail in the providers chapter.

Evolving toward an ever-expanding mandate

Payers sit at the heart of the US healthcare ecosystem—not just as financial services, but as influential architects of how care is accessed, priced, and prioritized. Over time, payers have evolved into powerful stakeholders that influence provider behavior, negotiate drug pricing, administer public programs, and design value-driven payment models. Their decisions ripple across the system, impacting government budgets, provider margins, employer-sponsored coverage strategies, and overall health system efficiency. Hence, payers must play a constructive, transparent, and collaborative role. The future demands more than reactive compliance or profit maximization; it requires stewardship. Whether it's through better data sharing, aligned incentives with providers, or thoughtful participation in public programs, payers must reimagine their role from gatekeepers to enablers of a more integrated and sustainable healthcare system.

Payers are already expanding their role in direct service delivery, offering integrated care options that combine medical, behavioral, and even social support services. Simultaneously, payers are leveraging data and analytics to improve member engagement—identifying high-risk patients, personalizing interventions, and closing care gaps to improve outcomes.

In the Medicaid space, payers have begun addressing social determinants of health more intentionally, recognizing housing, food security, and education are just as vital to health outcomes as clinical care. Innovative pilot programs are testing the integration of these services into benefit designs, particularly for vulnerable populations. Meanwhile, the specialty insurance markets—such as coverage for high-cost gene therapies or rare diseases—continue to challenge traditional cost-sharing and utilization strategies. In response, payers are exploring cost-containment tools, including outcomes-based contracting and reinsurance models, to maintain sustainability while ensuring access to breakthrough treatments.

As these trends converge, payers sit at a critical intersection of financial stewardship and care transformation. How they balance innovation, regulation, and member trust will define their relevance and resilience in the future and continue to have a strong influence on how patients are cared for across the country.

Notes

1 Field, M. J., & Shapiro, H. T. (Eds.). (1993). *Employment and health benefits: A connection at risk*. National Academies Press, Washington, DC.

2 Morrisey, M. A. (n.d.). *Health Insurance*. Health Administration Press, Association of University Programs in Health Administration (AUPHA) Press. (page 10).

3 *U.S. Health Insurance Industry Analysis Report*. (n.d.). National Association of Insurance Commissioners (NAIC).

4 Centers for Medicare & Medicaid Services (CMS) data.

5 Fang, H., Frean, M., Sylwestrzak, G., & Ukert, B. (2022). Trends in Disenrollment and Reenrollment Within US Commercial Health Insurance Plans, 2006–2018. *JAMA Network Open* 5(2):e220320.

6 Centers for Medicare & Medicaid Services (CMS) data; *Why are Americans paying more for healthcare?* (2024). Peter G. Peterson Foundation.

7 Robeznieks, A., (2023). *Once just a burden, prior authorization has become a nightmare*. American Medical Association.

8 Jaber, N. (2022). *Carvykti approval marks second CAR T-cell therapy for multiple myeloma*. National Cancer Institute.

9 Fowler, L., Rawal, P., Fogler, S., Waldersen, B., O'Connell, M., & Quinton, J. (2022). *The CMS Innovation Center's strategy to support person-centered, value-based specialty care*. Centers for Medicare & Medicaid Services.

10 *CMS announces increase in 2023 in organizations and beneficiaries benefiting from coordinated care in accountable care relationship.* (2023). Centers for Medicare & Medicaid Services.
11 Bond, A. M., Civelek, Y., Schpero, W. L., Casalino, L. P., Zhang, M., Pierre, R., & Khullar, D. (2025). Long-term spending of accountable care organizations in the Medicare Shared Savings Program. *JAMA* 333(21):1897–1905.
12 NHE Fact Sheet. (n.d.). Centers for Medicare & Medicaid Services (CMS).
13 Walker, B., Frytak, J., & Hayes, J. (2020). Evaluation of practice patterns among oncologists participating in the oncology care model. *JAMA Network Open* 3(5):e205165.

Chapter 5

Organized Providers

Patient Care at Scale

Matt Ruple and Joe Stevens

In the healthcare system, a "provider" is any individual or organization delivering medical services to patients. From independent physicians, nurse practitioners, and therapists, to large hospitals and specialty clinics, their primary role is diagnosing, treating, and supporting patients through direct clinical care. In this chapter, we will discuss:

- How providers have evolved into larger and larger organizations
- The types of providers most common in the United States
- Which factors drive large, organized providers' strategic decisions
- How the need to succeed as a business influences how these groups are structured and how they deliver care

Evolution of organized healthcare providers

Organized providers are groups of healthcare professionals and facilities that coordinate the delivery of patient-care services through a professional management structure and specialized administrative roles. This is in contrast to small practices, where administrative decisions are made by one or more physicians who spend most of their time on patient care. Organized providers' structure can be either legal (i.e., one corporation) or operational (i.e., a loose affiliation

DOI: 10.4324/9781003603597-5

of multiple organizations working together). Organized providers range from small group practices to massive health systems, but they strive to integrate some facets of people, processes, and technology to provide care more efficiently than fragmented solo arrangements.[1] These organizations usually attempt to serve as their own small healthcare *ecosystem*, aligning the patient's journey across different care settings (e.g., clinics, hospitals, labs) rather than each working in silos.

Organized provider systems have largely emerged because the complexity and costs of modern healthcare have outgrown the capabilities of the solo physician practice. Over the past few decades, delivering quality care has increasingly required expensive infrastructure—such as electronic health records (EHRs) and diagnostic equipment—along with teams of support staff and the ability to navigate complex insurance and regulatory demands. Small practices often struggle to manage these burdens alone. However, by organizing into larger groups or networks, providers can share overhead costs, centralize administrative functions, and invest in capabilities like data systems and care coordinators—resources that would be out of reach of individual physicians.[2] Larger organizations also gain greater leverage when negotiating with payers (and, more recently, directly with employers), helping them secure higher reimbursement rates and better contract terms than a solo practitioner could achieve. In short, organized provider systems arose to achieve economies of scale and scope—making healthcare delivery more cost-effective and easier to manage.

Another driving factor is the shift toward the value-based care (VBC) model, which rewards quality and outcomes over volume. As detailed in the chapter discussing payers, the Centers for Medicare and Medicaid Services (CMS) has spearheaded VBC innovation pilots over the last 10+ years to shift more care from fee-for-service to value-based payment models. Programs like Medicare's Accountable Care Organizations (ACOs)[3] and the Medicare Access and CHIP Reauthorization Act (MACRA)[4] payment reforms of 2015 explicitly encourage providers to coordinate across settings and take on population health management. A solo practitioner would struggle to succeed in these models, which require tracking extensive quality metrics and sometimes accepting financial risk for patient cost overruns. Larger, organized entities are better equipped to bear risk and meet value-based goals since they can pool patient populations and expertise. For instance, under the Affordable Care Act (ACA), many providers formed ACOs to align hospitals, primary care, and specialists—an effort that enhances care integration by aligning operational, clinical, and financial incentives across participants.

This chapter examines the different types of organized providers, their organizational objectives, and the financial incentives that shape their decisions. It concludes by introducing a framework for understanding how these factors come together to influence the evolution of provider organizations.

Types of organized provider organizations

Organized healthcare providers come in many forms and sizes, each with its own structure and purpose (see Figure 5.1). It is important to note that these forms are not mutually exclusive.

For instance, a hospital within a health system might also be a federally qualified health center (FQHC) or an academic medical center (**AMC**). Some of the key types of provider organizations within the US system are:

- **Group practices:** The simplest form of organized providers, where multiple physicians band together to share office space, staff, and business operations. Group practices can be single-specialty (e.g., Florida Cancer) or multispecialty—a mix of primary care and specialists under one practice entity. By pooling resources, group practitioners split fixed costs and benefit from mutual support. As of 2020, single-specialty group practices accounted for the largest share of US physicians (about 42.6%), far outnumbering those in solo practice.[5] These groups often negotiate collectively with insurers and can offer patients expanded services or extended hours compared with a solo office, as well as hire more specialized staff in areas such as finance or practice operations. However, decision-making in these practices is typically less centralized than in other organized provider models, with each physician operating independently within the practice.
- **Clinically integrated networks (CINs):** A CIN is a legal affiliation of healthcare providers—independent physician practices, clinics, and sometimes hospitals—that come together to improve quality and coordinate care for a defined population without fully merging into a single entity. Participants in a CIN agree on performance goals, share data, and implement clinical protocols collaboratively. This structure enables the network to negotiate contracts with payers as a unified group, often to pursue VBC arrangements. CIN allows independent providers to act together to enhance care and efficiency while maintaining autonomy.[6] To comply with antitrust law, CINs must demonstrate active collaboration focused on quality and not just price-setting. In 2009, the Federal Trade Commission (FTC) issued guidance to ensure CINs facilitate care coordination—a key objective of the ACA—without engaging in anticompetitive behavior. Today, CINs have become a launching pad for providers seeking benefits from integration (shared IT, care management) without an outright merger. For instance, a regional CIN might enable community physicians and a local hospital to jointly manage diabetic patients under a unified care plan, sharing in any savings from better outcomes. An example of a CIN is Advocate Physician Partners.

Figure 5.1 Types of provider organizations within the US health system

- **Integrated delivery networks (IDNs):** An IDN is a fully integrated network of healthcare facilities and providers operating under one parent organization. IDNs typically include hospitals, outpatient clinics, primary and specialty care offices, perhaps labs, pharmacies, and often an insurance plan or close partnership with an insurer. The goal is to provide a *"continuum of health care services"* under one umbrella.[7] By design, an IDN is a self-contained health system that can serve most patient needs internally—from preventive care to hospitalization to rehabilitation—coordinating each transition. Classic examples are Kaiser Permanente (which combines hospitals, medical groups, and a health plan) and large regional systems such as Intermountain Healthcare or University of Pittsburgh Medical Center. These organizations pursue logical integration instead of fragmentation, aiming to streamline referrals, unify electronic records, and promote population health management across their network. IDNs became more common as hospitals merged and acquired other care settings. Many IDNs adopt a variation on this model called Integrated Payer-Provider Networks (IPPN) or "Payvider," which is a healthcare system (IDN) where the payer (insurance provider) and the healthcare provider operate under one organizational structure. This model integrates the financing and delivery of healthcare services to improve care coordination, reduce costs, and enhance patient outcomes. IDNs have largely become IPPNs to hedge risk from traditional revenue sources. By the 2010s, the largest health systems in the United States each owned dozens of hospitals and hundreds of clinics.[8] However, IDNs can also command significant market power, which has raised concerns.
- **Academic Medical Centers (AMCs):** AMCs are healthcare organizations that integrate patient care, medical education, and research. According to the American Association of Medical Colleges, AMCs are anchored by a medical school and affiliated teaching hospitals, where they serve as hubs for training future healthcare professionals, conducting groundbreaking research, and delivering advanced medical care. AMCs are distinct from other healthcare providers due to their dual mission of education and research alongside patient care. They often handle complex tertiary and quaternary care, such as organ transplants and experimental treatments, while also serving as safety-net providers for underserved populations. Massachusetts General Hospital is an example of an AMC.
- **Academic health systems (AHSs):** An AHS is an extension of an AMC model encompassing broader clinical operations. These systems include networks of hospitals, faculty practice groups, outpatient clinics, and other entities organized to deliver coordinated care across multiple sites. They are increasingly oriented toward population health management, with the goal to improve health outcomes on a larger scale. Historically, many AMCs

operated as standalone teaching hospitals. However, in response to financial pressures and the evolving healthcare landscape, they have increasingly joined or formed larger health systems to remain competitive while preserving their academic focus. It is common for an AHS to also be an IDN.

- **Government-operated health providers:** The US government runs several organized healthcare systems (either directly or indirectly) serving specific populations:
  - **Veterans Health Administration (VA):** The VA operates the nation's largest integrated healthcare system, encompassing 170 medical centers and more than 1,000 outpatient sites across the country. It provides comprehensive care to more than 9 million enrolled military veterans. As a fully public health system, the VA both employs its physicians and owns its hospitals, functioning as a highly organized and centralized provider network. Established to ensure lifelong access to care for veterans, the VA's scale enables it to implement system-wide initiatives—such as unified EHRs across all facilities—that often serve as models for private healthcare systems.
  - **Indian health service (IHS):** The IHS provides healthcare to American Indians and Alaska Natives. According to the IHS, its network includes 43 hospitals, 383 health centers, and 101 health stations across 37 states, serving approximately 2.8 million individuals from 574 federally recognized tribes.[9]
  - **Federally Qualified Health Centers (FQHCs):** FQHCs are nonprofit community health centers that receive federal funding and designation to provide primary care in underserved areas. They form a national network of safety-net clinics that is highly organized through government support and oversight. As of 2023, more than 31 million people (about one in 10 Americans) relied on FQHCs for care.[10] These centers are patient-governed, offer sliding fee scales, and provide comprehensive services. Collectively, FQHCs and similar clinics comprise roughly 1,400 organizations operating at more than 14,000 sites. These exemplify organized care focused on health equity, often integrating medical, dental, and behavioral health services under one roof for vulnerable populations.
  - **Department of Defense (DoD) Healthcare System:** The DoD supports approximately 1.32 million active-duty military personnel, as well as their families, retirees, and reserve members, through the Military Health System. This system includes military treatment facilities, TRICARE health plans, and partnerships with civilian providers to ensure comprehensive medical care.
- **Specialized service provider organizations:** Not all organized healthcare providers are general health systems or clinics; some specialize in particular services nationwide. Two notable examples include:

- **Large dialysis organizations (LDOs):** Companies such as DaVita and Fresenius Medical Care operate extensive chains of dialysis clinics that treat patients with end-stage kidney disease. Dialysis is a niche but life-sustaining service, typically requiring visits up to three times per week. Over time, this sector consolidated heavily. By 2020, just two firms—DaVita and Fresenius—owned approximately 75% of US outpatient dialysis centers,[11] making them one of the most consolidated segments in healthcare. These LDOs are organized providers spanning all 50 states, operating hundreds of clinics under unified management. Their scale provides efficiencies in supply procurement and clinic operations; however, their size has raised concerns. Research found that after independent dialysis centers were acquired by large chains, patient outcomes worsened—hospitalization rates increased, survival rates declined modestly, and transplant referrals dropped.[12] Research has noted a strong focus on profit maximization in dialysis centers may have unintended negative consequences on patient care, potentially leading to increased hospitalization rates and lower transplant referrals. This example highlights both the power and peril of organized provider monopolies in a specialized field.
- **Home infusion therapy providers:** These organizations administer intravenous medications to patients at home or in outpatient infusion centers, rather than in a hospital. The availability of complex biologic drugs has widened the network of home infusion industry. The largest player, Option Care Health, describes itself as "the nation's largest independent provider of home and alternate site infusion services," with more than 7,500 employees and hundreds of pharmacy infusion centers.[13] These organizations coordinate with physicians to provide therapies for chronic conditions—antibiotics, nutrition, and immunotherapy—safely outside the hospital. As hospitals seek to outsource or partner on infusion services, which can be resource-intensive, these specialized providers have consolidated to negotiate better drug prices and standardize protocols across their networks.

Mission and goals of organized providers: An ever-increasing list of "aims"

Organized providers usually emphasize their mission of achieving broad healthcare goals. These goals are captured in the evolution from the "Triple Aim" to the "Quadruple Aim" and, more recently, the "Quintuple Aim." Understanding these aims helps clarify what organized systems strive to achieve.

The concept of Triple Aim, introduced by Donald Berwick et al., signifies three interdependent goals for optimizing health system performance: improving the patient care experience, improving the health of populations, and reducing per-capita costs.[14] In other words, care should be effective and satisfying for individuals, proactive in enhancing public health, and efficiently delivered to eliminate waste. Organized provider systems are often seen as a key integrator to achieve the Triple Aim—Berwick noted that an organization must accept responsibility for all three aims for a defined population.[15]

For example, an ACO or integrated health system can coordinate preventive, acute, and chronic care, whereas siloed providers might only optimize one component, leading to a suboptimal outcome on the others. The Triple Aim framework has guided many health system strategies and has been frequently referenced by health system executives (either implicitly or explicitly) when describing their goals. The premise is that these aims are synergistic when managed well: better population health can lower costs and a good care experience can improve adherence and outcomes. However, balancing all three is challenging, and some efforts have overemphasized cost reduction (due to financial pressure) or patient experience (due to market competition) without equal progress in population health. Still, the Triple Aim remains a foundational compass for organized care delivery, frequently referenced in mission statements, strategic plans, and discussions within the industry.

Additional aims have been added over the years. The Quadruple Aim emerged about six years later as healthcare leaders realized a critical element was missing: the well-being of the healthcare workforce. By 2014, burnout among physicians and nurses had reached alarming levels, partly due to the stressors of increased productivity demands, EHR documentation, and system changes. This addition acknowledges that without a satisfied, engaged, and resilient workforce, the other three aims suffer—unhappy, burned-out providers can lead to worse patient experiences, increased medical errors (hurting outcomes), and higher staff turnover (which is costly). The Quadruple Aim reframes the issue of provider burnout and morale as a quality imperative: A health system should aim to be a great place to work, not just a great place to receive care.

When this idea entered industry parlance around 2014, it was quickly embraced by many organized providers. Large health systems started appointing Chief Wellness Officers and implemented "joy in work" initiatives, recognizing employee experience had been historically neglected in improvement efforts. The logic was simple: Achieving the Triple Aim was proving difficult in practice, partly because the people delivering care were under immense strain.[16] In a sense, the fourth aim eclipses the others if not met—you can't have happy patients with miserable providers. This was a tacit admission that employee experience had long been an afterthought—historically, healthcare improvement efforts led by "bean counting administrators" focused on efficiency and patient outcomes, assuming clinicians would "do their job" regardless of personal toll.

The Quintuple Aim is the most recent evolution, pushing the framework further by explicitly adding health equity as a fifth aim. This shift emerged in response to persistent and glaring disparities in health outcomes among different populations, brought into sharp focus during the COVID-19 pandemic. While the original Triple Aim emphasized population health, it was often pursued in aggregate—measuring average improvements that sometimes masked gaps between subgroups. It became clear that one could achieve better overall outcomes yet still leave minority or marginalized communities behind, *unless equity was deliberately targeted.* In 2021-2022, thought leaders, including Dr. Kedar Mate and Dr. Lloyd Minor, and publications such as JAMA called for elevating equity to the same level as the other aims.[17] This means making the elimination of disparities a stated goal alongside cost, quality, patient experience, and provider well-being.

Health equity as the fifth aim means designing care improvements specifically to reduce disparities—for instance, tailoring interventions to high-risk groups, addressing social determinants, and involving community voices in care design. This is now driving organized providers to stratify quality data by race, ethnicity, socioeconomic status, geography, age, disability, and many other factors. They then use this data to drive investment in community health initiatives; and set specific equity targets (such as closing gaps in blood pressure control or maternal mortality). While this fifth aim has become a priority, many systems still struggle to deliver on these goals and continue to seek better interventions to make the needed impact.

Most large provider organizations today publicly commit to, at a minimum, the first three aims and are at least thinking about the other two. For instance, a health system may have a strategic plan that mentions "achieving the Triple Aim and becoming an employer of choice for our staff, while eliminating health inequities in our region"—essentially embracing all five aims. These frameworks serve as a narrative guide and performance checklist for organized providers. They also highlight *why* providers organize: It is arguably easier to pursue such ambitious, interconnected goals as a coordinated group than in isolation. A fragmented set of solo practitioners could hardly take responsibility for a community's health outcomes or their own collective burnout, or societal inequities. But an organized system with professional, dedicated leadership can set up programs to tackle each aim: for example, implementing patient experience training (aim 1), launching public health outreach (aim 2), adopting lean cost reduction (aim 3), creating wellness resources for staff (aim 4), and partnering with community organizations to address social needs (aim 5).

The ultimate promise of organized provider systems is that by being integrated and mission-driven, they can simultaneously improve care experiences, outcomes, cost-effectiveness, staff morale, *and* equity in ways that disjointed care cannot. Whether they fulfill this promise is one of the major ongoing stories of US healthcare reform.

Balancing lofty ambitions with the realities of business

Regardless of which version of the "aims" a health system follows, achieving these goals requires creating a large organization with many skilled employees, building expensive facilities, and equipping those facilities with costly equipment and technology. All of this requires substantial investment, and investors typically require a financial return. Healthcare has also consistently been the largest employer in the United States[18] and represents a significant portion of the economy. As a result, the business of healthcare—that is, ensuring revenue meets and hopefully exceeds costs—is a major driver of organizational strategy and decision-making in health systems.

Unfortunately, evidence suggests many health systems are not all that good at this. Excluding the volatile COVID-19 years, hospitals generally have an aggregate operating margin of only around 6%. Additionally, there is a wide distribution around this average with an amazing 39% of hospitals having *negative* operating margin in 2023.[19] These negative margins aren't necessarily the result of bad management. Low-margin hospitals tend to be small (low market share), rural, and/or high-Medicaid-share institutions, none of which are highly controllable by institutional leadership. However, it's undeniable that how to achieve and maintain a positive operating margin is a large driver of institutional decision-making. Unsurprisingly, high prices are a key driver of high operating margins. Thus, to understand how provider organizations behave, we must understand the drivers of how and how much they get paid.

How health systems get paid

The vast majority of revenue generated by a health system comes from payment for the services these health systems provide to patients. However, how those services are paid for depends on both the type of care being received and the type of service provided. At a high level, the types of fees a health system might receive can be thought of in the categories in Figure 5.2.

Facility fee
A charge for the use of the site and equipment provided by the health system. This is always collected by the health system (or other facility).

Professional fees (procedures and office visits)
The fee for an actual procedure performed on a patient. It can be received by the health system where the physician is employed or by the physician directly if they are in private practice but using health system facilities.

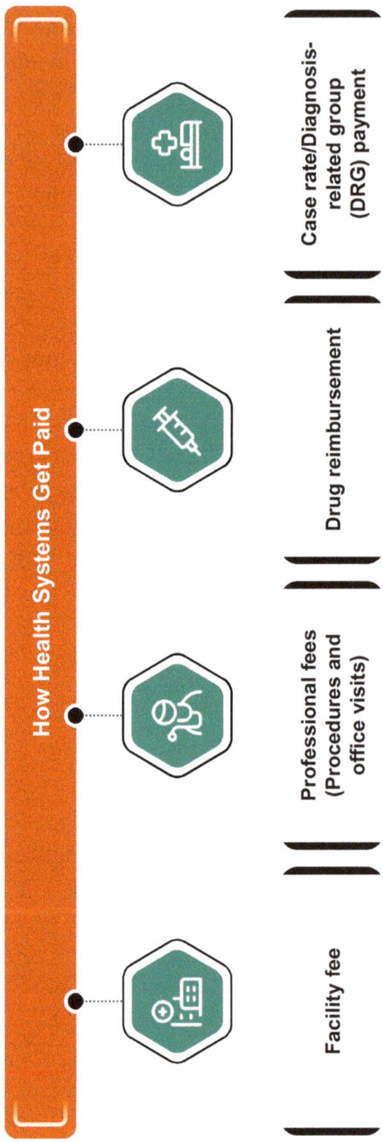

Figure 5.2 Types of fees health systems can receive

Drug reimbursement
Revenue from some of the drugs dispensed to patients. When a health system bills a patient and/or their insurance for a drug, the system can usually bill the price it paid for the drug plus a dispensing fee that the system keeps.

Case rate/diagnosis-related group **(DRG) payment**
Certain well-defined procedures—such as some organ transplants or some types of orthopedic surgery—are reimbursed at a fixed negotiated rate called a "case rate." Most inpatient hospital stays are also paid at a fixed per-day rate based on the diagnosis for which the patient was admitted, known as a DRG payment. This is a single payment designed to cover all charges for a given treatment (i.e., drugs, facility use, and procedures performed).

All else being equal, health systems prefer to be paid more

The structure of payments is important because a large part of succeeding financially as a health system is, of course, maximizing the revenue you generate under each of the above payment types. In turn, each of these payment types creates incentives for health system management that we must understand to adequately explain their behavior.

More facilities mean more facility fees
The renting of health care facilities through facility fees is probably the most straightforward health system business model and leads to the most straightforward outcome: Getting more facilities means serving more patients in more places and generating more fees. Additionally, larger health systems can usually negotiate higher fees for the same facility than smaller systems or individual hospitals. As a result, a large health system can often improve the profitability of a smaller facility—such as an ambulatory surgery center—simply by acquiring it and putting it under the corporate umbrella and fee structure.

An analysis[20] published in *Annals of Surgery* that looked at the change in cost of surgical claims between 2011 and 2017 found professional fees didn't change, while facility fees increased by 53% over the studied time. During this period, overall inflation was only about 10%,[21] but these facility fees increased the cost of surgeries by 29%. Clearly, health systems have done a good job of maximizing these payments.

More patients mean more professional fees
Today, around half of hospitals advertise their services directly to patients. A study comparing these hospitals to their non-advertising peers found advertising hospitals were bigger (i.e., had more beds) and made more money. Unsurprisingly, no meaningful difference was found in the quality of patient care across the two groups.[22]

An additional driver of advertising appears to be the positive impact it has on a patient's perception of the services they receive at a health system. In competitive hospital markets, the volume of advertising spend has been found to directly increase patient ratings in the Hospital Consumer Assessment of Healthcare Providers and Systems (HCAHPS) survey,[23] specifically, their overall rating of the hospital and likelihood to recommend it to others. It has often been noted that patients don't observe directly the quality of care they receive, because they don't have a reference point to compare it to—you go to the doctor or you don't, then you get better or you don't, never knowing how much of your recovery was attributable to the treatment you received versus your own natural healing. Thus, advertising can have a strong impact on "perceived quality," which helps attract and retain patients. CMS also links part of Medicare reimbursement to a hospital's HCAHPS scores, suggesting advertising can improve a hospital's revenue as well.

Vertical integration of pharmacy services drives revenue

According to the ZS Provider Organization Partnership Tracker, a 2022 survey of provider organizations' strategic objectives, 83% of health systems were either planning to expand or had already expanded their in-house pharmacy offerings. This generally involves dispensing more drugs and earning more revenue from the drugs dispensed.

Another analysis by the Drug Channels Institute found that between 2015 and 2019 large hospitals (600+ beds) owning a specialty pharmacy increased from 44% to 89%.[24] Many hospitals have also announced the opening of retail pharmacies on their campuses. These initiatives are designed to make things more convenient for the patient, allow for follow-up by health system staff (i.e., to ensure medication adherence), and capture the revenue that would otherwise be lost to a third party.

In addition to dispensing more drugs, these strategies can greatly increase the amount health systems get paid for the drugs they dispense. Similar to facility fees, as health systems get larger, they can often negotiate better reimbursement from payers. A ZS analysis of provider reimbursement data from Turquoise Health shows almost all clinics get reimbursed for the infused drug infliximab around 33%–85% over average selling price (ASP), depending on whether the branded or biosimilar version of the drug is used.[25] However, around 25% of hospital reimbursements are near the wholesale acquisition cost price, which is more than three times as expensive for the branded drug and more than five times as expensive for the biosimilar. Given the high cost of many drugs and public scrutiny of these costs, it surprises many people that hospitals can be reimbursed 3×–5× the ASP of the drug.

Driving these payments is the favorable contract that a large, powerful provider can negotiate with a payer. The same data reveals that the most common reimbursement mechanism for all types of clinics is ASP-based, while specialty pharmacies usually receive reimbursement based on the much higher average wholesale price (AWP/"list price") and outpatient hospitals can receive "billed charges," which more or less means whatever they decide to invoice.

In addition to being paid more for drugs, large health systems can drastically lower the acquisition cost of the drugs they procure. Of course, increasing scale brings more bargaining power with drug suppliers and with it, marginally lower costs. However, a much bigger driver of health system economics has been the federal government's 340B program.[26]

At a high level, this program requires drug manufacturers to sell their products to provider organizations that care for many low-income or uninsured patients at a large discount—often greater than 50%. Originally, CMS intended this program to increase the impact of federal spending for these patients by also lowering reimbursements to 22.5% below the ASP. However, in 2022, the US Supreme Court ruled this payment policy was unlawful and required CMS to reimburse providers at the standard rate of ASP plus 6%. But the ruling did not reverse the requirement of drug manufacturers to sell discounted drugs to these providers, creating a very large margin on the dispensing of 340B drugs.

Coding your way to success

DRG payment is commonly understood as a fixed payment designed to push the financial risk of treatment cost overruns onto the provider to encourage efficiency in care delivery. However, in practice, DRG payments are never as fixed as is generally believed.

In designing the DRG payment system, CMS accurately realized the cost to treat some patients greatly exceeded others. As a result, it devised a method for increasing payment for patients who had significant complications and comorbidities that increased the resources needed for care (e.g., a longer hospital stay was needed).[27] In theory, this should appropriately compensate providers when difficult patients use more resources than the average patient.

However, in reality, this leads to a situation in which the details of how a patient's condition is coded greatly impact how much the hospital is paid for that patient's care. In turn, this creates an incentive to aggressively find and identify the "right codes" to add to a patient's diagnosis, even when a comorbidity has a minimal impact on how the patient is treated. A 2020 study found that between 2012 and 2016, admissions that had been coded with a major complication or comorbidity rose in 15 of the top 20 DRG categories.[28] The study's authors could not detect any increase in the actual disease severity, but the coding of the additional comorbidities resulted in a more than $1.2 billion increase in payments from CMS.

Capturing these additional payments creates a significant administrative burden on health systems. This creates an advantage for large systems that can support large billing departments with the specialized knowledge necessary to maximize their reimbursement through coding. Additionally, an entire consulting industry has sprung up to help providers capture these benefits by analyzing their historical billings and locating areas where they could potentially be reimbursed more for the care they provide. While DRG coding is certainly not the only source of administrative overhead, it's a major contributor. The scale of the problem was illustrated by a recent study that showed the United States had the highest billing and coding costs across six countries studied, adding $215 to the cost of a typical inpatient surgery.[29] This was more than 35 times that of neighboring Canada, which had the lowest administrative costs in the group.

How these incentives drive the evolution of health systems

These payment dynamics have driven a series of decisions by large health systems that are more or less consistent across multiple institutions and geographies over the past two decades. These decisions can be viewed as an evolution, as health systems seek to capitalize on more of the economic opportunities offered by consolidation and sophistication. In general, this evolution also follows a specific order, where institutions first strive to achieve scale, then standardize operations, and finally shift to incorporating more patient-focused consumer services.

Achieving the advantages of scale

Implementing most of the modern strategies that drive health system success first requires a sufficiently large organization that operates across the spectrum of patient care. The proliferation of organized provider systems is not accidental—it has been propelled by distinct factors. Economic pressures, policy changes, and investor influence have all encouraged healthcare providers to consolidate into larger entities or networks. For this reason, the United States has seen more than 90 mergers and acquisitions each year between 2012 and 2019. While this slowed during the COVID-19 pandemic, these transactions have steadily increased since then, returning to more than 70 transactions in 2024.[30]

For a small hospital system, this usually means adding clinics that provide primary and specialty care to the same patients in the geographic area. This creates a captive referral network in which primary care clinics generate demand for specialty and acute care services. As systems grow, they can support a larger, dedicated billing and finance infrastructure to maximize their revenues through reimbursement and payment collection. Additionally, even a small health system can afford to invest in various enabling technologies (like integrated EHRs) and the dedicated, skilled staff to support them, which may be cost-prohibitive for independent clinics.

Even after a hospital has joined with its surrounding clinics, the incentive to continue to increase scale remains. As a health system has a greater market share in its local geography, it can negotiate better rates from payers. If a health system sees 10% of patients in a geography and its rates are too high, a payer might find it acceptable to not have a contract and allow it to go "out of network," forcing its patients to find other providers. If it sees 60% of patients in a geography, the payer will get strong pushback from the employers that are its customers if it doesn't include such a popular facility in its network—giving the payer a strong incentive to agree to a contract with a larger system even at a higher price. The Medicare Payment Advisory Commission confirmed that *larger physician groups obtain higher private insurance rates than smaller groups*, reflecting their enhanced bargaining position. Many mergers have been driven by the lure of such market power.

As health systems get larger, they can also buy supplies in bulk to achieve better pricing, lowering costs in addition to boosting revenue. Merging or organizing into a larger entity promises to eliminate redundancies and reduce per-unit costs. Hospitals joining a system can consolidate back-office functions (billing, supply chain) and negotiate volume discounts on supplies from manufacturers through group purchasing organizations. For example, when a hospital system acquires physician offices, it can integrate their IT and care management processes, avoiding duplication and smoothing patient handoffs. Scale can also support specialized personnel—for example, a large health system can employ data analysts to find care improvements, a cost that a small clinic would be unable to cover.

Given the large number of mergers, it's not surprising that regulators are paying close attention to provider consolidation. Antitrust authorities have ramped up challenges to mergers they believe will harm consumers through higher prices or reduced access. The FTC, under a mandate to promote competition in healthcare, has actively reviewed hospital and provider mergers in recent years and has blocked or forced the abandonment of several high-profile deals:

- In 2022, New Jersey's RWJ Barnabas Health (a 12-hospital system) had to scrap its planned acquisition of St. Peter's Healthcare System after the FTC filed suit, presenting evidence that the merger would reduce competition and likely raise prices in the region.[31] The health systems opted to call off the deal rather than fight in court.
- That same year, HCA Healthcare (the nation's largest for-profit hospital chain) halted its bid to buy five Utah hospitals from Steward Health Care when the FTC moved to block the transaction.[32] The combined entity would have controlled a dominant share of inpatient services in the area. The FTC argued this could lead to increased prices and lower quality, and HCA abandoned the deal under pressure.
- State attorneys general and the Department of Justice (DoJ) have also become more skeptical of large physician group acquisitions by hospital systems, although such deals are harder to regulate.

This enforcement trend signals that the era of unchecked consolidation may be ending. Regulators are essentially asking organized providers to prove how a merger benefits patients—if it's just about market power with *"no apparent consumer benefit,"* it's likely to be challenged. Industry defenders argue some mergers are necessary to maintain access in struggling areas, and scale can help control costs via efficiencies. But the FTC's leadership has explicitly stated they will not hesitate to act to protect healthcare consumers from deals that could undermine care access or affordability.

Standardizing across sites of care

Once a health system has reached a certain scale, scope of services, and level of infrastructure, it becomes capable of a much higher degree of centralized management. This is when it can begin to standardize how care is delivered across the many patients in the institution to improve outcomes, reduce costs of care, or both. The ability to harmonize care in this way facilitates participation in advanced payment models and VBC, which financially reward a health system for achieving improvements in these areas.

The EHR systems implemented in large providers are a key enabler of this standardization and administrative influence on how patient care is delivered. According to a 2022 survey,[33] 70% of health systems are using externally developed guidelines in their EHRs, which can be used to track whether physicians are treating according to best practices. Additionally, 52% of systems have implemented restrictive order sets to influence what diagnostics, procedures, and drugs a physician could order to ensure compliance with these guidelines. Furthermore, 61% of health systems implemented some type of provider scorecard that linked a physicians' treatment behavior to performance evaluation, with 40% having a direct link to physician's compensation (up from 11% in 2019).

In general, the goal of this influence is to *standardize best practices* across the network, invest time and energy in population health initiatives, and offer more comprehensive, coordinated care. For example, a large integrated system may implement a cardiometabolic management program that spans clinic visits, nutrition counseling, pharmacy support, and hospital care seamlessly for the patient. Organized groups also often provide extended patient access (after-hours clinics, call centers) and a broader range of services under one roof, improving both access and patient experience. Providers within systems can also benefit from shared knowledge and peer review, potentially elevating care quality. And during crises like the COVID-19 pandemic, large health systems could leverage these systems to flexibly move staff and resources where they were most needed.

Success stories certainly do exist: A case study by Kaiser Permanente indicates its integrated care model has led to improved preventive care outcomes and reduced hospitalization rates compared with non-integrated systems.[34] Similarly, some community hospitals that merged into larger systems gained access to specialty services (such as oncology or trauma care) that they couldn't have supported alone, benefiting local communities.

Together, standardizing best practices and eliminating unnecessary costs set up a health system well to participate in the various VBC and risk-sharing models available (which we discussed in the chapter on payers). Managing population health under fixed payments (such as in ACOs or capitated contracts) requires a broad network of services and sizable patient volume. A small practice will struggle to absorb the financial risk if a few patients require intensive care, whereas a large system can pool risk across tens of thousands of patients. The ACA's encouragement of ACOs explicitly pushed providers to integrate operationally and clinically.[35] Indeed, most Medicare ACOs involve hospital-physician partnerships or multi-provider networks, rather than standalone clinics. Additionally, advanced payment models often require significant reporting and data analytics, which an organized group can handle more readily. We can see this with independent primary care practices selling to larger entities to join Medicare Advantage networks or manage ACO contracts—they gain access to the infrastructure and patient base needed to succeed in VBC.

Unfortunately, this type of standardization can also sometimes turn care into a volume-driven, impersonal experience for the patient if not done thoughtfully. The example of dialysis chains mentioned earlier is a cautionary tale: As large for-profit organizations took over, their drive for efficiency and profit led to understaffing and overly standardized protocols that didn't suit all patients, ultimately harming outcomes. This undercuts the argument that consolidation inherently improves quality—it can, but only if the organization prioritizes reinvestment in care rather than just cost-cutting.

Another potential downside is innovation stagnation. Smaller practices and hospitals often differentiate themselves through personalized services or niche programs. When absorbed by large systems, there's a risk of homogenization and loss of local innovation. Large bureaucracies can be slower to change courses. If a health system monopolizes a region, new entrants (like a novel clinic model) may be kept out, potentially slowing the adoption of new approaches to care.

Health services as a consumer good

In the chapter on patients, we discussed how more patients were taking control of their own care journey. Health systems have been at the forefront of responding to this trend. The largest and most sophisticated systems, after achieving a level of standardization across care delivery, tend to shift to a variety of patient-focused programs that turn engaging with health systems into more of a consumer good. These large, successful systems tend to advertise more. Additionally, the way they describe their services tends to shift from "treating you when you are sick" to "providing a happy, healthy life." These systems can hire many nonphysician staff in patient-facing roles that increase the patient's quality of experience while reducing the institution's cost-per-patient. This is known as "practicing at the limit of the license"[36] (or more pejoratively, "down-skilling") and can only be achieved in an organization with strong protocols on how a patient should be cared for: when care can be handled by a physician assistant or nurse and when escalation to a physician is required. In many ways, this represents the logical conclusion of the standardization process. The institution sees itself as having reached the pinnacle of best practice in its operations, and its evolution therefore shifts focus toward bringing in a greater and greater number of patients into its established model.

Takeaways for working together with providers

Succeeding as a healthcare provider today often requires achieving sufficient scale to standardize care delivery according to best practices, reduce costs, and market yourself to patients effectively. With approximately 70% of general acute care hospitals and over 40% of all primary care physicians,[37] health systems are the largest and most sophisticated type of provider institution, influencing how a huge portion of patients are cared for in the United States. They are concerned with creating good clinical outcomes, pleasant patient experiences, and succeeding financially. One or more of these goals should usually be the basis for any type of partnership or program proposed to a provider. However, how a provider will care about each of these factors is influenced by the organization's priorities and stage of evolution. When seeking to work with a health system to achieve a shared objective, it's important to understand how those objectives fit into its broader goals. An innovation that is a "good idea" might not be adopted because the health system hasn't reached a level of maturity to accept it, or because other "even better" ideas are of greater focus.

Due to the relatively low operating margin of health systems and the large number in financial distress, the financial incentives created by both a health system's pricing and the structure of how systems are paid should be a particular focus. For the payer, modifying reimbursement models such as DRG payment or VBC is a way to immediately influence the provider. However, if not carefully considered, that influence may or may not generate the intended outcomes. For a manufacturer with an innovative product, a new product doesn't always need to lead to increased provider revenue. But it's important to understand how providers will be paid and do everything possible to avoid a situation in which a new innovation causes providers to lose money. Successfully navigating this complexity is the key to innovations that drive value for both the patient and for other ecosystem stakeholders.

Notes

1 Hart, J., & Russell, H. (2024). *Clinically integrated networks.* The Business of Primary Care.
2 Squires, D., & Blumenthal, D. (2016). *Do small physician practices have a future?* The Commonwealth Fund.
3 Accountable Care Organizations (ACOs) (n.d.). *General information.* Centers for Medicare & Medicaid Services (CMS).
4 AAPC. (n.d.). *What is MACRA?*
5 Kane, C. (2021). *Recent changes in physician practice characteristic.* American Medical Association.
6 Kaul, B., et al. (2023). *Health care provider consolidation and shortages.* Society of Actuaries Research Institute.
7 Goldsmith, J., et al. (2015). *Integrated delivery networks: In search of benefits and market effect.* National Academy of Social Insurance (NASI).
8 Squires, D., & Blumenthal, D. (2016). *Do small physician practices have a future?* The Commonwealth Fund.
9 Abdelhadi, O., et al. (2024). *Private equity ownership of physician practices is rising.* The National Institute for Health Care Management (NIHCM) Foundation.
10 Goldsmith, J., et al. (2015). *Integrated delivery networks: In search of benefits and market effect.* National Academy of Social Insurance (NASI).
11 Kaul, B., et al. (2023). *Health care provider consolidation and shortages.* Society of Actuaries Research Institute.
12 *As large chains grow to dominate dialysis, patient outcomes decline.* (2019). Duke University's Fuqua School of Business.
13 Option Care Health. (n.d.). *A history of extraordinary care.*
14 Berwick, D. M., Nolan, T. W., & Whittington, J. (2008). The triple aim: Care, health, and cost. *Health Affairs*, 27(3), 759–769.
15 Berwick, D. M., Nolan, T. W., & Whittington, J. (2008). The triple aim: Care, health, and cost. *Health Affairs*, 27(3), 759–769.
16 Olayiwola, J. N., & Rastetter, M. (2021). Aiming for health equity: The bullseye of the quadruple aim. *Journal of Hospital Management and Health Policy*, 5. https://jhmhp.amegroups.org/article/view/6519/html
17 Nundy, S., Cooper, L. A., Mate, K. S. (2022). The quintuple aim for health care improvement: A new imperative to advance health equity. *JAMA*, 327(6), 521–522. doi:10.1001/jama.2021.2518.
18 Dowell, E. K. P. (2020). *Health care still largest U.S. employer.* U.S. Census Bureau.
19 Levinson, Z., Godwin, J., & Neuman, T. (2024). *Hospital margins rebounded in 2023, but rural hospitals and those with high Medicaid shares were struggling more than others.* The Henry J. Kaiser Family Foundation.
20 Zheng, L., Liao, W., Luo, S., Li, B., Liu, D., Yun, Q., Zhao, Z., Zhao, J., Rong, J., Gong, Z., Sha, F., & Tang, J. (2024). Author manuscript, (2021), Final edits (2020). Association between alcohol consumption and incidence of dementia in current drinkers: Linear and non-linear Mendelian randomization analysis. *EClinicalMedicine*, 76, 102810.
21 U.S. Bureau of Labor Statistics. (2024). *Historical Consumer Price Index for All Urban Consumers (CPI-U): U.S. city average, all items index, 1913 to present* (Supplemental File).

22 Ndumele, C. D., Cohen, M. S., Solberg, M., Lollo, A., & Wallace, J. (2021). Characterization of U.S. hospital advertising and association with hospital performance, 2008–2016. *JAMA Network Open*, 4(7), e2115342.
23 Huppertz, J. W., Bowman, R. A., Bizer, G. Y., Sidhu, M. S., & McVeigh, C. (2017). Hospital advertising, competition, and HCAHPS: Does it pay to advertise? *Health Services Research*, 52(4), 1590–1611.
24 Fein, A. J. (2020). *Hospitals continue their startling expansion into specialty pharmacy.* Drug Channels.
25 Luan, W., O'Dell, C., & Slifer, M. (2025). *Drug pricing & reimbursement infusion confusion in 2025.* Turquoise Health.
26 U.S. Department of Health and Human Services, Health Resources and Services Administration. (2000, March 15). Notice regarding the Section 340B Drug Pricing Program—Program guidance clarification. *Federal Register*, 65(50), 13983–13985.
27 Centers for Medicare & Medicaid Services (CMS). (2024). *Design and development of the diagnosis related group (DRG).*
28 Gluckman, T. J., Spinelli, K. J., Wang, M., Yazdani, A., Grunkemeier, G., Bradley, S. M., Wasfy, J. H., Goyal, A., Oseran, A., & Joynt Maddox, K. E. (2020). Trends in diagnosis related groups for inpatient admissions and associated changes in payment from 2012 to 2016. *JAMA Network Open*, 3(12), e2028470.
29 Richman, B. D., Kaplan, R. S., Kohli, J., Purcell, D., Shah, M., Bonfrer, I., Golden, B., Hannam, R., Mitchell, W., Cehic, D., Crispin, G., & Schulman, K. A. (2022). Billing and insurance–related administrative costs: A cross–national analysis. *Health Affairs*, 41(8), 1098–1106.
30 Singh, A. (2024). *Hospital and health system M&A in review: Despite industry stabilization, numbers reveal ongoing distress in 2024.* Kaufman Hall.
31 Federal Trade Commission. (2022, June 2). In the matter of RWJ Barnabas Health/Saint Peter's Healthcare System (Docket No. 9409).
32 Morse, S. (2022). *Hospital mergers in Utah and New Jersey called off after FTC files complaints.* Healthcare Finance.
33 ZS Associates. (2022). *Provider organization control and partnership tracker wave 2.*
34 Kaiser Permanente Institute for Health Policy. (n.d.). *An overview of our integrated care model*; Kaiser Permanente International. (2020). *Demonstrating the value of integrated care: Managing the top 5%.*
35 Kaul, B., Larocque, A., Matson, T., & Sheppard, R. (2023). *Health care provider consolidation and shortages.* SOA Research Institute.
36 Jain, S. H (2022). *'Practicing at the top of your license' and the 'great' American healthcare labor arbitrage.* Forbes.
37 Furukawa, M. F., Machta, R. M., Barrett, K. A., Jones, D. J., Shortell, S. M., Scanlon, D. P., Lewis, V. A., O'Malley, A. J., Meara, E. R., & Rich, E. C. (2019). Landscape of health systems in the United States. *Medical Care Research and Review, 77*(4), 357–366.

Chapter 6

Physicians

Mainstay of Evolving Healthcare

Maria Whitman, Komal Gurnani, Karishma Trikha, Anush Khandelwal, and Amudha Sharma

At the heart of healthcare stands the physician—a trusted guide, decision-maker, and healer. Their role, rooted in deep expertise and human connections, remains central even as the landscape around them shifts. This chapter looks at the:

- Role of a physician as an expert caretaker on whom so many health decisions depend
- Continued evolution of the physician role in concert with the healthcare landscape
- Importance of other healthcare providers who work alongside physicians in care delivery

The evolution of what it means to be a physician

The role of physicians has evolved significantly over the past few decades, shaped by technological advancements, shifting patient expectations, cultural and economic events, and a changing policy landscape. The role's recent evolution can be broadly categorized across three eras—the early 2000s, the post-Affordable Care Act (ACA) era (2010–2019), and the post-COVID era (2020 and beyond).

DOI: 10.4324/9781003603597-6

Each of these eras has brought a unique set of changes and challenges, with more changes still on the horizon.

Early 2000s: Autonomy and authority

In the early 2000s, physicians primarily operated in an environment characterized by individual autonomy, with the majority (about 60%[1]) being independent physicians. The doctor–patient relationship was intimate, with physicians making decisions largely based on their expertise. Their recommendation was the often-uncontested determinant of the course of a patient's treatment.

During that time, information technology was not as pervasive in clinical settings, with medical records primarily maintained manually with paper files and fax machines (which, despite technological progress, still remain a reminder of this time in many practices). Physicians' focus was on direct patient care, and they maintained authority to lead treatment decisions on behalf of patients and caregivers.

Despite the autonomy and relatively straightforward practice model, early signs of strain in the healthcare system were evident. For example, during this period, we began to see concerns around physician shortages, particularly in primary care. By 2010, the number of American medical students entering primary care had already declined by over 50% from 1997.[2]

The economic model of healthcare during this era was largely fee-for-service (FFS), where physicians were reimbursed based on the volume of services provided. FFS incentivized a quantity-driven approach to care, as we have discussed in the chapter on payers. Doctors of this era succeeded as practicing physicians by finding and keeping many patients, who then would need many medical services. While this system was straightforward, it often resulted in overuse of healthcare resources and fragmented care, and as a result, higher healthcare costs without always achieving quality or efficiency. This placed great strain on the system and laid the foundations for change.

Post-ACA era (2010–2019): Quality, care, and business

The passage of the ACA in 2010 marked a pivotal moment in the healthcare ecosystem, setting the stage for significant transformation in both the role of physicians and in healthcare delivery more broadly. The ACA focused on expanding access to healthcare, improving quality, and reducing healthcare costs. These goals were hailed and recognized as steps in the right direction for the US healthcare system in terms of quality and patient experience.

At the same time, momentum was gaining for specialty-based healthcare.[3] Between 2005 and 2015, the physician-to-population ratio for non-primary care specialties increased by 52%,[4] while that for primary care remained stable. The participation of more specialists in a patient's care led to a greater need for care coordination across healthcare providers. Despite being an essential step toward improving patient outcomes, this added to the administrative burden, especially in the absence of seamless access to patient records and care across practices and specialties.

Since the ACA shifted incentives from FFS toward quality and efficiency, consolidation grew as a key way to bring care teams together to support common patient populations and drive greater efficiency across practices. As a result, in just a few years, physicians practicing independently declined significantly in share to about 40% by 2013.[5] The trend of consolidation continues even today, which we review in greater detail in the chapter discussing providers.

In the years following the ACA, a significant number of Americans received coverage.[6] This added patient volume, when combined with incentives and consolidation, led to a notable shift in many physicians' independence regarding how they cared for their patients. Physicians needed to adjust and align with organizational policies and protocols governing treatment, patient care, and outcomes measurement.

Success was no longer defined solely by clinical expertise and human counsel, but also by the ability to see more patients, deliver a wide range of services, and meticulously document and report data. For instance, physicians spent 44.9% of their time on administrative tasks such as inputting data into electronic health records, which highlights the burden on physicians.[7]

This new reality created tension between personalized care and efficiency in the provider-patient interaction. Physicians had less time to spend with each patient—dropping to an estimated 59% of the historic time spent per visit. For many physicians, compassionate, individualized care began to feel at odds with the business side of care. The strain was evident in measures of job satisfaction, burnout, and, worse yet, negative impact on quality of care. A meta-analysis of 47 studies involving more than 42,000 US physicians found that physician burnout doubled the risk of adverse patient safety incidents and led to poorer overall quality of care and lower patient satisfaction.[8] In this era, technology started to emerge that could enable some innovations to meet the challenges. But these technologies did not gain significant momentum until COVID-19 created an imperative for change.

Post-COVID era (2020 to now): Asynchronous care and AI

The COVID-19 pandemic disrupted healthcare at its core. The financial distress caused by the pandemic further accelerated healthcare system consolidation, with independent physicians declining to nearly 23% while approximately 77%[9] were employed by either hospitals or corporate entities by 2023. Further, the in-person nature of healthcare had to evolve during the pandemic as systems and physicians had to adapt rapidly to alternative methods of care delivery. Telemedicine surged, and policies were quickly altered to allow greater reach (for example, over state lines) to maintain access to care for a country in a new norm of individual isolation.

Hospitals and critical care centers remained in service with strict protocols, and we began to see more nurse practitioners (NPs) and physician assistants (PAs) on the front lines of care. In fact, after COVID, these two groups make up approximately 51%[10] of primary care providers (42.9% NPs and 8.2% PAs), collectively larger than physicians (48.8%). At the same time, emergency healthcare policies during this time, such as extended Medicaid enrollment and sustained coverage for virtual care with fair reimbursement, played a vital role in strengthening the foundation of healthcare delivery during this challenging period.[11]

These kinds of changes were not evenly distributed during the COVID years, and the impact has been felt by different patients in different ways. Cancer diagnosis took a dramatic step back during COVID, with diagnosed cancer incidence rates lower than expected by 9.4%[12] in 2020. But care continued, and many will forever be grateful to the thousands of "healthcare heroes"—doctors, nurses, surgeons, pharmacists, and others whose efforts came at great personal cost in health (physical and mental) and burnout. Although physician burnout rates have significantly fallen from 56% in 2021 to 43.2%[13] in 2024, it is still a matter of concern.

The pandemic exposed system inefficiencies while simultaneously accelerating innovation in care delivery, workforce flexibility, and digital integration—paving the way for a more resilient, tech-enabled healthcare future. The widespread adoption of telehealth and the asynchronous use of digital tools such as patient portals and applications were especially significant in primary care and mental health during this period. For instance, 23%[14] of psychiatrists delivered nearly all their visits through telehealth compared with less than 1% for physicians in other specialties, while more than 75%[15] of primary care physicians (PCPs) provided less than 10% of their services via telehealth.

Physicians now operate in a hybrid model, balancing in-person visits with virtual consultations and remote monitoring. This shift has broadly been beneficial and has come to be an expected part of the care patients receive across the country. Care delivery choices reduce the friction for many patients in receiving care, especially given the cost and hassle associated with system engagement, as explored in the chapter discussing patients. In the 2022 ZS Provider Organization Survey,[16] 85% of organizations focused on expanding virtual care delivery, digital and data infrastructure, and home health initiatives as a continued priority for their institution to "meet patients where they are."

Being a doctor in the age of AI

Analytics and AI were making inroads in care. Still, the advent of generative AI is redefining the post-COVID era and the future role and focus of physicians and other healthcare providers. AI-powered diagnostic tools, predictive analytics, and automated workflows are only a few examples of how technologies can and

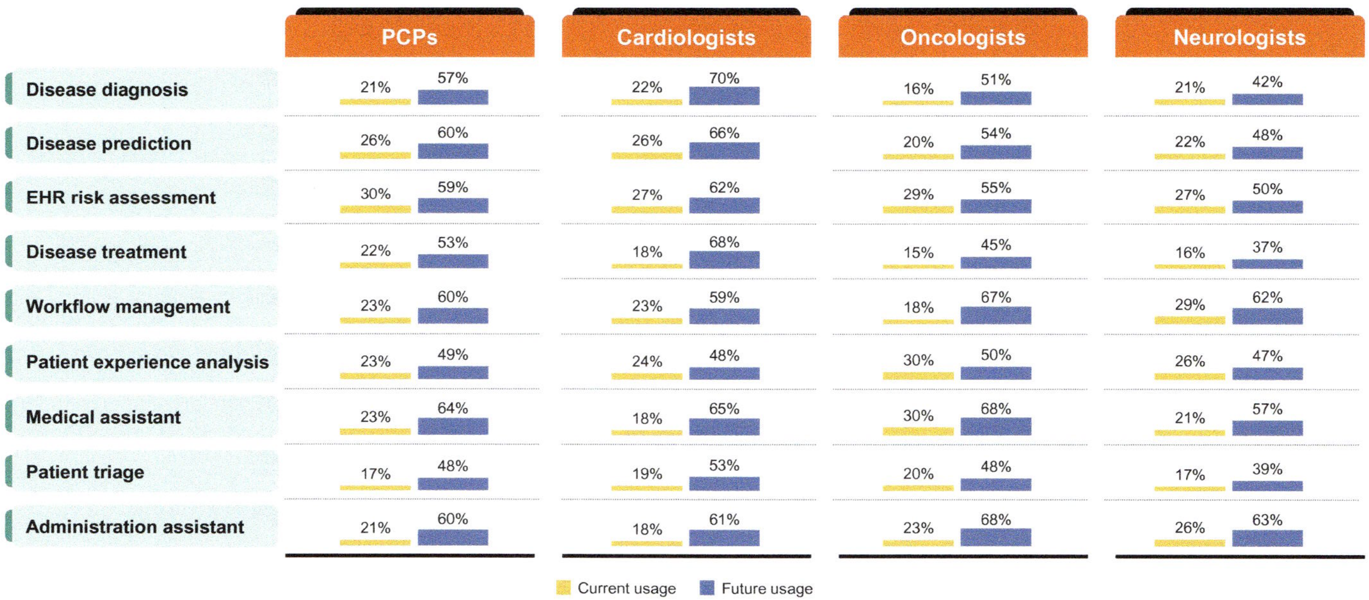

Figure 6.1 AI use across US PCPs and select US specialists

***Note*: Percentage of specialists who selected "aware and tried it" or "aware and consistently using it."**

***Source*: 2025 ZS Future of Health Report.**

will streamline processes, inform decisions, and improve patient engagement, experiences, and outcomes. Garnering these benefits requires physicians and their workflows to adapt accordingly. To be successful, physicians must now trust and leverage a growing range of information technology tools in addition to seeing many patients, reporting on their outcomes, and coordinating with other providers.

Encouragingly, many physicians have embraced this shift (see Figure 6.1). About nine in 10 physicians[17] want to spend more time with patients, deepen relationships, and focus on preventive care. AI and technology advancements are increasingly seen less as risks to their role, but more as opportunities to achieve these goals, putting their time and energy where the human is most needed. Overall adoption of and comfort with AI and digital tools are increasing with more than two-thirds of physicians,[18] who state AI has helped increase time for patient care by reducing administrative workload and are optimistic about its future potential.

According to the ZS 2025 Future of Health study, more than 60% of US PCPs are comfortable using AI for workflow management and administrative support.[19]

Uptake to date on more direct patient care-related uses is slower, but even there, we see a more positive attitude, particularly among specialists. There is some variance by specialty, but cardiologists are particularly optimistic about AI for diagnosis, prediction, and treatment, followed by oncologists. Neurologists are more conservative in these areas. In addition, physicians are increasingly willing to adopt AI-driven diagnostics for faster and more accurate results. While the implementation and adoption of these tools are in the early stages, some evidence of impact has started to emerge. For example, an AI system from Massachusetts General Hospital and MIT achieved 94% accuracy in detecting lung nodules, compared with 65% by human radiologists.[20]

While we focus on decoding the US healthcare system, much like COVID, the AI wave is truly global in its potential to support healthcare outcomes. As illustrated in Figure 6.2, while the United States is making progress, countries across the globe have already accelerated AI adoption for many tasks. For instance, current AI usage for workflow management is 47% in China and 69% in India, compared to just 23% in the United States.[21]

Despite the technological advances of this era, the physician demand-supply gap remains very real, with the United States projected to face a shortage of up to 86,000 physicians by 2036[22] (versus 37,000 in 2021). To help bridge this gap and better manage burnout, physicians and care settings are increasingly willing to work alongside "physician extenders," such as NPs and PAs, for care delivery. This trend is currently seen mostly in primary care, but is expected to expand to other specialties in the next few years. NPs and PAs represent the fastest-growing professions among healthcare providers. Projections show a 46% increase in NP roles and a 31% increase in PA roles over the next few years, signaling a substantial

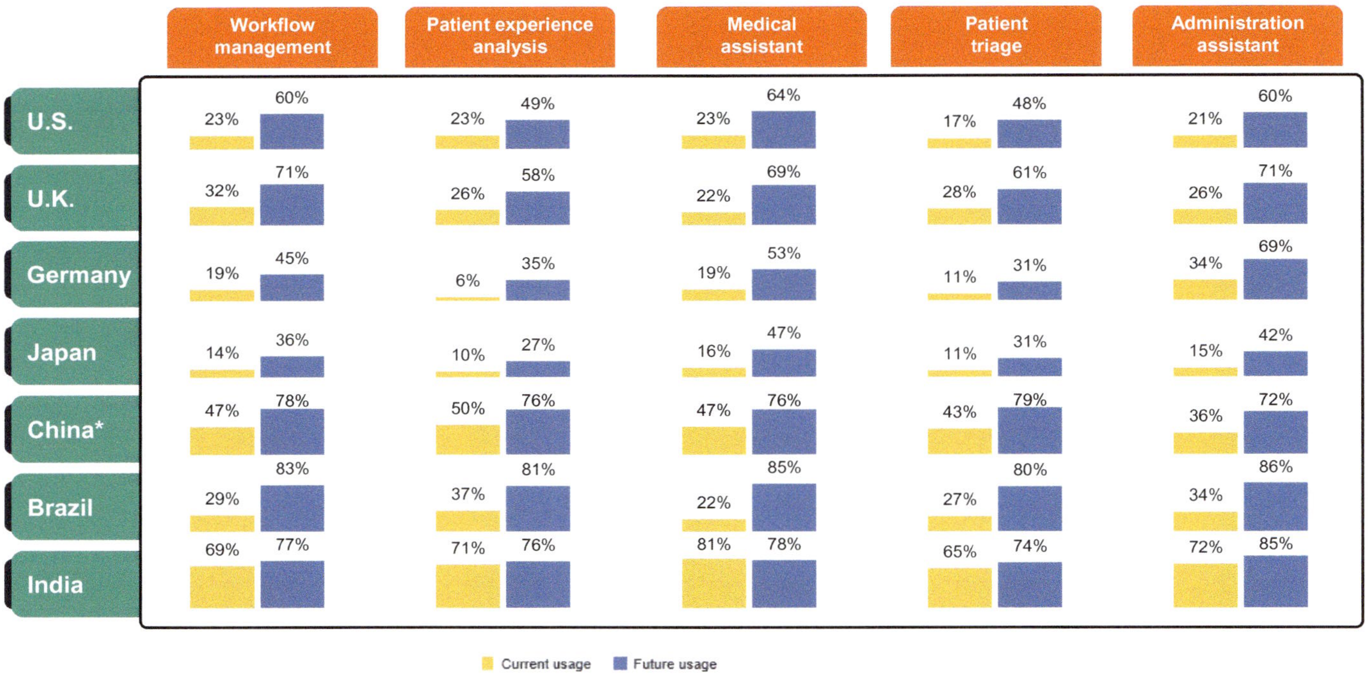

Figure 6.2 PCP-stated current and predicted future usage of AI in healthcare

Internal medicine practitioners in China.

Source: 2025 ZS Future of Health Report.

expansion by 2031.[23] They had some prescription authority in all 50 states and accounted for nearly 30%[24] of all retail prescriptions between 2021 and 2022. NPs and PAs provide more cost-effective care compared with physicians and their role is increasing even in specialized fields such as cardiology, orthopedics, and emergency medicine. Given the projected oncology physician shortage, the number of NPs and PAs in oncology has grown to an estimated 10,000[25] across the country.

In summary, physicians today must balance technological advancements, patient empowerment, and their own well-being. With AI integration, hybrid care models, and workforce shifts, the focus remains on delivering high-quality, personalized care while addressing the challenges of a strained workforce and an ever-growing demand for services. Yet each physician is striving for the best outcomes in their unique practice setting, diverse patient populations, and personal beliefs and experiences.

Decoding the physician of today

While the same macro forces impact most physicians to a greater or lesser extent, anyone looking to decode the healthcare ecosystem and deeply understand today's physicians needs to look under the surface: to where physicians practice, the dynamics of their specialty, patient populations, influencers, and how they make decisions. This gives us insights into not only what they do, but how they see themselves and how they practice as they face rapidly evolving options and increasingly heterogeneous patients.

Context of practice dynamics and workflows

Physician behaviors across settings are driven by resource availability, payer influence, patient complexity, and institutional priorities. Figure 6.3 denotes the four distinct market archetypes based on per-patient healthcare resource utilization and degree of market competitiveness as introduced in the healthcare landscape chapter. Each archetype depicts a unique care setting.

These dimensions and care setting dynamics impact the behavior of multiple stakeholders. When healthcare resource utilization is high, payer, provider, and pharma incentives are often aligned to accelerate use of advanced therapies sooner to reduce total per-patient healthcare cost across inpatient and outpatient settings. When healthcare resource utilization is lower, pharma is at one end and payers/providers are on the other end. In case of high competition and low resource utilization, payer and provider incentives can diverge, leading to dynamics where several options may seem to exist to improve the health of the patient, but not all options may be truly accessible given the differences in payer and provider priorities.

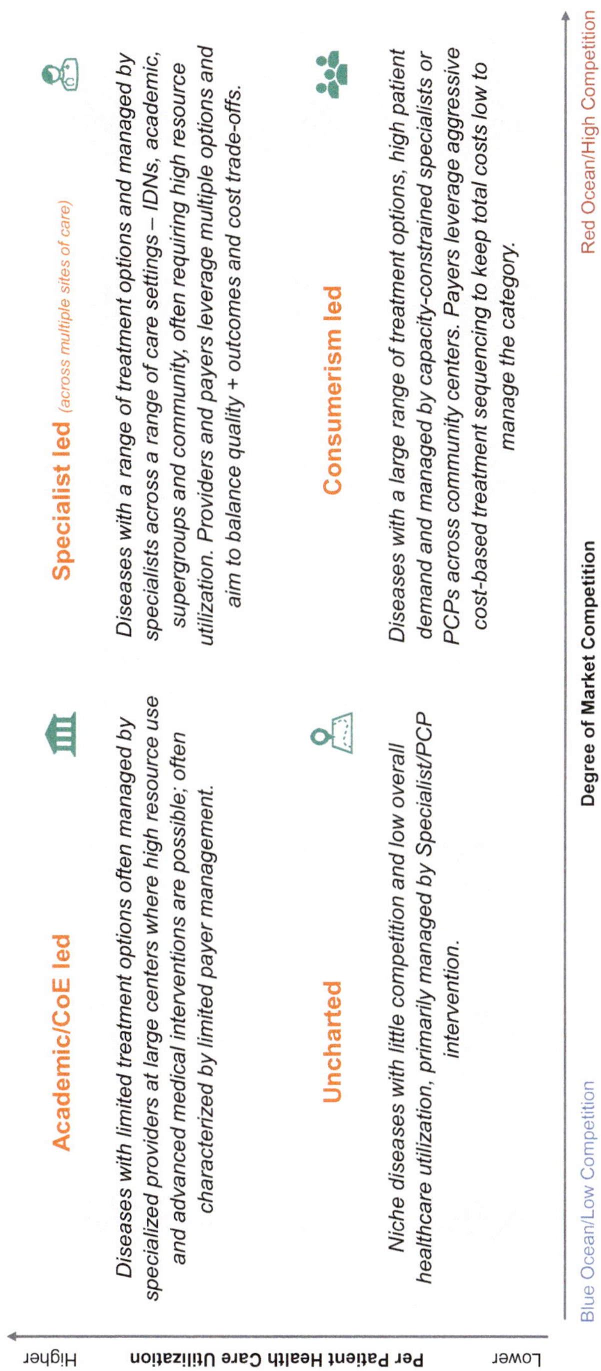

Figure 6.3 Four distinct market archetypes—each defined by a unique dynamic interplay

It is fundamentally important to understand the orientation of these stakeholders in a given disease state. Doing so highlights areas of win-win-win opportunity across payer-provider-pharma to drive outsized patient impact. But as we consider decoding physicians, their orientation in a given archetype can explain why and how they behave as they do.

Across these care settings, behavioral patterns shape clinical decision-making, patient engagement, and practice dynamics—offering a powerful lens into how physicians navigate diverse healthcare environments. We can understand this behavior by applying the lens of therapy area archetypes, as shown in Figure 6.4.

In **academic/CoE-led** settings, physicians are highly specialized, deeply involved in research, and focused on cutting-edge treatments for complex diseases with limited options. A key priority for these physicians is identifying the best possible outcomes and treatment for the most challenging diseases. They, therefore, are driven by the clear focus on enhancing patient outcomes and quality of life, spending significant time with patients due to the complexity of cases and the need for personalized care. While AI adoption is high in research applications, such as biomarker identification and clinical trial optimization, routine AI-driven automation is lower due to the criticality of physician judgment in rare diseases.

In **specialist-led** settings, providers operate across diverse care environments, balancing treatment efficacy, cost, and payer considerations. Time spent with patients is moderate as efficiency is emphasized, but case complexity still requires meaningful engagement. AI adoption is moderate to high, particularly for workflow optimization, predictive analytics, and prior authorization automation, though physician judgment remains central.

In **consumerism-led** settings, where diseases have a broad range of treatment options and are managed by capacity-constrained specialists or PCPs, physicians focus on efficiency and high patient volumes. A particular setting can become consumerism-led when physicians arrive at a consensus on what defines a good clinical outcome and how to achieve it. Given this, the intent of physicians is to treat a larger volume of patients and reduce the time spent on each interaction. In many cases, physicians are increasingly open to bringing in NPs and PAs to handle the day-to-day tasks while they focus on only the most valuable, critical aspects. Thus, time spent with patients is lower, with a reliance on standardized, often payer-driven treatment protocols. AI adoption is highest in this setting, particularly for automation in triage, decision support, and remote monitoring, to help streamline workflows and support patient self-management.

Not only does the setting define physician behavior, but it also varies within each therapy area, influencing how physicians diagnose, treat, and engage with patients.

- In cardiology, conditions like ATTR amyloidosis, which are CoE-led, have physicians focus on rare disease expertise, genetic testing, and innovative treatments. In contrast, heart failure is Specialist-led and requires

	Academic/CoE-led	Specialist-led	Consumerism-led
Site of care characteristics	• Large centers, CoEs with strong referral network across related specialties	• Range of care settings – IDNs, academic, supergroups and community (limited)	• Primarily community setting, PE-VC backed umbrella orgs, limited/no academic focus
Patient characteristics	• Progressive diseases with worsening prognosis	• Progressive diseases with controllable prognosis (at least for certain periods of time – 3-5 yr)	• Progressive diseases with well known/managed prognosis (for longer periods of time – 5-10 yr)
Provider characteristics	• **Type**: Mostly a KOL or a specialist expert • **Personal focus**: Clinical trials, Adv Rx • **Dept metrics**: Clinical Quality, Pt satisfaction • **Typical appt duration**: 1st - 40 to 60 mins, follows-ups 30 to 60 mins • **AI adoption**: High in research application	• **Type**: Mix of KOLs and specialists • **Personal focus**: Clinical trials, Adv Rx, care protocolization to improve safety/quality • **Dept metrics:** Clinical Quality and outcomes, practice productivity, Pt. Satisfaction • **Typical appt duration**: 1st – up to 45 mins, follows-ups 30mins • **AI adoption**: Moderate to high (workflow automation)	• **Type**: Community specialists & PCPs • **Personal focus**: Procedures and range of Rx (Early to Advanced) • **Dept metrics**: Pt. Satisfaction, practice productivity • **Typical appt duration**: 1st – up to 20 mins, follows-up 10mins, procedures can be longer • **AI adoption:** High (CDS, remote monitoring etc.)
Treatment philosophy	• Response-rate-driven mindset: Improve prognosis by leveraging advanced therapy options sooner	• Remission mindset with treat-to target/treat-to-failure approaches: Accelerate treatment to Adv Rx while navigating Prior Auths/Letters or Medical Necessity	• Improve patient satisfaction with treatment by leveraging 360-degree service mindset

Figure 6.4 Physicians' mindset across archetypes

strict adherence to guideline-directed medical therapy while addressing payer restrictions. Hypertension and hyperlipidemia are shifting to a Consumerism-led model where physicians act as coaches, supporting patients who use wearables, remote monitoring, and digital therapeutics. In the Uncharted space, conditions like NASH/NAFLD push physicians into an exploratory role, with unclear protocols and an increasing reliance on patient-reported outcomes.

- In oncology, physicians managing rare tumors in CoEs must stay at the forefront of research, clinical trials, and immunotherapy advancements to bring complex advancements like CAR-Ts to patients. For tumors with many more therapeutic options like breast cancer and non-small cell lung cancer, specialist oncologists navigate biomarker-driven treatment pathways while dealing with reimbursement challenges and access hurdles. In crowded tumor areas like prostate and early-stage breast cancer, patients are taking a more active role, using genomic testing and online decision tools and requiring physicians to interpret consumer-driven data and integrate it into care plans. In Uncharted tumor areas, such as neuroendocrine tumors, physicians must often advocate for experimental treatments or manage diagnostic ambiguity with limited guidelines.
- In neurology, CoEs dominate the management of complex disease states like spinal muscular atrophy, where neurologists manage gene therapy, specialized imaging, and complex multidisciplinary care. The gMG (generalized myasthenia gravis) treatment in specialist settings, on the other hand, requires physicians to optimize immunomodulatory therapies while navigating payer-driven access barriers. In migraines and mild cognitive impairment, the Consumerism-led model empowers patients with telemedicine, neuromodulation, and digital therapeutics, shifting physicians toward remote consultations and lifestyle-based interventions. Meanwhile, in Uncharted conditions like post-concussion syndrome, neurologists struggle with diagnostic clarity and treatment standardization, often facing patient skepticism and reliance on alternative care pathways.
- In immunology, conditions like polymyositis and dermatomyositis require CoE-led multispecialty coordination, with physicians balancing rheumatology, neurology, and dermatology insights to identify the right treatment approaches. In ulcerative colitis and Crohn's disease, specialists must sequence biologics, monitor disease progression, and navigate payer-imposed step therapies over the course of the patient's journey. In psoriasis and mild rheumatoid arthritis, telemedicine and patient-driven interventions are changing physician roles, shifting them toward virtual management and personalized lifestyle coaching. Meanwhile, in mast cell activation syndrome and chronic Lyme disease, physicians face uncertain diagnostic criteria, often debating between emerging science and patient-driven narratives in the Uncharted quadrant.

This results in heterogeneity among physicians, and we often observe a set of different archetypes that describe physician behavior and their engagement with their environment:

- **Visionaries** prioritize pushing the outcomes boundary and identifying or adopting better options. These physicians are often opinion leaders on the cutting edge of medical science.
- **Health system strategists** balance multiple treatment pathways while navigating payer constraints and cost effectiveness. They focus on pushing clinical care quality and outcomes with some ability to address patient satisfaction concerns. These physicians foster deeper relationships through shared decision-making, balancing clinical expertise with payer constraints.
- **Facilitators** are concerned with patient satisfaction and quality of clinical interactions as outcomes that are "table stakes" in their patients. These physicians engage in high-volume, patient-driven interactions, emphasizing accessibility and affordability, often leading to transactional relationships.

Each patient is unique, and so are their doctors

Physicians are not a homogeneous group of experts. The way they interact, deliver care, and connect with other parts of the system is deeply influenced by the myriad factors described in this chapter. Today's physician is no longer an independent medical scientist operating in a silo. Instead, they are a vital part of larger organizations that rely on multidisciplinary teams and advanced technology tools to help patients successfully navigate the complex healthcare ecosystem.

In managing patient care, a physician is heavily influenced by their: practice setup; team make-up; operating model around following and enforcing guidelines and ownership structures; key opinion leaders connections; payer guidelines that can highly inform services and drug choices; incoming patient's level of healthcare literacy and ability to advocate for themselves; healthcare ecosystem partners like specialty pharmacists and infusion service providers—as well as a variety of other factors.

Complementing this context of what makes a physician in practice, there is a human whose own lived experiences, beliefs, and attitudes, and what they see when they look across the table at each individual patient, shape their decisions and interactions each day. How they were trained, who they consult, and how the environment consistently (e.g., protocols and pathways) or acutely (e.g., staffing shortages) evolves can naturally change decisions. Decoding the physician and enabling them to derive and deliver the best possible treatment decisions for patients means understanding the person as much as the forces driving them.

Notes

1 Becker's Hospital Review. (2013, October 15). *42 statistics on independent physicians from 2000 to 2013.*

2 Carmichael, M. (2010). *Primary-care doctor shortage hurts our health.* Newsweek.

3 Miller, J. (2021). *Outpatient care in US shifts toward specialty care.* Healio.

4 Centers for Disease Control and Prevention. (2017). *Health, United States.* U.S. Department of Health and Human Services; Rice, T., Rosenau, P., Unruh, L. Y., & Barnes, A. J. (2020). *United States: Health system review 2020.* European Observatory on Health Systems and Policies.

5 Gamble, M. (2012). *42 statistics on independent physicians from 2000 to 2013.* Becker's Hospital Review.

6 Hest, R. (2025). *15 years of the Affordable Care Act: More Americans than ever have health insurance coverage.* State Health Access Data Assistance Center (SHADAC)

7 Toscano, F., O'Donnell, E., Broderick, J. E. et al. (2020). How physicians spend their work time: An ecological momentary assessment. *Journal of General Internal Medicine*, 35, 3166–3172. https://doi.org/10.1007/s11606-020-06087-4

8 Panagioti, M., Geraghty, K., Johnson, J., Zhou, A., Panagopoulou, E., Chew-Graham, C., Peters, D., Hodkinson, A., Riley, R., & Esmail, A. (2018). Association between physician burnout and patient safety, professionalism, and patient satisfaction: A systematic review and meta-analysis. *JAMA Internal Medicine*, 178(10), 1317–1331.

9 Avalere Health. (2024). *Updated report: Hospital and corporate acquisition of physician practices and physician employment 2019-2023.* Physician Advocacy Institute.

10 Davis, M. (2022). *Amid a physician shortage, 51% of primary care providers are nurse practitioners and physician assistants.* ValuePenguin.

11 Van Demark, D. C. (2020). *D. Secretary Azar calls on governors to modify regulations to expand healthcare workforce.* McDermott Will & Emery; National Academy for State Health Policy. (2020). *How the families first coronavirus response act affects state medicaid programs.*; Brooks, T. (2020). *Families first coronavirus response act freezes disenrollment in medicaid.* Georgetown University McCourt School of Public Policy.

12 Burus, T., Lei, F., Huang, B., Christian, W. J., Hull, P. C., Ellis, A. R., Slavova, S., Tucker, T. C., & Lang Kuhs, K. A. (2024). COVID-19 and rates of cancer diagnosis in the US. *JAMA Network Open*, 7(9), e2432288.

13 Berg, S. (2025). *U.S. physician burnout hits lowest rate since COVID-19.* AMA.

14 Yu, J., Civelek, Y. et al. (2024). *Telehealth delivery differs significantly by physician and practice characteristics.* Health Affairs; Olsen, E. (2024). *Female, nonrural physicians deliver more telehealth care study.* Healthcare Dive.

15 Yu, J., Civelek, Y. et al. (2024). *Telehealth delivery differs significantly by physician and practice characteristics.* Health Affairs; Thomas, N. (2024). *Telehealth delivery varies widely across physician age groups, practice areas.* Fierce Healthcare.

16 Stevens, J., Ruple, M., & Bhardwaj, M. (2023). *IDNs want to partner with life sciences to improve patient outcomes.* ZS Associates.

17 Jackson, C. (2025). *MDVIP/Ipsos primary care physicians survey 2024.* Ipsos.

18 Colturi, J., & Kim, A. (2023). *Can AI help increase time for patient care?* Op-Med.

19 ZS Associates. (2025). *ZS future of health report.*

20 Wilson, O. (2025). *AI diagnostics: Revolutionizing medical diagnosis in 2025.* Scispot.

21 ZS Associates. (2025). *ZS future of health report.*
22 Dall, T., et al. (2024). *The complexities of physician supply and demand: Projections from 2021 to 2036.* Association of American Medical Colleges.
23 Fastest Growing Occupations. (2022). U.S. Bureau of Labor Statistics. September 8.
24 Foster-Storch, S. (2023). *Tapping NPs and PAs in life sciences marketing.* PharmExec.com.
25 Braun-Inglis, C., Williams, E. L., Macchiaroli, A., Denicoff, A., & Gerber, D. E. (2022). Better late than never: Fully incorporating oncology advanced practice providers into cancer clinical trials. *JCO Oncology Practice*, 18(11): 729–732. https://pubmed.ncbi.nlm.nih.gov/35960907/

Chapter 7

Pharmaceuticals and Medical Devices

The Industry of Innovation

Howard Deutsch and Joe Stevens

The life sciences industry—encompassing pharmaceuticals, biotechnology, and medical technology—plays a central role in driving innovation, improving outcomes, and shaping healthcare costs. Yet, its inner workings often remain opaque to many outside it.

In this chapter, we will address some big questions about the life sciences industry:

- How does the industry determine which products to develop?
- How are drug prices set and why are there so many of them?
- What makes drug pricing such a hot-button topic?

While we will focus primarily on the pharmaceutical and biotechnology industry, much of what we discuss will also apply to many types of medical devices. However, the huge diversity of devices makes it difficult to make blanket statements for the entire industry. We will call out the most important differences as appropriate.

DOI: 10.4324/9781003603597-7

How the industry determines which products to develop

For a life sciences manufacturer, the product development approach is very simple in concept. The industry seeks to hit a sweet spot at the center of three areas, as shown in Figure 7.1.

While this schematic could describe nearly any industry, life sciences also have several features that shape investment choices to a greater or lesser extent, depending on the product. While each of these features may exist partially in other industries, the combination of these is unique to life sciences. Key characteristics that define the industry's investment landscape include:

- High uncertainty in product development
- Extremely long product development timelines
- Complex payment and intellectual property policies
- High development costs followed by low marginal cost of goods
- Heavy government regulation on product creation and commercialization
- The end customer and the payer are different

Let's take each of these in turn and describe how they shape product development decisions.

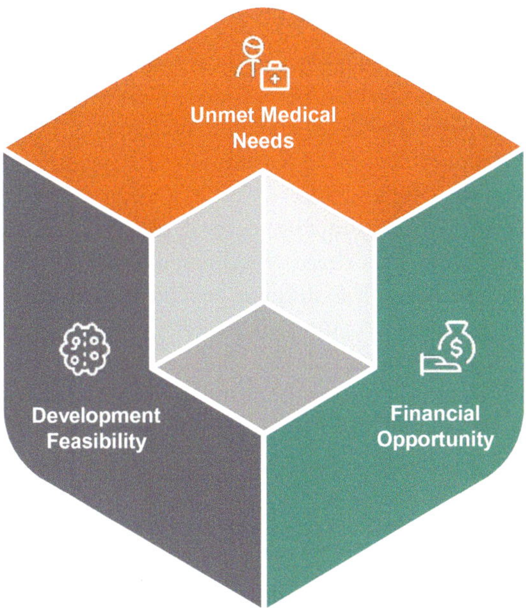

Figure 7.1 Strategic "sweet spot" for product development

High uncertainty in product development

Before a new drug ever reaches the market, it must overcome a series of scientific, regulatory, and financial hurdles—each steep and fraught with risk.

Exceedingly few drug candidates make it through the development gauntlet from discovery to regulatory approval. Only about 12% of preclinical candidates make it into human trials,[1] and only 13% of those drugs that start human trials get to approval, yielding an overall success rate of less than 2%.[2]

When accounting for the costs of both successful and failed trials, the average cost of bringing an approved medicine to market reaches several billion dollars. The most commonly cited estimate comes from the Tufts Center for the Study of Drug Development and was pegged at $2.6 billion in 2014—more than triple its 2003 estimate of $800 million. This trend suggests that by 2025, the true cost may far exceed even that.[3]

This level of uncertainty has two key industry implications. First, investors require a risk premium to compensate for the high likelihood of development failure. If industry revenues barely covered research and development costs, it would be unwise to invest in such a risky venture relative to investing in other sectors. Second, the required opportunity threshold for developing a drug is high. If the commercial opportunity for a new treatment is only small or moderate, it would be difficult to justify the development investment. In this sense, each successful drug must also "pay for" many failures.

Extremely long product development timelines

To make matters worse, developing a new drug is not only extremely risky, but it also takes an exceptionally long time. A drug usually goes through more than 10 years in human clinical trials (phases 1, 2, and 3), and if the preclinical phase is counted (as a product concept, or undergoing testing on animal models), the timeline to market can often double.

For the pharmaceutical company, even if the product succeeds clinically, the market it enters may look drastically different from the environment under which it was first conceived. This shift can be advantageous or challenging. Over the years, the prices a manufacturer could charge for a drug have been steadily increasing, boosting the value of almost all drugs under development (although simultaneously increasing pressure on patient out-of-pocket and insurer per-member-per-month costs). On the flip side, the emergence of unexpected discoveries or alternative uses of existing drugs during this long development period can reduce the unmet medical need by the time the original drug reaches the market, weakening its potential impact.

Complex payment and intellectual property policies

When assessing the commercial opportunity for a new product, an evaluation of unmet medical need is naturally paramount. How well-treated are patients with a particular disease? How much better might the new product candidate be, and in what ways? Is the new drug candidate more effective? For example, it might be easier for patients to tolerate or perhaps it is a tablet taken daily rather than an injection. But in addition to those considerations, intellectual property and payment policies place proverbial thumbs on the scale, favoring certain types of treatments over others.

Intellectual property for drugs in the United States is protected through an overlapping combination of patents and exclusivity rights. While many of the details of those regulations are beyond the scope of this chapter, we can call out some examples of how policy priorities shape drug development incentives. Perhaps the most prominent example is the Orphan Drug Act, enacted in 1983. The Orphan Drug Act provides a combination of incentives for companies to develop treatments for rare diseases. These include both tax credits for rare disease drug development and a longer exclusivity period post-approval: seven years for "orphan drugs" versus five years for typical drugs. The incentives embedded in the Orphan Drug Act led to significant industry investment in developing treatments for rare diseases, many of which may not have been commercially viable under prior policy.

Payment policies also influence commercial opportunity. The exact location in which a product is used has significant payment implications. Most medications are consumed in one of three types of settings:

1) Patients use the product themselves
2) Healthcare providers use the product on patients in a clinic or other outpatient facility
3) Healthcare providers use the product on patients in an inpatient facility

Each of these settings has its own pricing and reimbursement rules. For example, hospitals do not generally secure direct reimbursement for medicines that are administered on an inpatient basis. They are instead paid on a capitated basis, inclusive of all the care provided. The payment is tied to the specific reason for the patient's hospitalization, as specified in the diagnosis-related groups we discussed in detail in the payers chapter. This capitation creates a powerful disincentive for hospitals to adopt new expensive inpatient treatments unless those treatments can reduce other direct costs significantly, for example, by shortening a patient's inpatient stay. By contrast, drugs administered by healthcare providers in an outpatient setting are often profit drivers for those facilities. Drug developers understand these marketplace incentives and consequently invest less in inpatient therapies relative to outpatient therapies.

A more recent example of government incentives affecting drug development choices is the Inflation Reduction Act, passed in 2022. This law provided for direct government price-setting for Medicare and Medicaid populations once a drug has been commercially available for long enough. The law stipulated different time windows for non-biologic drugs (nine years) and biologic drugs (13 years) and included a special exemption for orphan drugs, but only when those drugs were approved for a single condition. The law shifted incentives for drugmakers, relatively discouraging the development of non-biologic treatments as well as studying orphan drugs for a second possible use. The implications of that policy change were both direct and public. Notably, Alnylam Pharmaceuticals announced in October 2022, two months after the passage of the Inflation Reduction Act, that it would no longer fund a late-stage trial for a second potential indication for its orphan drug, vutrisiran, while it "continues to evaluate the impact of the Inflation Reduction Act."[4]

High development costs followed by low marginal cost of goods

While bringing a drug candidate to market costs several billion dollars, once that candidate is approved, production costs tend to be quite low. There are exceptions, most notably advanced therapeutics like some cell therapies, but most treatments are quite inexpensive to manufacture relative to their prices. This dynamic is not unique to the pharmaceutical and biotechnology industries. For example, software applications also have significant upfront development costs, while additional copies of an application, once developed, cost almost nothing to produce.

High development cost followed by low-cost production has two implications. First, it makes the industry reliant on intellectual property protections. If anyone could produce copies of medicines once discovered by the intellectual property owner and approved by regulators, there would be no way to recoup the initial development investments. This makes patent length and enforcement policies critically important for supporting industry infrastructure. Second, this leads to a controversial global pricing dynamic in which the pharmaceutical and biotechnology industries are willing to accept lower prices outside the United States than inside the country. Without delving into country-specific nuances, the simple dynamic is that the value of pharmaceuticals can only exist when the intellectual property behind them is protected by a country's government. When that country then demands a price that is 50% or 75% lower than US prices, drug manufacturers prefer to acquiesce—both for the revenue opportunity and to mitigate the risk of intellectual property invalidation or other punitive action by the foreign government.

Heavy government regulation on product creation and commercialization

Almost all the layers under drug development and commercialization are heavily regulated. This regulatory regime provides substantial benefits to the pharmaceutical and biotechnology industry—but the costs are also quite clear. They include, but are not limited to, arduous clinical trials, complex regulatory filings for approval, personnel who interact with government agencies, and limitations on exactly how a drug's benefits can be communicated. The primary benefit is that government approval *means something*. The rigor of clinical trials and approval criteria mean that every drug approved today clears a high evidence bar. After a drug is approved, government oversight still doesn't end. Pharmaceutical companies are required to manufacture their drugs in facilities that adhere to strict process control and safety standards ("good manufacturing practices"), and remain alert even after their drug is on the market for any reports of unexpected risks to their patients (pharmacovigilance).

Before these processes existed, there were numerous examples of "snake-oil" drugs that didn't deliver any of the promised efficacy, and even drugs that were clearly harmful. While it's true that non-efficacious and/or harmful drugs have still made it to market despite government approval, the number and frequency of these cases have certainly declined. In this sense, the trust conveyed by government approval is as important for the development of the pharmaceutical market as intellectual property protection.

Engagement with this level of regulation is both costly and time-consuming. Additionally, regulatory policies influence the types of medicines developed and how evidence is generated. For example, it is increasingly understood that patients may suffer from "metabolic syndrome," which places them at high risk of diabetes, heart failure, and kidney disease. Many drugmakers have formed business units that combine two or more cardiovascular, renal, and metabolism therapy areas accordingly. Some medications initially developed to treat type 2 diabetes have shown efficacy in treating heart failure and kidney disease. However, we do not yet see medicines developed to treat metabolic syndrome because it is not currently recognized as a disease by the US FDA, so there is no regulatory approval pathway.

The end customer and the payer are different

One of the unusual features of the healthcare market is that the consumer—the patient—tends to pay only a small percentage of the costs while another entity—the health insurer, or payer—covers the rest. That payer, consequently, plays a significant role in influencing the types of care the patient receives.

To be commercially successful, new drug candidates must satisfy three different constituencies with overlapping but different priorities: patients, prescribers, and payers.

- **Patients** seek convenient treatments that will improve their health and/or quality of life with few unpleasant side effects or safety risks, and at low prices.
- **Prescribers** seek treatments that will improve patient health and require little work on their part for patients to get.

Table 7.1 Market dynamics across stakeholders for select therapeutic areas

Category	*Patient Perspective*	*Prescriber Perspective*	*Payer Perspective*	*Result*
Insomnia	Many options already exist across nondrug, over-the-counter, and generic drug remedies: None are perfect but many patients are satisfied with existing options	Prescribers recognize some of the downsides of existing treatments, but it is an area of high concern for many of them	Many effective existing options are quite inexpensive, making it a low priority to spend more on new medicines	Limited commercial opportunity, absent truly groundbreaking innovation
Obesity	While many options have long existed, most non-surgical treatments don't work for patients while the newest prescription medications work very well, leading to extremely high demand	Prescribers are impressed with the effectiveness of the newest obesity medicines, but worry about difficulties in patient coverage and their own effort required to help patients get started	Large eligible populations and high prices cause significant affordability fears, even though today's treatments represent major clinical improvements	Significant commercial opportunity, though with big challenges in enabling most eligible patients to benefit
Cancer	Needs vary by disease type and patient situation, but most patients seek better treatments that can extend and improve quality of life	Oncologists are regularly looking for innovation and the best possible treatments to extend patient life	Payers are hesitant to limit cancer medication coverage, given disease severity	The market remains extremely positive for new treatment innovations that promise even modest improvements

- **Payers** seek treatments that will improve patient health as long as they are not too expensive relative to other available options.

If any of these three constituencies says "no" to a medication, the patient will not receive it. This complex dynamic significantly influences the types of medications drugmakers study. We can look at a few different drug categories as examples (see Table 7.1) to see how they play out differently and how that influences focus areas for investment.

Each major stakeholder's priorities must align sufficiently for a drug candidate to have strong commercial prospects. This has been a key driver for the evolution in the pharmaceutical and biotechnology industry's investment areas in less common severe diseases over the past 20 years.

Considerations differ between drugs, medical devices, and commodities

Myriad specialized medical products are used in providing patient care, and the dynamics of all these do not function in the same way. At a high level, it's often useful to consider three categories of products: pharmaceuticals, medical devices, and commodities (see Table 7.2).

Table 7.2 Applicability of healthcare market factors across products

	Pharmaceuticals	*Medical Devices*	*Commodities used in healthcare*
High development uncertainty	✓	×	×
Long development timeline	✓	×	×
Complex payment and intellectual property	✓	Sometimes	×
Costly development followed by low COGS	✓	Sometimes	×
Heavy government regulation	✓	✓	Sometimes
Different end customer and payer	✓	Sometimes	Sometimes

Pharmaceuticals are a relatively easy category to understand. Any substance administered to a patient for the purpose of influencing some biological process can be thought of as a drug. In general, each of the six key industry characteristics will usually be true of drugs to a greater or lesser extent. In this way, drugs are the most distinctive of the products made for healthcare, which is why they have been the major focus of this chapter.

There is also a great deal of technology used in healthcare that isn't a drug. We collectively refer to these technologies as "medical devices," but the category is so broad it defies easy description. This can include extremely large capital equipment such as an MRI machine, an implantable device used in surgery such as a stent, or a device used at home by a patient, such as a blood glucose monitor. Across this spectrum, we can think of the dynamics of medical devices as more or less like drugs.

The most "drug-like" medical devices are items like blood glucose monitors. They are generally prescribed by a physician, paid for by a patient's insurance, and often "dispensed" by the patient's pharmacy. Most of the unique features of healthcare products are present, although some are not. For example, this type of device usually has a much shorter development timeline than a drug and much less uncertainty. Depending on the device, many also have a higher marginal cost of goods (as a percentage of its value) than drugs do.

Products used during surgery, such as stents or orthopedic implants, have many of the same market drivers as drug-like blood glucose monitors; however, the purchasing dynamics are very different. For example, the healthcare provider tends to choose the products used during a procedure. Since the patient's insurance will usually pay the healthcare provider a predetermined fee for a given procedure, the provider alone determines which products to use and the payer's perspective ceases to be a factor in decision-making. In this way, the market for these devices is more like a traditional "business-to-business" transaction for some type of supply used in its operation. This is also true of the capital equipment used in healthcare facilities—which include such items as an MRI machine, surgical robot, or plasma exchange machine. Even though these items are used in patient care, the market dynamics are more similar to capital equipment purchases in any other industry. Some unique facets of the healthcare market apply—for example, intellectual property is important, devices are usually still highly regulated, and clearance by the FDA is needed before they can be used—but most do not.

Finally, many commodities are used in healthcare delivery, including such items as personal protective equipment (PPE), hand sanitizer, and thermometers. This market may be somewhat regulated (e.g., hand sanitizer must contain a certain percentage of alcohol and PPE must adhere to certain specifications). Still, it is not subject to significant intellectual property or payer dynamics. The best way to think about these commodity products is not as "healthcare products" as much as "regular products that happen to be used in healthcare."

Importantly, many products don't fit cleanly into one of these three groups (for example, interesting drug-device combinations such as the drug-eluting stent or drugs packaged in a unique inhaler or autoinjector). In these cases, it's impossible to pinpoint if a product is a "drug, device, or commodity," but it's still useful to think about which of the six healthcare market factors apply when attempting to understand how they operate.

Price as a driver of financial opportunity and investment decisions

Thinking back to the drivers of investment decisions—unmet medical needs, development feasibility, and financial opportunity—the last of these three deserves a bit more consideration, as it is the one most directly shaped by the stakeholders in the ecosystem.

"Unmet medical needs" refers to the degree to which care for a given condition is less than ideal today. This is essentially a function of medical best practices, the availability of skilled staff, and technological capability. "Development feasibility" is fundamentally an engineering and operational question: Can we achieve a given goal in a reasonable time and cost? While both can be influenced (e.g., by discovering a better medical practice or by changing the regulations around what is required for drug approval), that influence is usually indirect and difficult to achieve. These two topics are also not the focus of this book.

"Financial opportunity," how much money you can make off a product, is a function of price and access. Price is, of course, how much each patient will pay or have paid on their behalf for a particular product. Access refers to how easy or difficult it is for patients who need a product to get it paid for (by themselves or their insurance) and is usually highly dependent upon price. Both are directly impacted by the various ecosystem stakeholders that are the focus of this book. For this reason, it is worth examining the question of pricing in a bit more detail, using the example of drugs as the quintessential healthcare product.

How drug prices are set and why there are so many of them

Drug pricing is, in a word, complicated. If we added another word, it might be "fraught," since drug pricing often elicits strong emotions from people inside and outside the industry. In this section, we seek to demystify many aspects of drug pricing. In particular, we will address the following questions:

1) How do drugmakers set prices in the United States?
2) How does US drug pricing contrast with pricing in other countries?

3) What are some of the different types of US prices?
4) How do drug prices relate to what a patient pays at the pharmacy?

How drugmakers set prices in the United States

In the United States, unlike in most other markets, drugmakers theoretically can select a list price without much interference from the government—they're free to choose whatever price they want. Practically, however, drugmakers often encounter either hard or soft constraints on pricing decisions.

Drugmakers in the United States will generally consider several criteria when determining a new drug candidate's list price. These include, though are not limited to:

- The level of therapeutic advance over alternative options. A new drug candidate that works more effectively than existing competitors, for example, may be priced at a premium to that of the competition.
- Prices for drugs in other categories that offer similar types of benefits. This is a common set of guideposts in categories with limited competition, such as in many rare diseases.
- Payers' willingness to cover the treatment. Drugmakers will conduct extensive market research to understand how insurers will cover a drug at different potential price points. For example, if a new cardiovascular treatment is perceived to be too expensive, payers may require cardiologists to complete laborious paperwork before the treatment is authorized for a patient, thereby reducing the number of patients who may benefit.
- The cost of manufacturing and distribution, especially for advanced therapies that are expensive to produce.
- The patient population size, which impacts the total cost for payers (and likewise the total revenue available to the manufacturer).
- Organizational pricing philosophy and internal benchmarks. Many drugmakers have articulated pricing philosophies that guide pricing decisions.

The reason drugmakers consider the abovementioned factors is that payers have various mechanisms to push back against prices perceived to be "out of line" and, thus, reduce an improperly priced drug's marketability. In most cases, this is through utilization management tools (discussed extensively in the payers chapter), but can also be driven by decisions made by the healthcare provider or patient, depending on the market.

In competitive categories, the prices that payers already pay for existing treatments serve to constrain a new entrant's price. If a new drug candidate is substantially more expensive than existing treatments, and in a way that is not justified by the degree of therapeutic advance, health insurers may relegate that treatment to usage only for a small subset of patients who fail on one or several other treatments, or they may decline to cover the new drug candidate altogether.

Even with limited or no competitors, softer constraints exist. First is the drugmaker's pricing philosophy and internal assessment of the relationship between a drug's value and its price. Second is concern about backlash and reputation risk from a pricing decision that others consider inappropriate. That backlash could come from health insurers, medical experts, patient groups, and government officials. In one prominent example from 2012, expert oncologists from Memorial Sloan Kettering, in the opinion pages of *The New York Times*, declared a new cancer treatment, Zaltrap, would not be used in their facility because it was too expensive relative to a clinically comparable alternative.[5] The PCSK9 inhibitor category is another example of an aggressive pricing backlash, this time from payers. This category of drugs is exceptionally effective at reducing LDL cholesterol, far outshining statin therapies such as atorvastatin (Lipitor) and rosuvastatin (Crestor). However, the statin drugs were available generically for pennies each day. Even before PCSK9 inhibitors were approved, concerns about their affordability had already surfaced. ExpressScripts' Chief Medical Officer, Dr. Steve Miller, stated on the evening of the drug's approval that the class could become "the most costly therapy our country has seen." When those treatments were approved, utilization restrictions were extraordinarily aggressive, sharply dampening market demand. Aside from the demand risk, corporate leaders are also protective of their organizations' reputations and want to avoid being perceived as high-price outliers.

However, payers can't push back against high prices in all cases. Severe diseases with only one treatment option, particularly if present in children, are a common case where drug manufacturers have extremely strong pricing power. For example, Spark Therapeutics made headlines in 2018 when it launched a gene therapy to treat a rare form of hereditary blindness at $850,000 per patient.[6] While undoubtedly expensive, health insurers had little choice but to foot the bill because the therapy worked and no other options existed to bring sight back to these patients.

How US drug pricing contrasts with pricing in other countries

The approach to pricing in the United States, where the interplay between multiple stakeholders determines the price of a drug, is different from how new drugs are priced in most other developed countries. Most other major pharmaceutical markets use one of three primary pricing mechanisms, all driven by government bodies:

1. **Comparative effectiveness:** In this approach, a government-designated body will compare the data for a new drug candidate with other available options. A price is determined for the drug by assessing how much better (if

at all) it may be and then setting a price relative to those alternatives. France is an example of a country that uses such a mechanism.

2. **Health economics:** In this approach, a government-designated body assesses the clinical value provided by a new drug according to a framework or formula, and then assigns a financial value to that clinical value. For example, if a new cancer treatment can extend a patient's life by a year, that one year has a prespecified economic value. A drug will be covered if its price is below the economic threshold set for its clinical impact. The United Kingdom uses health economics assessments for its drug coverage and price determination.
3. **International price referencing:** Some countries, rather than doing their own clinical and economic assessments, rely on pricing benchmarks from other countries. The exact nations that make up the price references may vary from one country that employs this approach to another. Switzerland is one country that uses international price referencing.

The consistent appeal of such pricing approaches is apparent: Politicians see them as a way to rein in pharmaceutical companies' pricing power. For example, as we wrote this chapter, an executive order called for various US federal agencies to "communicate most-favored-nation price targets to pharmaceutical manufacturers to bring prices for American patients in line with comparably developed nations"[7]—an example of international price referencing. Other attempts have been made to integrate versions of these approaches in the United States, most notably by the non-profit Institute for Clinical and Economic Review, which promotes a health economics-driven methodology. While adoption may yet happen, currently, none of these approaches impacts pharmaceutical pricing or payer coverage policy in a meaningful way in the United States.

The different types of US prices

While a drugmaker sets a drug's list price in the United States, the net price the drugmaker realizes is often quite different, as is the effective price that actually gets paid for a patient receiving care. Complicating this are several different measures of price in the marketplace, usually with confusing acronyms. The list price is usually referred to as the wholesale acquisition cost (WAC). From here, several different market segments are legally mandated to receive discounts. The largest such segments are state Medicaid programs, and drugs sourced to a pharmacy affiliated with health systems that qualify for 340B pricing. Both Medicaid and 340B sales volume have a discount formula that accounts for a drug's list price, any history of drug price increases, and any discounts available to other market segments.

In addition to WAC, drugs have "list" prices through other parts of the supply chain, and these are measured in terms of historical averages. Some often-used examples are the average manufacturer's price, the average price at which wholesalers purchase drugs from a manufacturer, and the average wholesale price (AWP), the list price wholesalers charge to pharmacies and other downstream purchasers of the drug. Although discounts are provided through the supply chain to both wholesalers and retailers, markup also occurs. AWP, in particular, is prone to price inflation and can often be significantly higher than the WAC for a particular drug.

All market segments may also receive discounts or rebates at the drugmaker's discretion. The most common such situation is where drugmakers negotiate rebates with pharmacy benefit managers (PBMs) and other health insurers in exchange for favorable coverage of their treatments or limitations on the coverage of competing treatments. One typical form of this negotiation is when a PBM tells all drugmakers in a category it will only select one or two treatments for favorable coverage and heavily restrict others. The PBM then solicits rebate bids from all competing drugmakers to identify which treatments will be readily available to patients. It is common in many competitive categories for such rebates to exceed 50% of a drug's WAC.

In certain situations, healthcare providers receive direct discounts or rebates from manufacturers as well, particularly for treatments that are administered by those providers, rather than self-administered by patients. Average sales price (ASP) is the term for the historical measure of the actual price paid by providers for these products, after factoring in any discount.

Taken together, the array of discounts and rebates—both legally mandated and discretionary—result in a system in which the drugmaker has significant control over the WAC price, but far less over the net price it realizes for a medicine and even less over what a patient actually pays. As intermediaries in the ecosystem like PBMs have consolidated and garnered greater power, their negotiation leverage has created an environment where the average unit net price for medicines has declined year-over-year for many drugmakers. A study by the Drug Channels Institute found the average reduction from list price exceeded 50% for a basket of five major pharma manufacturers.[8]

The discount negotiations with different intermediaries are also proprietary, leading to varied coverage and discounts for a single drug depending on a patient's insurance coverage. These variations also play an important role in the out-of-pocket price a patient pays at the pharmacy when filling a prescription, as we describe in more detail in the following section.

How drug prices relate to what a patient pays at the pharmacy

Are drug prices related to what patients pay at the proverbial pharmacy counter? They are, but that out-of-pocket price is one of several interconnected factors. Collectively, these factors are the major drivers when we think of "access," as they represent how easy or difficult it is for the patient to receive a particular drug (although the word "access" can refer to other, less common barriers as well). These factors include:

- The structure of the patient's health plan, often referred to as the "benefit design"
- The drug's list price
- The drug's coverage within the patient's health plan, often referred to as "formulary position"
- The availability of co-pay discounts for the drug, and the patient's eligibility for those discounts

When taken together, the result is a very wide variation in the exact prices different patients see for the same prescription medicine (or even the prices the same patient may see at different times), ranging from free to prices that exceed the medicine's list price.

A patient's benefit design describes their out-of-pocket responsibilities for medicines. The benefit may include a deductible, or the amount a patient must spend in a given year before insurance coverage kicks in. Beyond the existence and size of the deductible, there is typically a set of drug tiers with different associated co-pay levels. Sometimes, those tiers have a flat co-pay level (e.g., $10 for a generic medicine, $50 for a preferred branded medicine, and $100 for a non-preferred branded medicine). Other benefit designs include coinsurance tiers that specify patient prices as a percentage of the drug's retail price (e.g., 30% of WAC). Benefit designs also include a maximum annual out-of-pocket spend level, above which the patient no longer shoulders co-pay responsibilities.

A drug's list price has a direct bearing on a patient's out-of-pocket costs in situations where the drug is placed on a patient's coinsurance tier. In other cases, the drug price and discounts indirectly affect the patient's out-of-pocket responsibility through the contracting process that determines the drug's formulary position.

Finally, drugmakers commonly offer co-pay discounts for branded medicines. These discounts typically take the form of "pay no more than $x" with caps on the total discount available. For example, consider a drug with a retail price of $500 and a co-pay program in which a patient pays no more than $10, with a maximum monthly discount of $100. In this example, if the patient does not have a deductible and the drug is covered on their plan with a co-pay of $50, they only pay $10. If the patient has a $1,000 deductible and this medicine is their first prescription for the year, the co-pay discount will be the maximum level of $100, leaving the patient with a cost of $400. It is also important to note that only patients with private insurance are eligible for most co-pay discount programs. Patients on different government plans (Medicare and Medicaid, primarily) are ineligible for them due to regulations that make such assistance illegal.

What makes drug pricing such a hot-button topic?

Public approval of the pharmaceutical and biotechnology industry is very poor, as annual Gallup surveys can attest. Each year, Gallup asks Americans for their opinions on 25 different industries, and in the most recent poll in August 2024, the industry ranked dead last: Only 20% of respondents reported a positive opinion versus 61% with a negative one.[9] This –41% net positive rating made it the only industry to have lower public approval than the federal government (–32%). While public opinion of the pharmaceutical and biotechnology industry has been poor for decades, it has dipped sharply in recent years. Some of this has surely been driven by the political environment, particularly around the COVID-19 pandemic and vaccines. However, drug pricing is a long-standing and prominent lightning rod for the industry's critics.

In this section, we describe the most common criticisms of drug pricing and explain some of the dynamics that cause those pricing situations. This is not intended to be read as either an attack on, or defense of, industry practices, but rather a description of what is happening and why.

Drug pricing critics in the United States typically make three different, albeit related, claims:

1. Drug prices are dramatically higher than manufacturing costs
2. The United States pays much higher prices for drugs than other countries do
3. Patients struggle to afford their medicines because drugmakers charge so much

In one recent prominent example, Vermont Senator Bernie Sanders made all three of these points in March 2024 when talking about the Novo Nordisk drug, Ozempic:

> Today, a new Yale study found that Ozempic costs less than $5 a month to manufacture. And yet, Novo Nordisk charges Americans nearly $1,000 a month for this drug, while the same exact product can be purchased for just $155 a month in Canada and just $59 in Germany… A prescription drug is not safe or effective for a patient who cannot afford it.

Let's look at each of these three claims in more detail.

Drug prices are dramatically higher than manufacturing costs

The most common form of this drug pricing criticism suggests drugmakers gouge the public by charging many multiples of the cost of making a medicine. While there are exceptions, most notably with advanced therapies such as CAR-Ts, the core claim is true. The cost of manufacturing tends to be a small percentage of a drug's price, often lower than 10%. The implication is that drugmakers could make strong profits while charging much lower prices, and the purportedly inflated prices are evidence of unchecked corporate greed.

The pharmaceutical and biotechnology industry often pushes back on this critique by noting that drug profit margins for post-commercial approval must cover the high pre-approval development costs. Less often stated is that drugs are far from unique in having this sort of pricing structure. In fact, it is a common feature of industries with high upfront intellectual property development costs. For example, developing a new software product may be expensive, but once it is created, "manufacturing" an instance of the software product for a new user is almost cost-free. Ebooks are another great example. As of this writing, Senator Sanders' ebook, *It's Okay to be Angry About Capitalism*, is available on Amazon's Kindle E-reader for $8.99. The cost of manufacturing a version of that book on any reader's device is quite close to zero, and yet there is little outrage about this particular markup because we understand intuitively that if ebooks were priced near their manufacturing costs, few people could affordably write them.

Why then is the public not angrier about Senator Sanders' ebook not being free? The answer lies in the belief that consuming healthcare is not the same as most of the other goods we buy. While we have a choice whether or not to buy an ebook, when a patient is sick and wants to get well, it is easy for them to feel as if they are at the mercy of the medical system with no choice but to pay whatever is required.

The United States pays much higher prices for drugs than other countries do

This critique is pervasive across the political spectrum in the United States. If drugmakers are willing to sell their medicines at much lower prices in other countries, why are prices so high in the United States?

The pharmaceutical and biotechnology industry will sometimes argue that the differences in drug pricing between the United States and other countries are overstated because the comparisons focus on gross prices, while many drugs are heavily discounted in the United States. While true, researchers find that even when accounting for those discounts, US prices for branded drugs are substantially higher than prices in other countries. A RAND study from early 2024 found gross prices for branded drugs in the United States are 422% of the prices in other high-income countries. Once accounting for discounts, that number dropped but remained above 300%.[10] While the exact price ratio and list of comparable countries can be debated, in all cases, it's clear that the United States pays much more than almost everywhere else.

When assessing this critique, there are two important pieces of context to consider. First, drugs are not the only component of healthcare that is priced differently in the United States than in other countries. Most components of healthcare are more expensive in the United States than elsewhere and differences in drug spending explain only a small percentage of the higher healthcare spending levels observed.

Second, the lower prices paid by other countries are, on their own, insufficient to fund a vibrant industry that continues to invest in new treatments. The rate of return on investment for pharma R&D varies by time and measurement method, but is usually less than 10%. The United States alone accounts for more than 60% of the sales of new, innovative pharmaceuticals.[11] It's easy to see why an even small decline in US market potential could turn the average ROI negative, causing pharma companies to fund fewer, lower-risk assets, eventually leading to fewer innovative drugs that can improve treatment for patients.

A drugmaker may be willing to sell a medicine at a much lower price in, say, France than it does in the United States because commercializing in France may be more profitable than not doing so, given the medicine already exists. However, if the US price declined to match that of the French price, the entire commercial potential may not justify developing the drug in the first place. In this case, it is true that Americans shoulder more of the cost burden for medications than patients in other countries do. And it is reasonable to find this unfair. However, it's unclear what action can be taken to improve the situation. Policies that seek to match US prices to the lower prices of other nations could cause the industry to develop many fewer drugs. While this might reduce costs, this isn't necessarily an optimal outcome for the United States, which is able and willing to devote significant resources to pharmaceutical innovation and better health. On the other hand, denying innovative therapies to patients in a country that cannot or will not pay the US price is both bad for those patients and reduces total revenue for pharma. As we've discussed, the entire pharma and biotech market exists due to intellectual property protection and the trust conveyed by regulatory approval. A country that denied innovative pharmaceuticals could also just grant another group the right to ignore the patent. This process, often referred to as "compulsory licensing," has already occurred for several branded pharmaceuticals in India.[12]

Patients struggle to afford their medicines because drugmakers charge so much

Senator Sanders is, of course, correct that a patient who cannot afford their medication is unable to benefit from it. The Kaiser Family Foundation found in 2023 that over a quarter of adults report struggling to afford their medications.[13] In the same survey, 82% of respondents "say the cost of prescription drugs is unreasonable." Further, those respondents think they know whom to blame. The most commonly cited "major factor contributing to the price of prescription drugs" was industry profit.

With prescription medication comprising only a modest percentage of total US healthcare spending, why are drug prices such a focus for affordability concerns? One possible driver is that patients pay a higher percentage of drug costs directly, while health insurance picks up more of the tab elsewhere. Federal health spending data lends some credence to this claim. In 2023, the United States spent $450 billion on prescription medications with patient out-of-pocket spending contributing $58 billion of that figure (13%). By contrast, the US's spending on hospital care was more than three times higher at $1,520 billion, but patients paid only $38 billion of that out-of-pocket (2.5%).[14] These differences in out-of-pocket responsibility may lead to misperceptions about sources of healthcare costs.

Patients also naturally infer that when prices at the pharmacy counter are high, the reason is that drugmakers charge high prices and realize outsized profits. That is not, however, entirely true. Often, prices are high for reasons that have little to do with the drugmaker's profit. In research conducted by ZS in 2022, more than half of drug affordability issues reported by patients were associated with generic drugs, that is, those for which the original drug developer was no longer responsible for the price.[15] While some generic treatments remain expensive due to limited supply or other complexities, most such medicines have very low wholesale prices. However, retail prices at the pharmacy are marked up dramatically. Patients may be correct that they are "getting gouged," while being incorrect about exactly who is doing that gouging.

None of these observations suggests that the pharmaceutical and biotechnology industry bears no responsibility for perceptions of unfair or inappropriate pricing. But the broader context can help explain why medicines in particular are subject to outsized public ire. Those perceptions do create significant risk for drugmakers as they provide fodder across the political spectrum in the United States for drug price control advocacy. Both major US political parties have pursued such price controls in recent years, albeit in different ways. The Democratic Party passed the Inflation Reduction Act in 2022, providing for direct government price controls on some medicines through a negotiation mechanism. A few years later, in early 2025, a Republican president issued an executive order to sell drugs to the United States at "most favored nation" pricing to eliminate the disparity between costs in the United States and other countries, although the way this will be implemented remains unclear as of this book's writing. While the market environment remains strong for new drug candidates in early 2025, significant changes to drug pricing policy in the United States are a major risk for investors.

Working with manufacturers

This chapter provided an overview of some of the environmental forces influencing drug and medical device development decisions, an introduction to drug pricing, and a review of why those prices are so controversial. While far from exhaustive, readers can now better appreciate some of the "hows and whys" behind the industry's foundational behaviors. Pharmaceutical and medical device manufacturers operate in a very unique market environment. The general criticism of these companies is that while the innovations they create are valuable, they come at too high a cost to the patient and society. Just asking these companies to behave differently ignores the reasons why their innovations are expensive in the first place, and that some of these reasons are beyond the manufacturers' control. Life sciences manufacturers, however, recognize that their innovations are meaningless if price makes them inaccessible to patients. When working with these companies, a practical approach to identifying and creating solutions to patient access challenges remains the best way to get things done.

Notes

1 That's Nice. (2016). *Preclinical development: The safety hurdle prior to human trials.* American Pharmaceutical Review.
2 Yamaguchi, S., Kaneko, M., & Narukawa, M. (2021). *Approval success rates of drug candidates based on target, action, modality, application, and their combinations.* Clinical and Translational Science.
3 DiMasi, J., Grabowski, H., & Hansen, R. (2016). Innovation in the pharmaceutical industry: New estimates of R&D costs. *Journal of Health Economics*, 47, 20–33.
4 Alnylam Pharmaceuticals. (2022). *Q3 Report.*
5 Bach, P. B., Saltz, L. B., & Wittes, R. E. (2012). In cancer care, cost matters. *The New York Times.*
6 Spark's gene therapy price tag: $850,000. Nature Biotechnology, 36, 122 (2018). https://doi.org/10.1038/nbt0218-122
7 *Executive Orders. Delivering Most-Favored-Nation Prescription Drug Pricing to American Patients.* (2025). The White House. www.whitehouse.gov/presidential-actions/2025/05/delivering-most-favored-nation-prescription-drug-pricing-to-american-patients/
8 Fein, A. (2019). *Half-off sale! Five major drugmakers reveal vast gross-to-net price gaps—and why rebate reform is still needed.* Drug Channels.
9 Gallup. (n.d.). *Business and industry sector ratings.*
10 Mulcahy, A. W., Schwam, D., & Lovejoy, S. L. (2021). *International prescription drug price comparisons* (Research Report No. RRA788-3). RAND Corporation.

11 European Federation of Pharmaceutical Industries and Associations. (2023). *The pharmaceutical industry in figures: Key data 2023*.
12 Shah, R. (2021). *Compulsory license: India*. Kluwer Patent Blog.
13 Sparks, G., Kirzinger, A., Montero, A., Valdes, I., & Hame, L. (2024). *Public opinion on prescription drugs and their prices*. KFF.
14 Centers for Medicare & Medicaid Services. (n.d.). *National health expenditure data: Historical (NHE Tables – Table 4)*. U.S. Department of Health and Human Services.
15 Deutsch, H., & Sadiua, M. (2022). *Working toward a comprehensive affordability agenda: How to end the drug price blame game* (Research Report). ZS Associates.

Chapter 8

Intermediaries

The Glue that Holds It All Together

Ricky Yuen, Sean Scobell, Harshil Gagnani, and Joe Stevens

In healthcare, intermediaries are entities that operate between two or more primary stakeholders—such as patients, providers, payers, manufacturers, and government agencies—to manage specific administrative, logistical, or financial functions. They are not directly involved in the delivery of medical care but play a crucial role in how care is accessed, paid for, and regulated. Examples include pharmacy benefit managers (PBMs) that manage drug formularies and rebates, group purchasing organizations (GPOs) that negotiate bulk purchasing for hospitals, and third-party administrators (TPAs) that handle insurance claims and benefits. In this chapter, we will learn:

- How intermediaries emerged and evolved in the US healthcare system
- Who the core (direct) intermediaries are and what roles they play (e.g., PBMs, GPOs, TPAs)
- The functions and influence of other (indirect) intermediaries in the healthcare value chain
- Real-world examples that illustrate how intermediaries impact cost, access, and efficiency
- Key themes and considerations for engaging in or working effectively with intermediaries

DOI: 10.4324/9781003603597-8

Intermediaries and their types

With increasing complexity in treatments, regulations, and reimbursement models, intermediaries have become a critical part of the healthcare ecosystem. Their initial purpose was to improve efficiency, quality, and financial coordination by facilitating and managing interactions, contracts, and services across the system. However, that is not all they do. Some intermediaries have shifted from enabling value to extracting it, adding administrative burden, increasing costs, and leveraging their central position for financial gain.

Today, intermediaries hold significant influence across the healthcare value chain, often at the expense of affordability, patient access, and system sustainability. Understanding their evolving role (see Figure 8.1) is essential for identifying reform opportunities and promoting transparency.

Types of intermediaries

Intermediaries can be broadly categorized based on their influence in the drug value chain as Direct (Core) or Indirect (Other) intermediaries.

Direct/core intermediaries: Entities that directly shape the drug value chain by influencing operations, pricing, access, and efficiency—such as PBMs, payers, and distributors.

Indirect/other intermediaries: Entities that do not operate within the core value chain but still impact it by influencing supporting functions like policy, technology, data, and compliance.

Let's explore each of these in more detail.

Direct/core intermediaries

Wholesalers and distributors became essential intermediaries in the healthcare system as the products used in patient care increased in scale and complexity. For example, in the early 20th century, pharmaceutical manufacturers typically supplied hospitals and physicians directly. However, as drug production expanded and healthcare providers continued to grow and become more geographically dispersed, the need arose for specialized entities to manage inventory, logistics, and distribution. Pharmaceutical wholesalers centralized product distribution, enabling healthcare facilities to efficiently access a broad range of pharmaceuticals and medical supplies. By the latter half of the 20th century, advancements in logistics and information systems further optimized their role, making wholesalers critical to ensuring the timely and reliable delivery of healthcare products. Today, wholesalers and distributors continue to serve as key facilitators in the pharmaceutical supply chain (see Figure 8.2), balancing cost efficiency with supply chain resilience.[1]

GPOs originated from informal collaborations among hospitals to form centralized purchasing functions and became more structured after World War

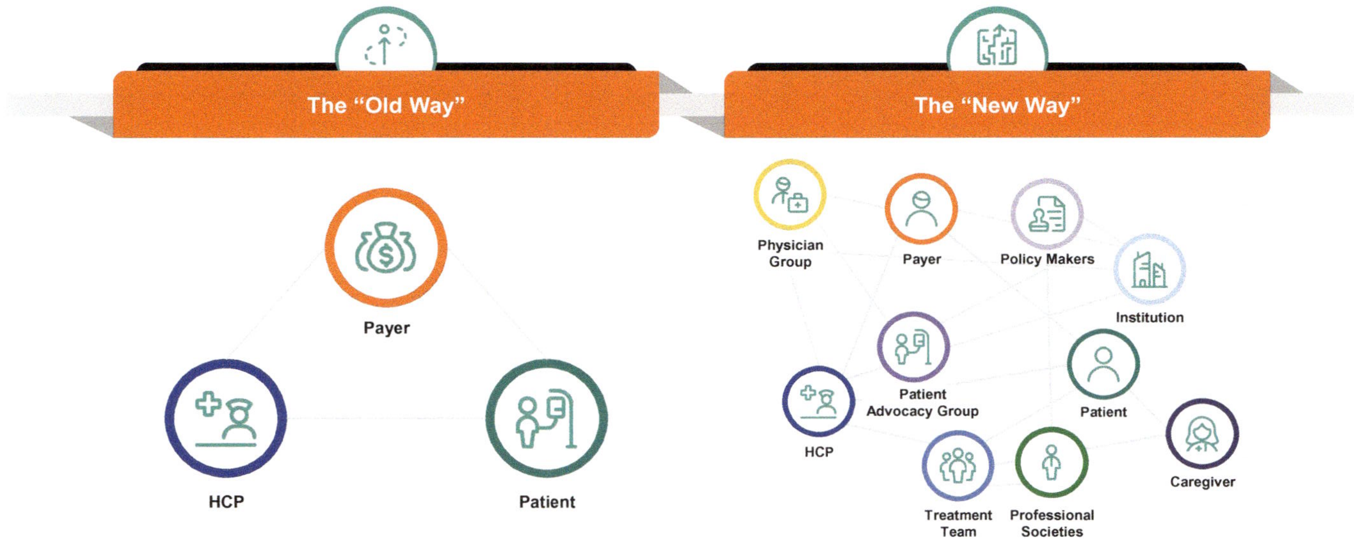

Figure 8.1 Healthcare landscape becoming more complex with emergence of new stakeholders

II as medical facility expansion and technological advancements increased the demand for supplies. By the 1960s and 1970s, they played a key role in reducing procurement costs amid rising healthcare expenses and supply chain complexities. Over time, their scope expanded beyond purchasing to contract management, supply chain optimization, and data analytics. Specialty GPOs also emerged to focus specifically on high-cost therapies managed by similarly specialized providers such as oncologists and rheumatologists. Today, GPOs remain central to healthcare procurement, influencing pricing and distribution while facing scrutiny over their market impact.[2]

PBMs emerged within the US healthcare system in response to the rising costs and complexities of managing prescription drug benefits. Before their widespread adoption, employers and insurers managed pharmacy benefits directly, a practice that became increasingly unsustainable by the late 20th century. PBMs started as TPAs, with their role limited to processing claims and negotiating discounts with pharmacies through bulk purchasing. However, as prescription drug spending surged due to the availability of new pharmaceuticals and expanding healthcare coverage, PBMs evolved to oversee formulary management, price negotiations, rebate structures, and drug utilization reviews. Their influence expanded significantly, shaping drug coverage and cost-sharing structures for insurers, employers, and government programs. While PBMs were designed to control costs and improve efficiency, their role has faced increasing scrutiny due to concerns over pricing transparency, rebate structures, and their impact on medication affordability.[3]

Specialty pharmacies (SPs) emerged to address the growing need for specialized handling and distribution of high-cost, complex medications ("specialty drugs"). These medications, which include biologics and many treatments for rare conditions, require specialized storage, preparation, administration, and patient management services that traditional retail pharmacies were not equipped to manage. By the 1990s and 2000s, as more of these therapies entered the market, SPs played an increasingly significant role in coordinating medication delivery, navigating the challenging health insurance reimbursement landscape, data collection, and patient counseling and support programs. The rising cost of specialty therapies and the goal of offering integrated care for patients with complex conditions have driven PBMs and health systems to consolidate networks and develop their own SP solutions.[4]

The role of core intermediaries

As we've discussed, intermediaries in the pharmaceutical supply chain emerged with the intent to streamline operations, reduce costs, and enhance access to medications. Initially, wholesalers, PBMs, GPOs, and SPs had a distinct role in improving efficiency, negotiating pricing, and ensuring product availability. However, over time, market dynamics, regulatory shifts, and industry

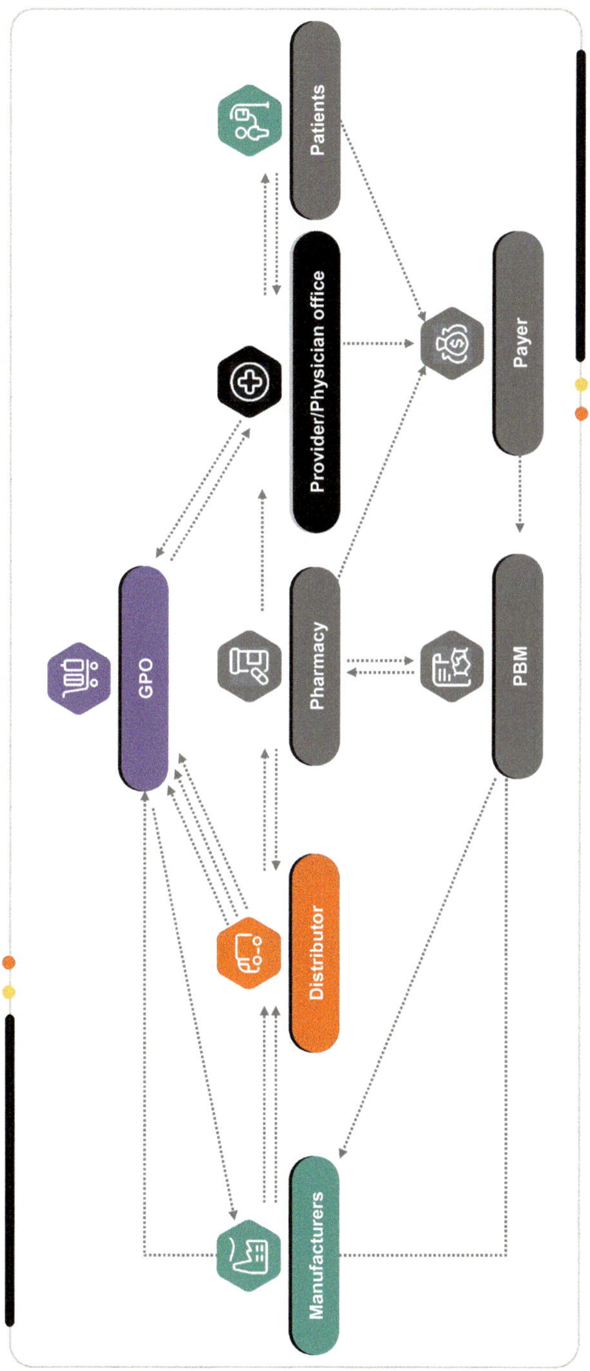

Figure 8.2 The complex pharmaceutical supply chain post-introduction of intermediaries

consolidation reshaped their business models, expanding their influence on cost structures and accessibility, and sometimes leading to inefficiency. In this section, we will explore who these intermediaries are, how their business models function, and the ways in which they shape drug pricing, market access, and healthcare delivery. We will also examine how their roles have evolved, whether through consolidation or service expansion, and the broader implications of these changes on the healthcare ecosystem today.

Wholesalers and distributors

Wholesalers and distributors have been pivotal in the pharmaceutical supply chain, acting as intermediaries that purchase supplies such as medications in bulk from manufacturers and distribute them to various healthcare providers, including pharmacies, hospitals, clinics, and GPOs. This central role ensures medications are efficiently delivered, maintaining the integrity and reliability of the supply chain. The terms wholesaler and distributor are used interchangeably here, as both serve similar roles in facilitating the movement of pharmaceuticals from manufacturers to healthcare providers.

Core functions and market influence

The core function of a pharmaceutical wholesaler centers on streamlining logistics and easing operational burdens for both manufacturers and providers. However, as the pharmaceutical landscape grew more complex, these entities expanded beyond transactional functions to offer value-added services such as inventory management, regulatory compliance, and data-driven analytics. The following sections explore the transformation of their business model from its origins to its current state (see Figure 8.3), shaped by consolidation, technological advancements, and new service offerings. Today, their role primarily focuses on:

- **Cost efficiency**: Leveraging bulk purchasing to secure lower prices and pass on cost savings to pharmacies and providers
- **Access**: Centralizing distribution to expand the reach of pharmaceutical products, ensuring even remote healthcare providers have access to necessary medications
- **Operational efficiency**: Alleviating the logistical burden on manufacturers and healthcare providers, managing warehousing, order fulfillment, and transportation
- **Supply chain reliability**: Maintaining large inventories to reduce the risk of shortages and delays, improving patient access to medications

Historically, wholesalers focused on distributing non-specialty drugs, playing a key role in ensuring broad access to routine medications. Their business model was centered on purchasing products from manufacturers either at wholesale

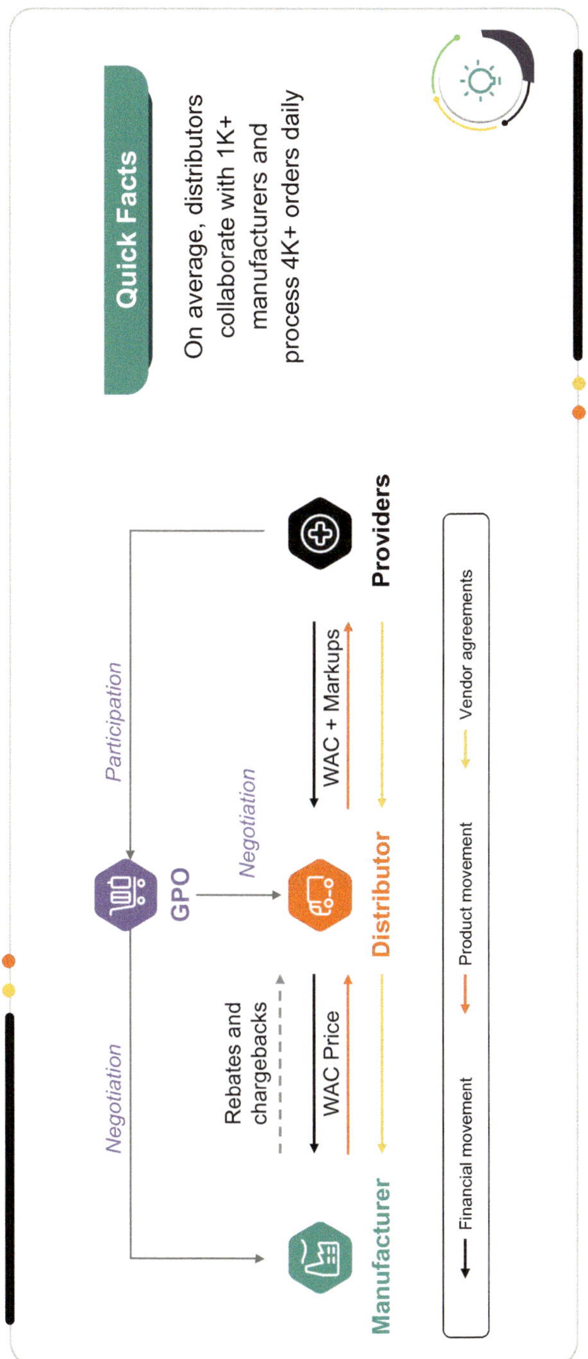

Figure 8.3 Business model of wholesalers and distributors

acquisition cost (WAC) or at negotiated discounts and reselling them to pharmacies and providers with a markup. Revenue was further supported through distribution service agreements, typically calculated as a percentage of WAC and often tied to specific performance metrics. Operating under a fee-for-service (FFS) model, wholesalers charged manufacturers for logistics, distribution, and payment collection. Over time, they began offering operational support to providers, including inventory and material management, compliance assistance, data analytics, and customer service. Additional incentives such as prompt-payment discounts helped solidify their relationships with healthcare providers.

These intermediaries can be classified as full-line and specialized distributors.

Full-line distributors: Offer a broad range of healthcare products, including pharmaceuticals, surgical tools, over the counter (OTC) medications, long-term care items, and wellness supplies.

Specialized distributors: Cater to a specific niche such as pharmacy services, medical equipment, or nutritional and wellness products.

Market landscape and key players

The US pharmaceutical distribution market is primarily led by three major full-line distributors —McKesson, Cardinal Health, and Cencora (formerly AmerisourceBergen)—which collectively account for approximately 95% of all prescription drug sales (see Figure 8.4).[5] These companies operate large-scale distribution networks and offer a range of services, including logistics, supply chain management, reimbursement support, and specialty drug distribution. As the industry evolves with changing regulations, pricing models, and the growing demand for specialty medications, these distributors continue to adapt by incorporating digital tools, automation, and additional services to support manufacturers, healthcare providers, and pharmacies.[6]

The wholesale and distribution sectors have undergone significant transformation due to five key factors:

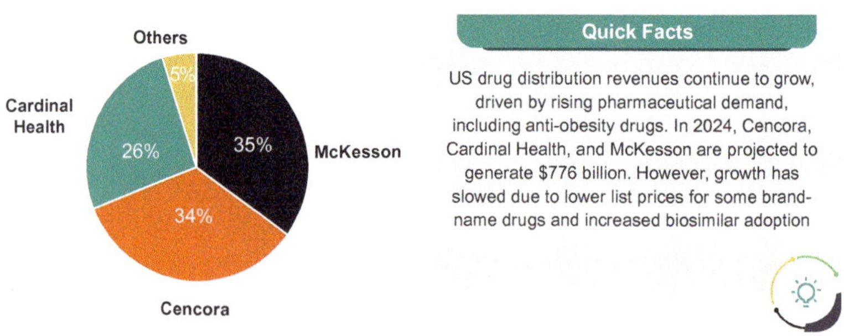

Figure 8.4 Key wholesalers and distributors

- **Strategic partnerships and vertical integration:** The US drug distribution market is undergoing consolidation, streamlining supply chains, improving economies of scale, and strengthening negotiating power with manufacturers and healthcare providers. Major distributors like McKesson, Cencora, and Cardinal Health are acquiring cancer specialist networks, such as Cardinal's acquisition of Integrated Oncology Network (ION) and McKesson's acquisition of a majority stake in the holding company for Florida Cancer Specialists, to enhance patient care coordination and drug supply management.[7] These strategic moves improve procurement efficiency, expand distribution capabilities, and drive cost savings, ultimately enhancing access to pharmaceutical products.
- **Pricing pressures:** Increased scrutiny on drug pricing has translated to pressure on list price, which directly impacts the profits wholesalers and distributors realize, given that discounts and service agreements are based on a percentage of WAC.
- **Rise of specialty drugs**: The demand for biologics, gene therapies, and high-cost specialty treatments is growing. Wholesalers have established dedicated specialty distribution networks and limited distribution models to accommodate these medications' unique handling and storage requirements.
- **Technology integration**: Innovative approaches such as AI-driven predictive analytics, blockchain-enabled supply chain tracking, and automated fulfillment processes are improving efficiency, accuracy, and transparency in drug distribution.
- **Expansion of value-added services**: Beyond traditional distribution, wholesalers offer services such as supply chain analytics, inventory management, reimbursement support, and regulatory compliance assistance to enhance efficiency for healthcare providers and manufacturers.

Evolving business models

To sustain competitiveness and profitability, McKesson, Cencora, and Cardinal Health are expanding into adjacent services such as retail and SP, GPOs, PSAOs (Pharmacy Services Administrative Organizations), and provider services. These entities:

- Operate or partner with provider networks (e.g., US Oncology Network, GI Alliance, OneOncology)
- Offer specialty-focused GPOs in oncology, rheumatology, and ophthalmology
- Provide tools for independent pharmacies, covering purchasing, PBM negotiations, and patient support
- Provide services to pharmaceutical manufacturers, such as hub services and benefits verification, to help patients get on therapy

This integrated approach (see Figure 8.5) not only deepens relationships with providers and pharmacies, diversifies revenue streams, and enhances supply chain control but also invites regulatory scrutiny over market consolidation and transparency.

In summary, pharmaceutical wholesalers and distributors have evolved from basic intermediaries to sophisticated entities integral to many different parts of the healthcare ecosystem. Their ability to adapt to industry changes, technological advancements, and shifting market demands underscores their essential role in the efficient and reliable delivery of medications. Wholesalers and distributors play a vital role in ensuring seamless pharmaceutical supply, but rising costs and shrinking margins require continuous efficiency improvements and strategic adaptations. Their high-volume, low-margin model remains sustainable due to automation, supply chain efficiencies, and an evolving product mix toward specialty drugs.

Group purchasing organizations

GPOs serve as intermediaries between healthcare providers and manufacturers, leveraging collective purchasing power across their members to negotiate pricing agreements with manufacturers and wholesalers (see Figure 8.6). In addition to cost savings, GPOs provide strategic sourcing, supply chain optimization, and data-driven insights to enhance inventory management and procurement. For this section, we will focus on provider GPOs as opposed to PBM GPOs, which we will cover in the PBM section.

Core functions and market influence

The primary functions of a GPO include:

- **Contract negotiation and administration**: Evaluate supplier capabilities, negotiate contract terms, and establish supplier partnerships to ensure stable, cost-effective product access.
- **Clinical and therapeutic insights**: Leverage data analytics to provide clinical benchmarking, drug utilization reports, and evidence-based recommendations to improve formulary management.
- **Regulatory compliance**: Help providers meet industry and government standards, including pricing transparency laws, anti-kickback regulations, and federal procurement policies.
- **Consulting services**: Support providers with cost-control strategies, supply chain optimization, and procurement best practices.
- **Market analytics**: Provide data-driven insights to optimize procurement strategies.

Vertical Alignment Within Wholesale Distribution Channels

	Cencora	Cardinal Health	McKesson
Manufacturer	Bluepoint Laboratories	Major Rugby	NorthStar Rx
Wholesale distribution	Cencora	Cardinal Health	McKesson
Specialty pharmacy	-	-	Biologics By McKesson
Retail pharmacy	Good Neighbor Pharmacy	The Medicine Shoppe Pharmacy	Rx Health Mart
PSAO	Elevate Provider Network	LeaderNET	Rx Health Mart Atlas
GPO	Cencora Specialty GPOs	Specialty GPOs	Onmark Unity
Provider	One Oncology; RETINA Consultants of America	Navista; GI Alliance	The US Oncology Network
Patient access services	Patient access and adherence support	Sonexus	covermymeds

Figure 8.5 Vertical alignment within wholesale distribution channels

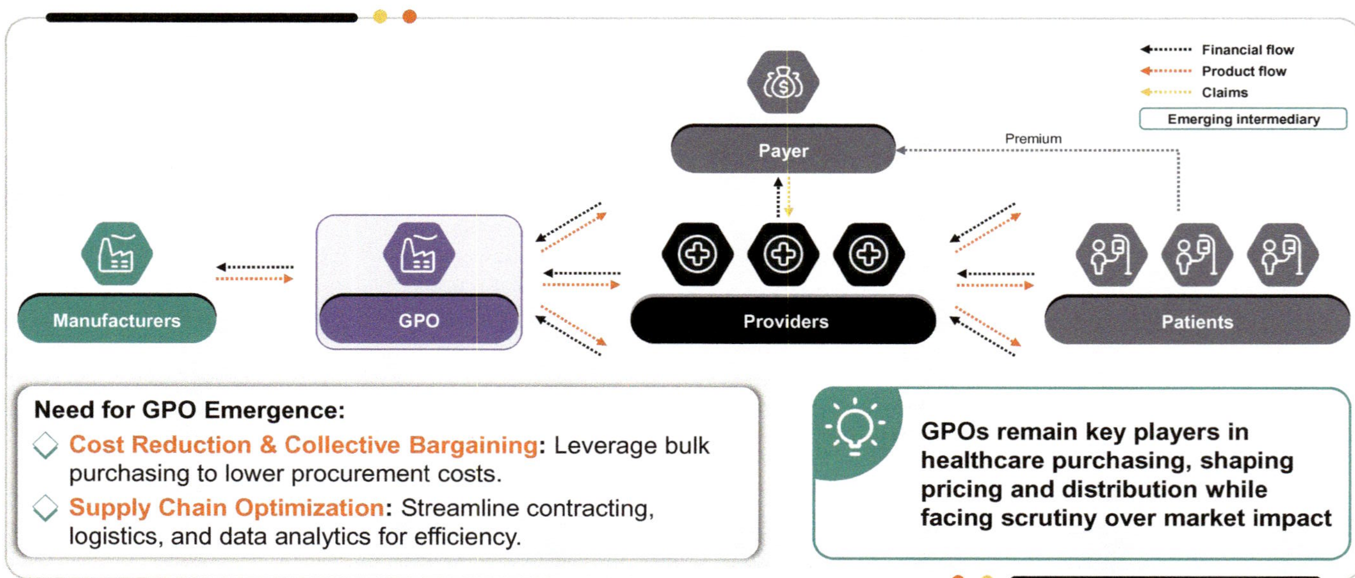

Figure 8.6 Role of GPOs in pharma supply chain

GPOs vary in structure (see Table 8.1):

- **Scope**: Hospital vs. specialty
- **Geography**: National vs. regional operations
- **Ownership**: Independent vs. provider-owned
- **Engagement**: Full-service vs. FFS consulting

Market landscape and key players

Facilitating around $300 billion in annual purchases, GPOs play a pivotal role in sourcing, especially for specialty drugs, biosimilars, and value-based contracts. Their relevance continues to grow due to the rise of biologics, precision medicine, and limited-distribution drugs (LDDs), which demand more sophisticated procurement approaches.[8]

Key players

The US GPO market is dominated by a few major entities (see Figure 8.7) that collectively influence procurement for around 80% of total staffed hospital beds:

- Vizient: The largest GPO, serving over 65% of acute care providers and 97% of academic medical centers, covering more than 452,000 staffed beds. Key members in 2023 included University of California Health, Sutter Health, and WJ Barnabas Health Inc.
- Premier Inc.: Supports more than 4,400 hospitals and health systems, managing 334,000 staffed beds. In 2023, it divested its non-healthcare group purchasing operations to OMNIA Partners.[9]
- HealthTrust Performance Group: Manages approximately 184,000 staffed beds, with affiliated members such as Appalachian Regional Healthcare and Aspen Mountain Medical Center.
- Cardinal Health: While primarily focused on pharmaceutical distribution, it also plays a role in group purchasing, managing 180,939 staffed beds and holding an 18% market share in pharmacy services and retail drugstores. Cardinal has several specialty GPOs serving different therapeutic areas: VitalSource (oncology and urology), Cornerstone Rheumatology (rheumatology), Acuity GPO (opthamology), Renal Purchasing Group (nephrology), MosaicGPO (gastroenterology), multispecialty infusion centers (neurology, allergy, and asthma), and Traverse GPO (for outpatient clinics owned by a health system).
- McKesson: A dominant entity in pharmaceutical distribution, with a 25% market shares in the pharmacy services and retail drugstore industry. McKesson also has several specialty GPOs serving different needs: PACT (serves hospitals/health systems), Onmark (community-based medical practices specializing in oncology, rheumatology, gastroenterology,

Table 8.1 GPO classification

Classification Based on	*Category*	*Description*	*Examples*
Offering	Hospital GPO	Large customer-based organizations dealing in broad supplies across all therapy areas	Premier, Vizient, HealthTrust
	Specialty GPO	Serve providers of specialty products, typically supporting small or niche practices	Onmark, UroGPO
Tier/Region	National GPO (tier 1)	Provide products and services across the entire United States; the most common type	Premier, Vizient, HealthTrust
	Regional GPO (tier 2)	Offer products and services limited to a specific geographic area	AllSpire Health, GNYHA, Roi
Ownership	Other entity-owned GPO	Operated by healthcare-related entities like distributors or providers	—
	Independent GPO	Standalone entities not owned by other ecosystem players	AllSpire Health, GNYHA, Roi
Engagement Model	Committed	Limited number of manufacturers. Member providers do not have the freedom to contract with any other GPO	HealthTrust
	At will	Can contract with as many manufacturers as they want. Member providers have the freedom to choose their GPOs	Premier, Vizient

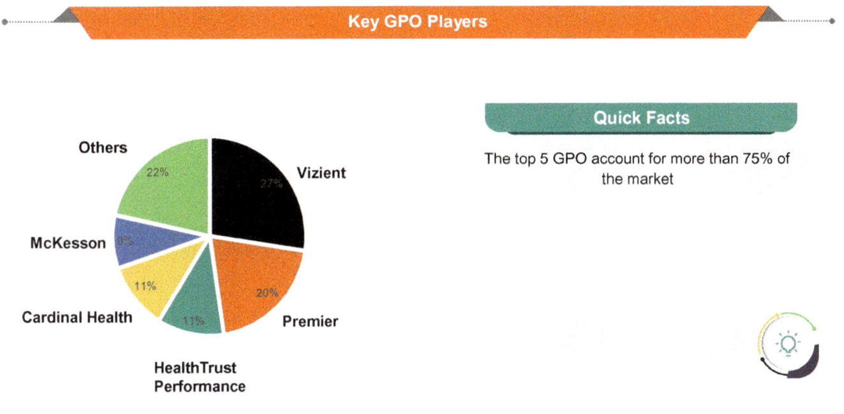

Figure 8.7 Key GPO players

opthalmology, dialysis/nephrology, and urology), and PlasmaRx (intravenous immunoglobulin IVIG, albumin and blood factor products).

These players offer tailored services for general procurement as well as specialized contracts with manufacturers. Several of the major GPO players are owned by wholesalers, and their strategies to vertically integrate stem from numerous factors, including managing cost and margin pressures, gaining greater control over the supply chain, enhancing operational efficiencies, and expanding into new revenue streams. This integration has strengthened partnerships with physician practices through both specialty distribution and access to competitive pricing through negotiated rebates and discounts.

GPOs operate as membership-driven organizations, tailoring their services to align with healthcare providers' specific procurement needs. Membership is not exclusive, and a single provider can be a member of multiple GPOs, choosing to buy through whichever offers the best price. A typical GPO consists of multiple teams handling different aspects of operations. The contracting team manages supplier agreements and pricing negotiations, while the sales team engages with suppliers and industry partners. The account team provides direct support to member organizations, ensuring their procurement needs are met. Additional support functions, such as data analytics and compliance, contribute to operational efficiency.

Most GPOs do not charge membership fees to provider members but may have minimum volume requirements. Larger or key members often receive greater rebates, invitations to participate in pilot programs, and a voice on the advisory board, which can influence the GPO's strategic direction. GPOs' profitability is influenced by contract structures, purchasing volume, and administrative fees. GPOs generate revenue through administrative fees paid by manufacturers, typically ranging from 1% to 3% of the purchase price. Additional financial factors include discounts and rebates negotiated with manufacturers. Manufacturers contracting on the inpatient/hospital side often offer off-invoice discounts, which can be significant, sometimes reaching 50% for specific hospital-use products. Some contracts include performance-based discounts, structured as incentives for providers meeting specific purchasing or utilization targets.[10]

GPOs are expanding their impact beyond bulk buying, becoming strategic intermediaries in pharmaceutical procurement, especially in specialty drug contracting, biosimilars, and value-based purchasing (see Figure 8.8.)

Modern GPOs—such as Vizient, Premier, HealthTrust, and wholesaler-aligned GPOs like Onmark (Cencora), ION (McKesson), and VitalSource (Cardinal)—now influence:

- Contracting for specialty therapies with manufacturers (e.g., oncology, nephrology)
- Clinical pathway design and prescribing behavior
- Data-driven benchmarking and decision support
- Integration with SP and hub services
- White-/brown-bagging models that shape drug administration settings

As healthcare providers seek greater financial sustainability, GPOs will play an increasingly strategic role in driving cost efficiencies, supply chain resilience, and data-driven procurement solutions. Their expanding influence in biosimilar adoption, specialty drug contracting, and innovative approaches such as AI-powered procurement underscores their importance in the evolving pharmaceutical ecosystem.

Pharmacy benefit managers

PBMs emerged as intermediaries in the pharmaceutical supply chain to streamline drug distribution and manage prescription benefits. Initially, their core functions included negotiating prices with manufacturers on behalf of payers, managing formularies, and processing claims for health plans. PBMs connect manufacturers (upstream), pharmacies (midstream), and payers such as insurers, employers, unions, and government programs (downstream), supporting a broad range of health plans including commercial insurance, Medicare Part D, and Medicaid managed care.

Core functions and market influence

PBMs play a central role in the healthcare system by managing relationships with key stakeholders.

- **Insurance companies:** PBMs design and administer prescription drug benefits, create formularies, negotiate drug prices, and process claims. They

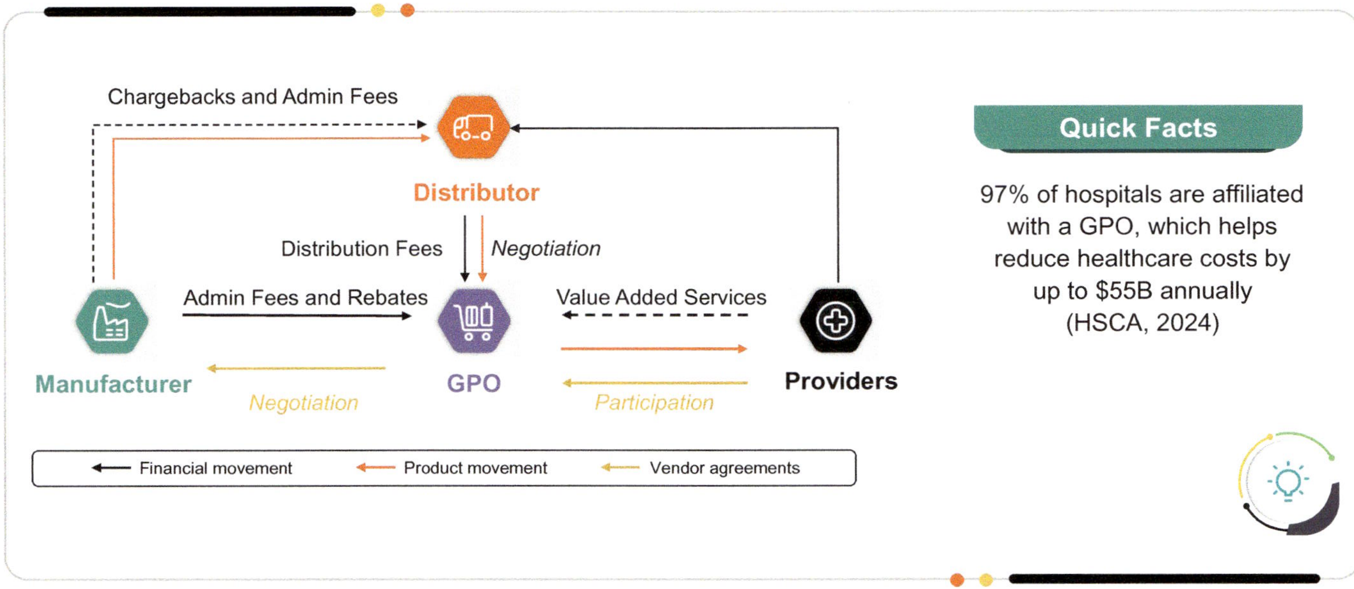

Figure 8.8 Business model of GPOs

reduce the administrative burden on health plans by administering their formulary, and their scale creates bargaining power that helps insurers control drug spending while ensuring coverage aligns with cost-effectiveness and clinical appropriateness.

- **Pharmacies:** PBMs establish pharmacy networks and negotiate reimbursement rates, which influence where and at what cost patients can access medications. Their network strategies, whether open, limited, or preferred, can steer prescription volume toward certain pharmacies in exchange for cost concessions. They maintain real-time IT systems that adjudicate claims, enforce formulary compliance, and manage utilization and rebates.
- **Pharmaceutical manufacturers:** PBMs negotiate rebate contracts with drug manufacturers to secure discounts in exchange for favorable formulary placement. The rise of PBM-affiliated rebate aggregators has further centralized these negotiations, increasing PBM leverage over pricing and contract terms.

As the pharmaceutical industry grew more complex, PBMs began to consolidate power through mergers, acquisitions, and vertical integration with insurers and pharmacy chains. This shift transformed their role from cost managers to industry gatekeepers. Today, PBMs' business model (see Figure 8.9) has evolved into a complex structure with both positive and controversial impacts. The competition among pharmacies and drug manufacturers directly influences drug pricing and reimbursement rates. PBMs play a key role in shaping these dynamics by designing pharmacy networks that steer patients toward preferred or affiliated pharmacies. This strategy helps PBMs control drug spending, manage formularies, and streamline reimbursement processes. While these efforts can reduce costs for insurers, they also have a profound impact on patient care, with both benefits and drawbacks.

Cost management versus hidden fees:

- While PBMs negotiate substantial discounts, they often retain a portion of the rebates rather than passing full savings on to insurers or patients (see Figure 8.10)
- Spread pricing—charging payers more than they reimburse pharmacies—has led to rising drug costs for employers and consumers

Patient access and formularies:

- PBMs determine which drugs make it onto insurance formularies, often prioritizing higher-rebate drugs over more affordable alternatives
- Exclusive arrangements with preferred pharmacies can limit patient choice and influence prescription fulfillment patterns

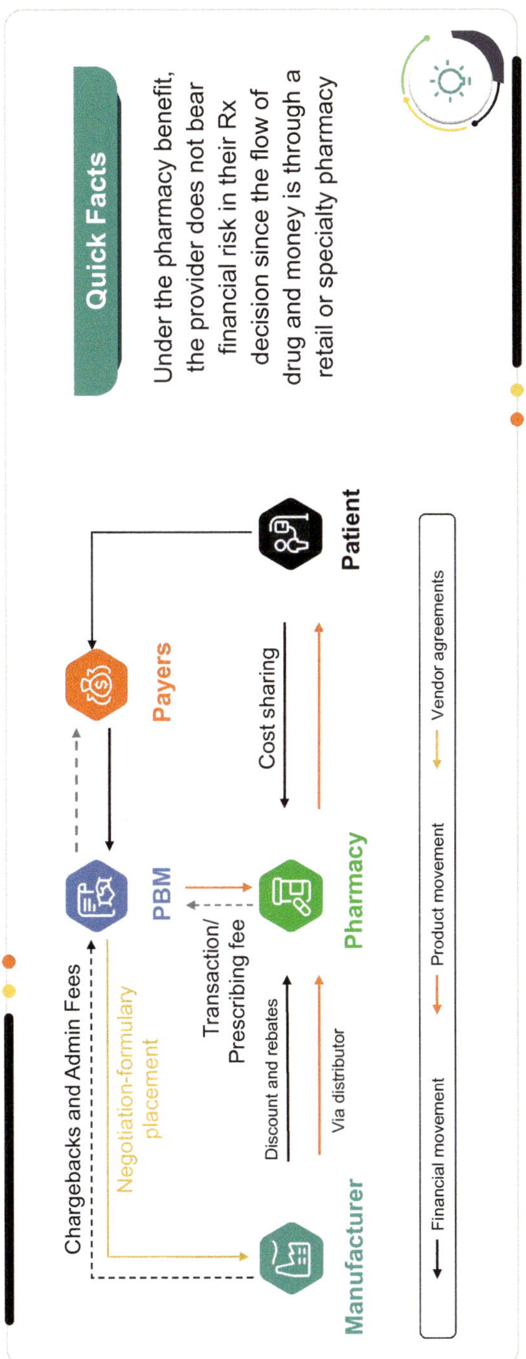

Figure 8.9 Business model of PBMs

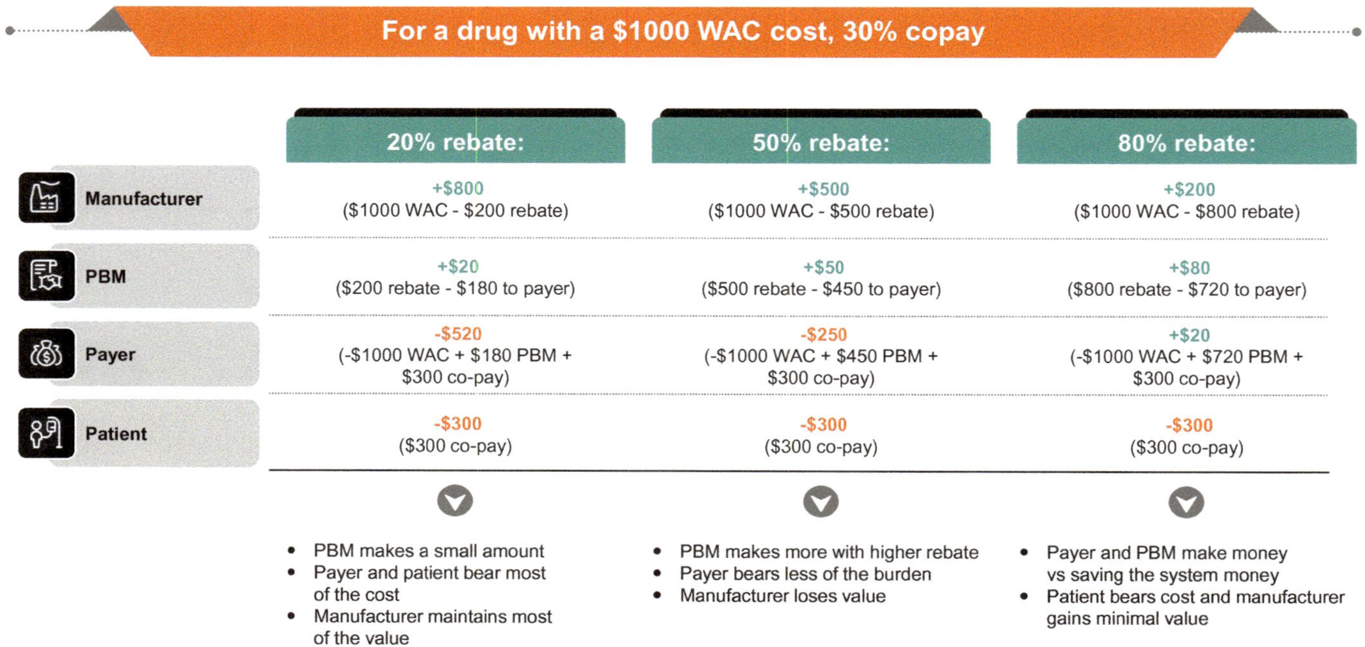

Figure 8.10 Illustration of PBM revenue generation

Operational efficiencies versus transparency issues:

- Advanced data analytics allow PBMs to optimize pricing and formulary decisions, improving operational efficiency

However, the lack of pricing transparency has sparked criticism, with regulators and policymakers demanding clearer disclosures on PBM earnings and rebate structures.[11]

While PBMs were originally designed to facilitate cost-effective drug access, their growing influence has led to concerns about affordability and transparency. Their pricing strategies and rebate structures, while intended to reduce overall drug costs, have drawn criticism for potentially driving up prices and shifting financial burdens onto patients. These concerns have intensified calls for greater transparency and regulatory oversight to ensure cost savings do not come at the expense of patient care.

Market landscape and key players

The PBM market is highly concentrated, with three major players—Caremark (owned by CVS Health), Express Scripts (a subsidiary of Cigna), and Optum Rx (owned by UnitedHealth Group)—controlling nearly 80% of all prescription claims in the United States (see Figure 8.11). Their dominance has raised concerns about competition, pricing transparency, and the negotiating power of smaller pharmacies and payers. As regulatory efforts continue to evolve, policymakers seek to address these concerns and enhance fairness in drug pricing and reimbursement practices.[12]

As policy changes such as increased transparency requirements and potential rebate safe-harbor eliminations creates risks for the major PBMs, they restructured their operations by creating separate, affiliated entities known as PBM GPOs or rebate aggregators. These entities were offshored and shifted their revenue models from rebates to administrative fees, data fees, and other incremental charges.

Unlike traditional GPOs that procure drugs and medical supplies for healthcare providers, these rebate aggregators negotiate contracts and rebates with drug manufacturers—a function previously handled directly by PBMs. The three major PBM GPOs (see Figure 8.12) are Ascent (affiliated with Express Scripts and Prime, and also serving Humana Pharmacy Solutions), Zinc (affiliated with CVS), and Emisar (affiliated with OptumRx). Rather than creating a new segment of the pharmaceutical supply chain, these entities were formed through corporate restructuring of existing entities.

PBMs argue these rebate aggregators enhance their bargaining power by aggregating purchasing volume to secure greater savings from pharmaceutical manufacturers. However, industry experts and members of Congress suggest these entities primarily serve to drive PBM revenue through new fee structures. A former OptumRx executive stated that the goal of these rebate aggregators

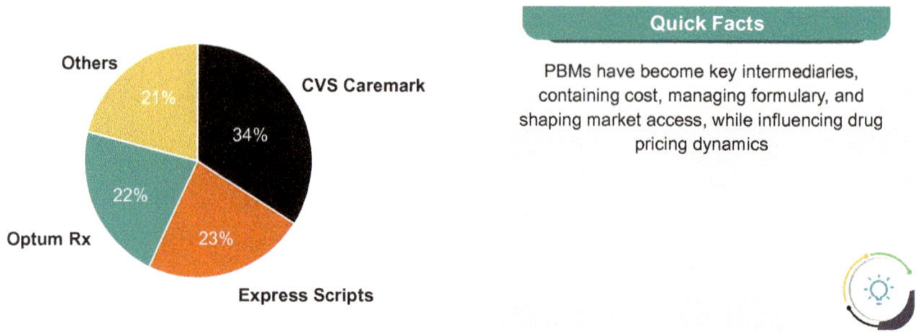

Figure 8.11 PBM market share by total equivalent claims managed

PBM GPO/ Rebate Aggregators	*Parent/Owner*	*Year Established*	*Headquarters Location*	*Selected Clients*
Ascent Health Services	Cigna (ESI), Prime, Kroger	2019	Switzerland	ESI, Prime, Kroger, HPS
Zinc Health Services	CVS	2020	United States	CVS Caremark
Emisar Pharma Services	United (OptumRx)	2021	Ireland	OptumRx

Figure 8.12 Overview of PBM GPOs or rebate aggregators

is to create fees that can be retained rather than passed on to clients.[13] Internal PBM documents reveal new methods of fee generation (such as data fees), with reports estimating these entities have extracted billions of dollars from drug manufacturers since their formation.

Consolidation and integration of PBMs

Over the past two decades, the US PBM industry has undergone significant horizontal and vertical consolidation (see Figure 8.13). The top three PBMs—CVS Caremark, Express Scripts, and OptumRx—now manage over 75% of all prescription claims, serving around 270 million people. Along with Humana, MedImpact, and Prime, the "Big 6" PBMs control more than 90% of claims, operating within vertically integrated conglomerates that span retail, SPs, health insurers, distributors, and provider networks.

This deep integration has led to unprecedented control over drug pricing and distribution. Four major healthcare entities—UnitedHealth Group, CVS Health,

Parent/Owner	*CVS Health Corporation*	*The Cigna Group*	*UnitedHealth Group Inc.*	*Humana Inc.*	*MedImpact Holdings Inc.*	*19 BlueCross BlueShield plans*
Drug Private Labeler	Cordavis Limited	Quallent Pharmaceuticals	Nuvaila			
Healthcare Provider	Minute Clinic, Signify Health, Oak St.	Evernorth Care Group, MD Live, Vilage MD	Optum Health	CenterWell, Conviva		
PBM	**34%**	**23%**	**22%**	**7%**	**5%**	**3%**
"PBM GPO"/ Rebate Aggregator	Zinc	Ascent Health Services	Emisar Pharma services	Ascent (via contract)	Prescient Holdings Group LLC	Synergie (medical benefit drug) Ascent (via contract)
Pharmacy Retail/LTC	CVS Pharmacy Omnicare		Genoa Healthcare Pharmascript			
Pharmacy Mail Order	CVS Caremark Mail Service Pharmacy	Express Scripts Pharmacy	OptumRx Mail Service Pharmacy	CenterWell Pharmacy	Birdi, Inc.	Prime Therapeutics Pharmacy
Pharmacy Specialty	CVS Specialty Pharmacy	Accredo, Freedom Fertility	Optum Specialty Pharmacy	CenterWell Specialty Pharmacy	Specialty by Birdi	Accredo (via contract)
Health Insurer	Aetna	Cigna Healthcare	United Healthcare	Humana		19 BlueCross BlueShield Plans

Figure 8.13 PBM ownership and vertical integration

Cigna, and Humana—now account for more than $1 trillion in combined annual revenue, or 22% of US national health expenditures, with profits rising by over 150% from 2016 to 2023, largely driven by more than 190 mergers and acquisitions and the growth of revenue from internal affiliates.

Impact of vertical integration

Increased integration has also drawn scrutiny. The Federal Trade Commission (FTC) launched a multi-phase inquiry into PBMs, citing anticompetitive practices such as:[14]

- Self-preferencing of PBM-owned pharmacies
- Exclusion of lower-cost drugs from formularies in favor of higher-cost branded drugs due to rebate-driven incentives
- Imposition of unfair contract terms on independent pharmacies
- Use of spread pricing and excessive markups, especially for specialty generics

These practices inflate costs for patients, employers, and taxpayers.[15] Several investigative reports have highlighted stark examples where drugs were significantly more expensive through insurance than through direct wholesale or retail purchases.[16]

Emerging models: private label biosimilars

PBMs are increasingly favoring private-label biosimilars—branded generics under PBM-affiliated labels—to capture additional margins. Deals, such as CVS's Cordavis with Sandoz (Hyrimoz), Cigna's Quallent with Boehringer Ingelheim (Cyltezo), and UHG's Nuvaila with Amgen (Amjevita), have replaced Humira on formularies, accelerating biosimilar adoption. However, this shift raises concerns:

- Employers and plan sponsors may lack visibility into the financial terms
- Competing biosimilars without PBM partnerships face limited access
- Narrow margins and access barriers may stifle future biosimilar innovation

This evolving PBM model underscores a growing need for transparency, competition, and reforms that prioritize patient and payer value over intermediary profits.

Regulatory scrutiny and legislative pushback

As PBMs have grown in power, they have also attracted scrutiny from policymakers and regulators. Key developments include:

- **Federal oversight:** The FTC and the Department of Health and Human Services have initiated investigations into PBM pricing strategies and potential anticompetitive behavior, focusing on issues like spread pricing, rebate manipulation, and market consolidation.

- **Pharmacy Benefit Manager Transparency Act of 2023:** This legislation, currently under discussion by Congress, seeks to prohibit PBMs from charging health plans more than they reimburse pharmacies, increasing transparency and promoting fair competition in drug pricing.
- **State-level reforms:** Many states have enacted laws targeting spread pricing, requiring PBMs to disclose rebate structures, and banning practices that restrict independent pharmacy participation in provider networks. All 50 states have enacted at least one law regulating PBMs. In 2023 alone, 43 states considered PBM reform bills, resulting in more than 20 new state laws. Many states now prohibit PBMs from imposing "gag clauses" on contract pharmacies, allowing pharmacy employees to freely inform patients about lower-cost drug options.[17]
- **Proposed federal legislation:** Ongoing congressional efforts aim to realign PBM incentives, ensuring a greater portion of manufacturer rebates benefits patients and insurers rather than being retained by PBMs.

By managing these relationships, PBMs shape drug pricing, reimbursement, and patient access. However, their evolving role as powerful intermediaries continues to spark debate. As regulatory scrutiny increases, the future of PBMs will depend on their ability to balance profit-driven models with patient-first policies, ensuring cost savings and access to quality care are not mutually exclusive.

Specialty pharmacy

SPs emerged to manage the dispensing of complex and high-cost medications, often referred to as specialty drugs. These medications require specialized handling, close patient monitoring, and adherence support. SPs were designed to ensure proper medication management while improving patient outcomes and reducing healthcare costs.

Core functions and market influence

SPs differ significantly from retail pharmacies in the types of medications they dispense, the level of patient support they provide, and their role in managing complex conditions (see Table 8.2).

Retail pharmacies are designed for convenience and accessibility, making them the preferred choice for common prescriptions. However, for patients with complex or rare conditions requiring specialized medications, financial assistance, and ongoing clinical support, SPs serve as important healthcare partners. The added services they provide—such as personalized patient care, medication adherence programs, and 24/7 clinical support—make them a critical part of the healthcare ecosystem.

Table 8.2 Retail pharmacy versus specialty pharmacy

Feature	Retail Pharmacy	Specialty Pharmacy
Scope	Common chronic & acute medications (e.g., antibiotics, blood pressure meds)	High-cost, complex therapies for chronic/rare diseases
Patient Support	Basic counseling at the counter	Disease-specific education, adherence programs, and side effect management
Financial Navigation	Standard insurance processing	Assistance with prior authorizations, copay support, and financial aid
Accessibility	Walk-in convenience, local stores	Often mail-order, limited distribution, requires coordination
Pharmacist Expertise	General medication guidance	Disease-specialized pharmacists available 24/7

SPs operate within a distinct business model centered around high-touch patient care and complex medication management (see Figure 8.14). Their revenue streams primarily come from:

- **Drug reimbursement:** SPs procure medications at negotiated rates and are reimbursed by payers (insurance companies, PBMs, or government programs) at a markup.
- **Service fees:** SPs offer patient support services such as adherence programs, prior authorization assistance, and patient education, often receiving fees from manufacturers and/or healthcare providers.
- **Pharma partnerships:** Many SPs collaborate with pharmaceutical companies on LDDs, gaining exclusive or semi-exclusive rights to dispense high-cost specialty therapies.
- **Data and analytics services:** SPs collect real-world data on drug efficacy, adherence, and outcomes, monetizing insights through partnerships with pharma companies and payers.
- **Medical benefit management:** Some SPs operate under a medical benefit model, managing infusion services and provider-administered therapies in clinical settings.

SPs are crucial for dispensing self-administered or provider-administered medications for complex, chronic, and rare conditions. Many manage multiple therapy areas, although some are more common than others. For example, oncology is supported by 431 dedicated SPs. Other key areas for SPs include blood disorders, HIV/AIDS, arthritis, and multiple sclerosis. These pharmacies tackle the challenges of complex medications through clinical expertise, personalized patient support, and operational efficiencies:

- **Clinical expertise:** Pharmacists with specialized knowledge in oncology, HIV, autoimmune diseases, and other complex conditions ensure appropriate medication dispensing, monitor for drug interactions, and manage side effects.
- **Patient education and adherence support:** Dedicated teams provide instruction on administration techniques, side effect management, and disease understanding. Medication adherence programs—including follow-ups, reminders, and counseling—help patients stay on track.
- **Care coordination:** Close collaboration with physicians and specialists ensures treatment regimens align with overall care plans, optimizing dosing schedules and minimizing risks.
- **Specialized medication handling:** Many specialty drugs require strict storage and transportation conditions, such as refrigeration or light protection. SPs implement secure distribution methods to maintain efficacy.

Figure 8.14 Role of specialty pharmacies in the pharma supply chain

- **Insurance and financial assistance:** Given the high costs of specialty medications, SPs assist with insurance navigation, prior authorizations, and access to financial aid programs, reducing the burden on patients.
- **Ongoing patient monitoring:** Regular assessments, lab tracking, and symptom evaluations help measure treatment effectiveness and allow timely adjustments to therapy.[18]

Specialty drugs usually require specialized handling and distribution to ensure quality and appropriate administration of the medication. SPs are directly involved in several distribution models (see Figure 8.15):

- **Brown bagging:** The SP ships the drug to the patient's home, who then carries it into the physician's office for administration.
- **White bagging:** SPs act as intermediaries between healthcare providers and payers. These SPs stock and distribute drugs to the healthcare provider, then collect reimbursement from payers, removing the need for the patient to handle the drug directly.
- **Clear bagging:** A relatively new model, drugs are purchased by the SP affiliated with an IDN. The IDN SP takes on the financial risk and reimbursement process.

In contrast to these, in the **Buy-and-Bill** model (see Figure 8.16), healthcare providers buy drugs from manufacturers or wholesalers and then bill payers for reimbursement once the drugs have been prescribed. In this model, SPs are not involved.

Market landscape and key players

Approximately 68% of total prescription revenues for pharmacy-dispensed specialty drugs came from the top three PBM-owned SPs in 2023.[19] Key players include:

Payer and PBM-owned SPs: Payers and PBMs are increasingly directing specialty drug distribution through their owned or affiliated SPs to contain costs while maintaining control over specialty drug distribution. This achieves several goals:

- **Reduce hospital markups**: Shifting dispensing away from hospitals prevents inflated costs associated with hospital-administered specialty drugs.
- **Retain revenue**: Capturing dispensing fees within payer-owned pharmacies reduces reliance on independent pharmacies and strengthens financial control.

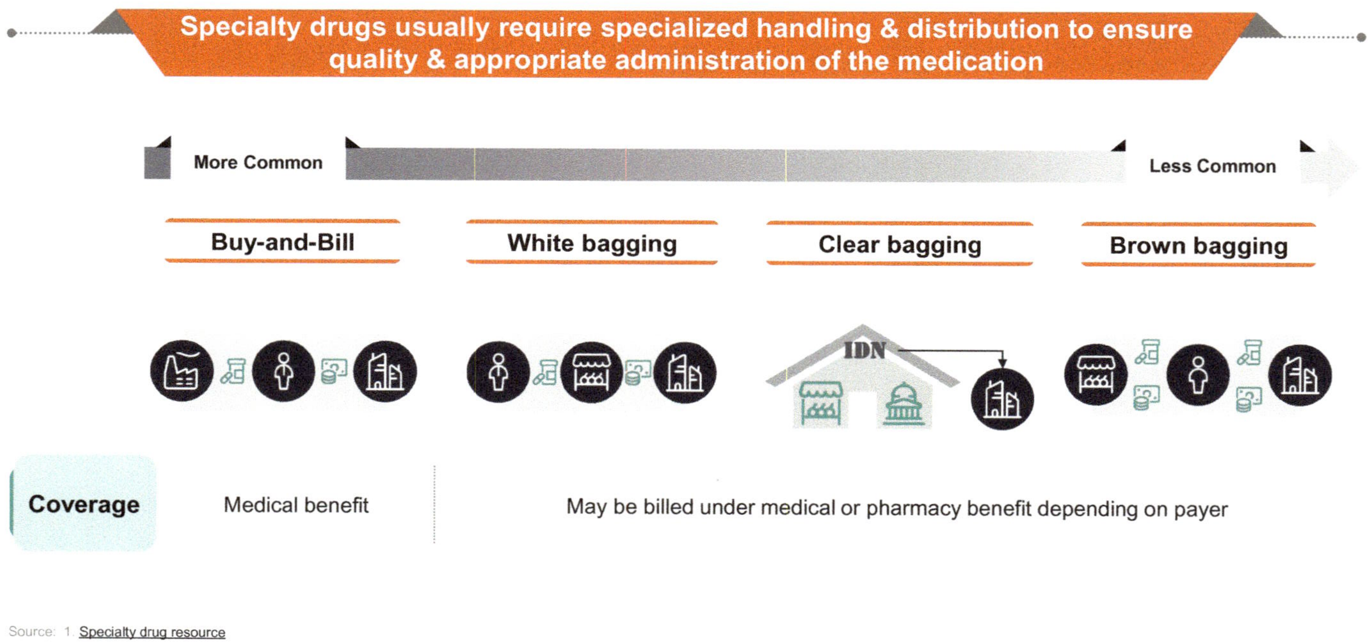

Figure 8.15 Specialty pharmacy distribution channels

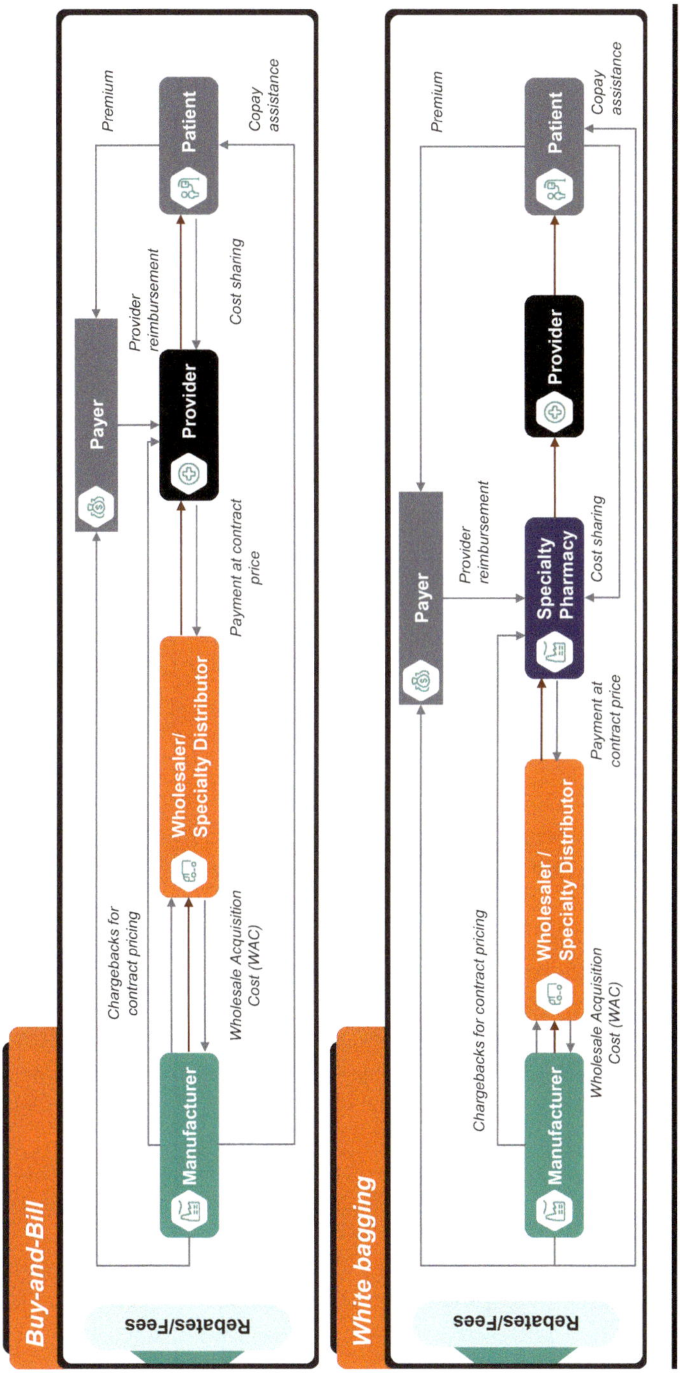

Figure 8.16 Business model of specialty pharmacy

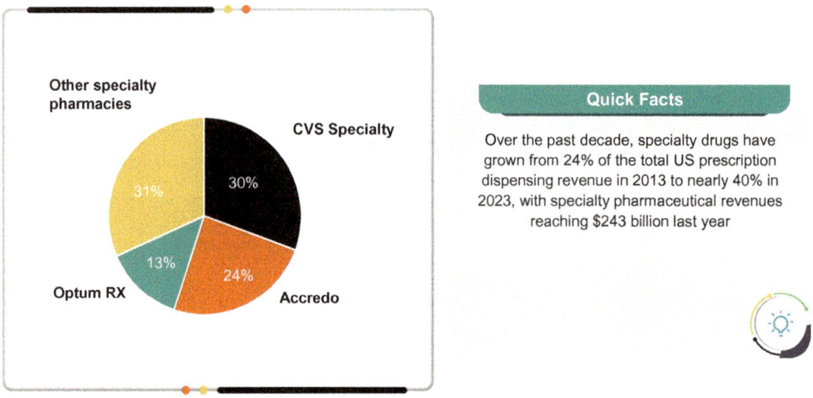

Figure 8.17 Top specialty pharmacies in the United States by market share

- **Enhance negotiating power**: Higher prescription volumes enable payers to secure better pricing from manufacturers and wholesalers.
- **Improve cost transparency**: Greater visibility into drug pricing, rebates, and utilization helps enforce cost-control measures and minimize inefficiencies.

These entities dominate the market and control a significant share (see Figure 8.17). Leading companies in this segment include CVS Specialty, Accredo, and Optum Rx.

Health system-owned SPs: These pharmacies are integrated within healthcare systems, providing seamless medication dispensing at the site of care. Approximately 40% of the nearly 1,800 dispensing sites with SP accreditation are owned by hospitals, physician practices, and other healthcare providers. Meanwhile, health system-owned SPs are emerging as key players. By integrating directly with hospitals and clinics, these pharmacies offer:

- **On-site dispensing**: Providing medications at the point of care reduces logistical barriers, enhances patient adherence, and ensures timely access to treatment.
- **Seamless care coordination**: Integrating with electronic health records streamlines therapy management, reduces duplication, and enhances provider collaboration.
- **Cost efficiency**: Integrated Health System Specialty Pharmacy models have demonstrated a 13% reduction in overall healthcare costs, lowering medication-related expenses and hospital readmissions.[20]

- **340B drug pricing benefits**: Eligible health systems can purchase drugs at discounted rates, reinvesting savings to expand medication access and improve care for underserved populations.

By combining clinical integration, financial incentives, and advanced data systems, health system-owned SPs attempt to enhance medication access, improve adherence, and contribute to better patient outcomes. Many major health systems operate this kind of SP.

Independent SPs: These are privately owned and often focus on niche markets, offering flexibility and personalized patient care. Unlike PBM-owned pharmacies, they are not bound by strict formulary adherence, which allows for more customized treatment approaches. However, they face challenges due to limited resources and restrictions on accessing certain LDDs. Prominent independent SPs include PANTHERx Rare Pharmacy, CarepathRx, and Senderra.[21]

In summary, SPs have undergone a significant transformation. Initially focused on dispensing high-cost, complex therapies (e.g., biologics, orphan drugs), SPs now act as critical patient engagement and care coordination hubs—particularly for chronic and rare diseases.

Today, their expanded role includes:

- Benefit verification and prior authorization support
- Patient education, adherence monitoring, and compliance with FDA-mandated Risk Evaluation and Mitigation Strategy
- Financial assistance and support services
- Data sharing with manufacturers and payers on real-world outcomes
- Nursing services and home infusion logistics

Many SPs are vertically integrated with PBMs (e.g., Accredo with Express Scripts, Optum Specialty Pharmacy, CVS Specialty), wholesalers (e.g., Biologics by McKesson, Onco360 by Cencora), or GPOs, leading to closed distribution networks that control therapy access. This ownership structure raises conflicts of interest. SPs may favor therapies linked to parent PBMs or GPOs, limiting competition and manufacturer flexibility. Furthermore, white-bagging practices where SPs ship drugs to provider sites have caused tensions with health systems, affecting control over inventory and reimbursement. SPs increasingly partner with manufacturers for LDDs, making them central to product launch strategies, patient onboarding, and adherence metrics (Figure 8.18).

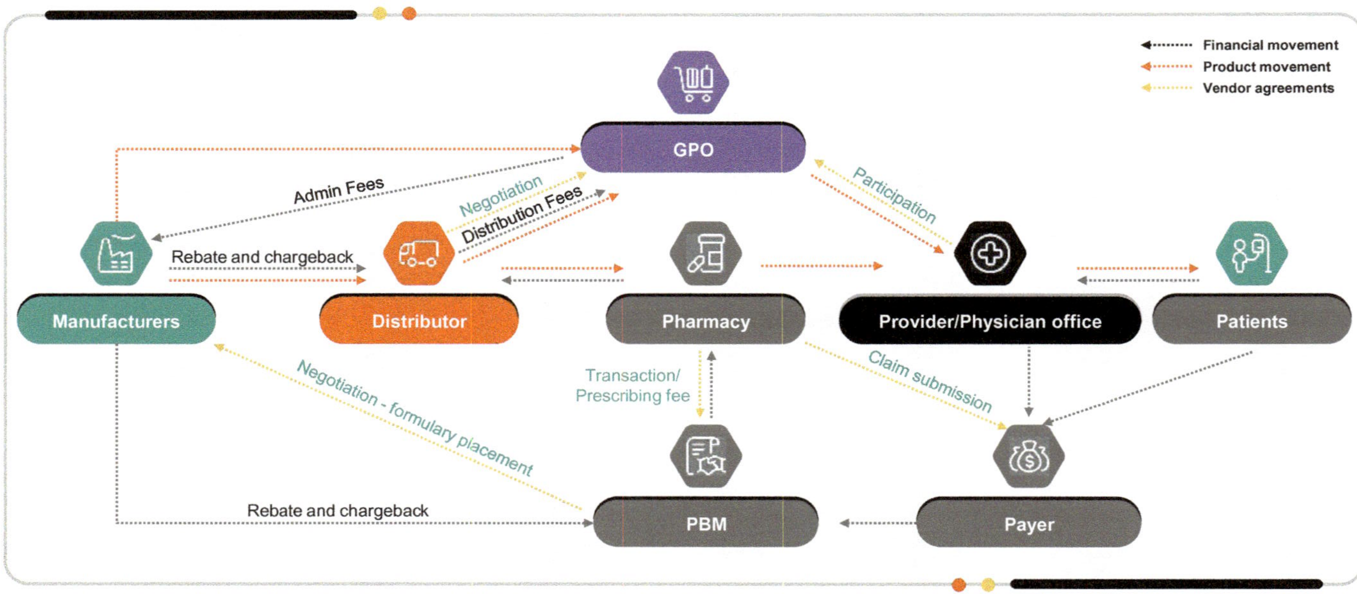

Figure 8.18 Pharmaceutical supply chain post-introduction of intermediaries

Indirect/other intermediaries

Indirect or other intermediaries do not directly handle the drug value chain or money flow but play a role in influencing operations, costs, access, and efficiency. They can further be categorized in four ways:

- **Ownership organizations**
  - **Private equity (PE)**: **PE** firms have become integral to the US pharma supply chain, driving growth, innovation, and efficiency across the industry with their strategic investments and operational improvements. In outpatient care, the eye care sector led activity in 2023 with 35 deals, more than double primary care and orthopedics (15 each). Unifeye Vision Partners (Waud Capital) and InFocus Eyecare (Regal Healthcare) drove 43% of transactions. Gastroenterology followed with 14 deals, including the buyout of United Digestive, a 200-provider network, by Kohlberg & Company, ending its affiliation with Frazier Healthcare, which originally established it in 2018.[22]
- **Service providers**
  - **Management service organizations (MSOs):** An MSO is a business entity that oversees the nonclinical functions of a medical practice. MSOs may be owned by hospitals, physician groups, insurers, non-healthcare investors, or formed as joint ventures between hospitals and physicians. They offer vital administrative and operational support to help medical practices run more efficiently. Medical practices have increasingly started turning to MSOs for their administrative needs such as support in billing, coding, and operations management, enabling physicians to focus on their patients' care. Some of the key players operating in the market include MedVanta, Envolve Health, One Oncology, Vanguard Health Solutions, Neolytix, Argusmso, Cority, and HealthSm.[23]
  - **Provider aggregators:** Within the primary care space, provider aggregators are providing vital support to manage value-based care initiatives. Their rise is driven by providers seeking an alternate business model, with greater upside, external financial backing, and less administrative burden. For example, major drug distributor McKesson has expanded into the provider space by acquiring oncology practices. In 2010, McKesson purchased US Oncology, significantly increasing its presence in cancer care. This move allows McKesson to secure its customer base and control the supply chain of cancer medications. Cencora (another distributor) has invested in oncology practices to strengthen its market position. In partnership with TPG Inc., Cencora acquired OneOncology, a network of cancer care providers, to enhance its service offerings and protect against competition.[24]

- **TPAs:** A TPA is an organization that provides administrative services to entities such as insurance companies, self-insured employers, and healthcare providers. These services often include claims processing, employee benefits management, and other operational tasks. TPAs are commonly used by self-funded health plans to manage claims and ensure compliance with regulatory requirements. TPAs share more similarities with PBMs due to their focus on administrative services, operational tasks, and compliance management.[25]
- **Retail pharmacies:** Retail pharmacies act as a bridge between healthcare providers and patients. They dispense medications, offer health consultations, and provide various health-related services. Consumer trust in providers in nontraditional primary care settings is high, with approximately 60% of patients likely to seek non-emergency healthcare at pharmacies. The urgency of COVID-19 vaccines during the global pandemic helped accelerate the transformation of retail pharmacies as a trusted site of care for many patients. During the next 5–10 years, retail pharmacies are projected to become the preferred administration site for all adult and adolescent vaccines.[26]
- **Non-dispensing pharmacies/digital pharmacies/hub service**: A non-dispensing pharmacy offers clinical pharmacy services without physically managing or distributing prescription drugs or medical devices. These services typically include medication therapy management, evaluating drug therapies, managing chronic conditions, and coordinating patient care. The primary aim is to improve a patient's medication outcomes through collaboration with both the patient and their primary care provider. Examples of such pharmacies include BlinkRx and RxLightning: BlinkRx simplifies prescription management by helping patients find the lowest prices, handling prior authorizations, and offering free home delivery, which improve affordability and access to medications; RxLightning digitizes specialty medication enrollment, accelerating therapy access for patients and supporting 500+ provider organizations to reduce administrative burdens, enhance adherence, and improve affordability through digital onboarding and patient engagement tools.[27]

- **Coalitions/advocacy organizations/partnerships/foundations**
  - **Buying groups:** Physician buying groups, like GPOs, are organizations that negotiate discounts on pharmaceuticals, medical supplies, and vaccines for independent physician practices and clinics. Atlantic Health Partners is recognized as one of the largest vaccine-buying groups in the United States, collaborating with all major vaccine manufacturers to offer favorable pricing and comprehensive support to physician practices, health systems, and clinics. These organizations play a role in supporting healthcare providers by reducing operational costs and improving access to essential supplies.[28]

- **Payer/employer payment models (FFS, VBC):** Companies such as Collective Health and Accolade are transforming self-funded employer health plans by streamlining administration, reducing costs, and improving efficiency through data integration and digital platforms. Collective Health integrates fragmented back-office functions, combining claims, people data, and program utilization to lower per-member medical costs. It serves around 200,000 members across major companies like Uber and Pinterest. Accolade provides personalized healthcare advocacy for 1.5 million patients, using digital engagement to enhance care navigation. Its partnership with Humana strengthens cost control for self-funded plans. Employers are increasingly adopting Direct Primary Care models over traditional FFS, paying $25–$100 per employee monthly for improved access. Care is delivered via on-site, near-site, or virtual clinics.
- **Medicaid buying groups**: Medicaid purchasing pools are multi-state collaborations that help states negotiate better drug pricing and rebates for their Medicaid programs. The National Medicaid Pooling Initiative and Top Dollar Program, both administered by Magellan Rx Management, allow states to collectively leverage purchasing power. The Sovereign States Drug Consortium enables individual state negotiations while benefiting from a collective pool. The Northwest Prescription Drug Consortium is a regional collaboration between Oregon and Washington, and MMCAP operates as a cooperative GPO for state agencies and government facilities. These pools play a role in reducing prescription drug costs and optimizing Medicaid expenditures.
- **Medicare administrative contractors (MACs)**: MACs are private entities contracted by the Centers for Medicare & Medicaid Services to handle tasks such as processing Medicare claims, enrolling providers, and managing other administrative functions. They help ensure claims are processed accurately and efficiently while also aiming to reduce the administrative workload for healthcare providers.[29]

- **Tech enablers**
  - Amazon and Apple are attempting to transform the healthcare industry by leveraging technology to enhance patient experiences and streamline healthcare services. As tech disruptors, they are introducing innovative solutions such as virtual care platforms, AI-driven diagnostics, and wearable health monitoring devices, which are shifting traditional healthcare models toward more personalized and proactive care. Amazon expanded into primary care with its One Medical acquisition and offers online prescriptions via Amazon Pharmacy (formerly PillPack). Amazon Web Services powers digital transformation in healthcare, while the Halo Band provides health tracking. Apple focuses on health data integration through HealthKit and its Health App, empowering users to manage medical records. Apple Watch advances proactive care with heart health

tracking and appears to be developing glucose monitoring capability. Meanwhile, AI-driven diagnostics and remote monitoring investments signal Apple's commitment to reshaping healthcare delivery.[30]

Understanding the common themes to work effectively with intermediaries

This chapter has introduced the large and diverse number of intermediaries in the US healthcare system, as well as identified several common themes in the business models of these groups. Specifically:

1. **The most powerful intermediaries are large and in concentrated markets**
   This chapter has shown that the core intermediaries are all operating in markets where a small number of intermediaries tend to control the majority of the volume.
2. **Many of the intermediaries are integrated with a major wholesaler or PBM**
   These core intermediaries tend to be owned by or affiliated with either a major wholesaler or major PBM, which allows them to capture value from more portions of the drug supply chain and influence decision-making.
3. **Intermediaries leverage their scale to achieve bargaining power**
   Many intermediaries use their scale to influence the use of a large volume of something (be it a drug, device, or service), to get a better price from somebody (like a manufacturer or a provider).
4. **Their business model involves adding a fee for their services**
   Usually, intermediaries will add a fee that is directly or indirectly related to the total value that flows through them (e.g., a percentage of a drug's WAC).
5. **They leverage data to refine and expand their business**
   Most intermediaries are interested in leveraging their position and volume to collect data that allows them to improve some aspect of healthcare delivery.

So what does this mean for someone attempting to work together with an intermediary? Since intermediaries are usually not responsible for any of the main roles in patient care, they are often thought of as a group that is "in the way." However, for any given group in the healthcare ecosystem, their view of intermediaries is likely to be influenced by whether that intermediary works "for" or "against" them. For example, a payer whose PBM gets them a large rebate stream, or a provider whose GPO gets them a low price, will certainly appreciate these groups' existence. On the other hand, the manufacturer providing the rebate or discount is likely to appreciate their existence much less.

To a great extent, these entities' structures codify how the healthcare ecosystem operates today. They can create a barrier to change if that change doesn't fit with their existing systems or business model. The scale and influence of intermediaries, particularly in the core, is large enough that anywhere they are involved, they must be understood and engaged.

The future of intermediaries in the US healthcare ecosystem is poised for significant change. Ongoing reforms targeting PBM transparency, the implications of vertical integration, and the adoption of innovative business models like private label biosimilars will collectively influence drug pricing, accessibility, and the overall dynamics of the healthcare market.[31]

Notes

1 *The evolution of pharmaceutical sales channels in the USA.* (n.d.). Mapple Valley Pharmacy; *The vital role of a distributor in the U.S. pharmaceutical supply chain.* (2025), AmerisourceBergen.
2 What is a GPO. (n.d.). Healthcare Supply Chain Association Website; *A primer on group purchasing organizations.* (n.d.). Healthcare Supply Chain Association.
3 Mattingly, T.J., Hyman, D.A., Bai, G. Pharmacy Benefit Managers: History, Business Practices, Economics, and Policy. *JAMA Health Forum.* 2023;4(11):e233804.
4 Schachte, J. (2016). Reflecting on the history of specialty pharmacy. *Pharmacy Times*; Suchanek, D. (2005). *The rise and role of specialty pharmacy.* Biotechnology Healthcare. pp. 31–35.
5 Fein, A.J. (2019). The big three wholesalers: revenues and channel share up, profits down. Drug Channels; *HDA factbook: prescription sales through traditional healthcare distributors remain strong in 2023.* (2024). HDA.
6 Fein, A. (2024). *The 2024–25 economic report on pharmaceutical wholesalers and specialty distributors.* Drug Channels Institute.
7 Mass, A. (2024). *Drug channels predicts more wholesaler vertical integration over next couple of years.* AIS Health.
8 *Top 10 GPOs by staffed beds.* (2024). Definitive Healthcare.
9 Muoio, D. (2023). *Premier Inc. carving off non-healthcare group purchasing business in $800M cash deal.* Fierce Healthcare.
10 *Effects of IDN & GPO consolidation on the healthcare supply chain.* (2020). Definitive Healthcare.
11 Fein, A. (2024). PBM power: the gross-to-net bubble reached $334 billion in 2023—but will soon start deflating. Drug Channels.
12 Fein, A. (2024). The top pharmacy benefit managers of 2023: market share and trends for the biggest companies—and what's ahead. Drug Channels.
13 *Pharmacy benefit managers: the powerful middlemen inflating drug costs and squeezing main street pharmacies* (Interim Staff Report). (2024). U.S. Federal Trade Commission; Modafferi, M., Levitt, F. (2024). *Federal Trade Commission investigating rebate aggregators' retention of money from drug manufacturers.* Frier Levitt Attorneys at Law.
14 *Pharmacy benefit managers: the powerful middlemen inflating drug costs and squeezing main street pharmacies.* (2024). Federal Trade Commission.
15 *Pharmacy benefit managers: the powerful middlemen inflating drug costs and squeezing main street pharmacies.* (2024). Federal Trade Commission.

16 Robbins, R., Abelson, R. (2024). The opaque industry secretly inflating prices for prescription drugs. *New York Times*; *FTC releases second interim staff report on prescription drug middlemen.* (2025). Federal Trade Commission.

17 *Pharmacy benefit managers: current legal framework* (Report No. LSB11080). (2023). Congressional Research Service.

18 *Top specialty pharmacy therapy areas.* (2020). Definitive Healthcare.

19 *The top 15 specialty pharmacies of 2023: market shares and revenues at the biggest PBMs, health plans, and independents.* Drug Channels.

20 *How specialty pharmacy can support value-based care and population health.* Shields Health Solutions.

21 Shelley, S. (2024). Specialty pharmacy: the trends shaping best practices. Pharmaceutical Commerce Website.

22 Bugbee, M., O'Grady, E., Fenne, M. (2023). Private equity in U.S. healthcare: trends in 2023 deal activity. Private Equity Stakeholder Project Website; Olsen, E. (2024). After decline, private equity investment in healthcare reaches turning point: PitchBook. Healthcare Dive; *Private equity's role in health care.* (2023). The Commonwealth Fund.

23 *An introduction to management services organizations (MSOs).* (n.d.). Premier Physician Support Services; Management service organization. (n.d.). Definitive Healthcare; *Global healthcare management service organization market size & trends report segmented by services (operations management, network management, quality management, other services), ownership (hospitals, physician groups, investors, others) forecasts to 2030.* (n.d.). Mid-Tech Insights.

24 Wainer, D. (2024). Why drug distributors are buying cancer specialists. *The Wall Street Journal*; Why drug distributors are buying cancer specialists. (2024). The Student Doctor Network Website.

25 What is a third-party administrator in health insurance. (2025). Healthee; Kagan, J. (2025). Third-party administrator (TPA): definition and types. Investopedia; Third party administrator: what is a TPA in health insurance? (2022). Collective Health Website.

26 Rebelo, A. (2023). *Wolters Kluwer's Pharmacy Next survey shows 58% of Americans likely to first seek non-emergency healthcare at pharmacies.* Wolters Kluwer; Natu, A., Burgess, T., Hakmeh, B., Singh, A. (2023). *The evolution of the retail pharmacy in vaccinations* (Whitepaper). ZS Associates; Samios, G. (2025). How retail pharmacies can help improve healthcare outcomes. *Forbes.*

27 Innovations: Wholesale drug importation under the spotlight [Newsletter]. (2021). National Association of Boards of Pharmacy. Vol 50, No. 6; BlinkRX homepage. BlinkRX.

28 Leveraging vaccine purchasing to help create greater operational efficiencies. Atlantic Health Partners Website.

29 What's a MAC. (n.d.). Centers for Medicare & Medicaid Services; Medicare administrative contractors: who they are and what they do. (2023). Crossroads Health.

30 Balasubramanian, S. (2022). Amazon's growth in healthcare is unparalleled. *Forbes*; Google, Facebook, Amazon, and Apple: how big tech is going to disrupt healthcare, big time. MD Connect Website; Sookhoo, R. (2023). Healthcare disruptors of 2023: the future of healthcare innovation. Healthcare Triangle Website.

31 Jeremias, S. (2024). Breaking down biosimilar barriers: payer and PBM policies. AJMC Website.

Chapter 9

The Journey of Healthcare Data

Records to Revolution

Asheesh Shukla, Himanshu Patni, and Anush Khandelwal

Having explored the structural components of the US healthcare system, including payers, providers, physicians, patients, and the incentives that impact them, we shift our focus in this chapter to a foundational yet often less visible element: healthcare data. Data already plays a critical role in how decisions are made, care is delivered, and outcomes are measured. However, recent technological developments mean the ecosystem interactions we have described in this book now each leave a "digital footprint," which has created an unprecedented volume and level of detail in available healthcare data. Today, many stakeholders are rushing to take advantage of this emerging data landscape in a variety of ways. As the digital transformation happens across the industry, data is emerging as the backbone of innovation in care delivery, operational efficiency, and policy reform.

In this chapter, we will explore:

- The healthcare industry's ongoing digital transformation, with advancements in electronic health records (EHRs), wearables, and remote monitoring, leading patients to actively participate and share their data, enhancing care coordination and outcomes.

DOI: 10.4324/9781003603597-9

- Fragmentation of care, with decentralized IT infrastructure and insufficient care coordination hindering seamless patient experiences.
- The need for regulatory agility that accelerates healthcare innovation and proactive policy frameworks to support future disruptions.
- Partnerships across healthcare providers, payers, and manufacturers that are crucial for leveraging data and technology to drive innovation, improve patient outcomes, and reduce costs.

Expanding the "digital shadow"

One of the clearest manifestations of digital transformation is unfolding within the provider landscape, where data-driven efficiencies and economic pressures are reshaping care delivery models. The rising operating costs of running a provider system and periodic supply–demand gaps have created significant disruption and attracted private equity firms into the provider space. As we discussed in the providers chapter, the trend is to achieve scale through various forms of provider consolidation with a focus on improving the economics of care delivery. While a primary goal is to create a commercially viable economic model, these efforts are also driving significant efficiencies, standardization, and EHR system adoption, as well as creating a digital footprint of the patient journey from intake to discharge.

As a result, the quality of patient structured and unstructured data on treatment, disease management, procedures, and distribution is rich and remains accessible over an extended patient journey as each patient engages with healthcare providers. An efficiency-driven approach is reshaping the broader health services landscape, driving consolidations but bringing various entities like pharmacies, pharmacy benefits managers, and other parts of the value chain together with increasingly vertically integrated payers. Such mergers aim to create more coordinated treatment pathways for patients and reduce inefficiencies, administrative costs, and resource wastage. This trend is creating an improved experience for patients as they engage with healthcare services and allows them to connect their own data to generate even more improvements through personalization of the services they receive.

Across the industry, the cycle of consolidation, driving data generation that drives operational improvements, is creating significant value and paving the way to cross-functional realization of healthcare outcomes.

Evolution of the US healthcare data landscape

This proliferation of available healthcare data is a recent phenomenon. Until the early 2000s, healthcare data was largely stored on paper. Clinical notes, prescriptions, and patient records existed in silos, often stored in physical folders or sometimes disconnected local information systems. This changed dramatically with the passage of the Health Information Technology for Economic and Clinical Health (HITECH) Act in 2009, which incentivized hospitals and physician practices to adopt EHRs. Healthcare's subsequent digital transformation unfolded through three seismic shifts.

Paper to digital

The first wave emerged in the pharmacy, with e-prescribing adoption skyrocketing from just a few thousand prescribers in the 2000s to greater than 90% of all prescriptions being filled electronically by the early 2020s. This transformation created unprecedented prescription intelligence (e.g., allowing pharmaceutical companies to track prescribing patterns), but offered little clinical utility or benefit to the patient.

Claims and administrative data emerge

The second surge came through electronic claims processing, where electronic transactions surpassed greater than 90% adoption across payers by 2020. These billing codes were breadcrumbs that could be used to trace patient journeys through a reimbursement—recording what insurers paid for, but not why interventions succeeded or failed. Additionally, each insurer switch fractured these narratives into discontinuous timelines, making long-term care history difficult to follow. Claims data became the healthcare equivalent of restaurant receipts: detailing transactions but with little insight into the meal's nutritional value and no information on whether it was tasty.

Adoption of EHRs

The third and most profound transformation came through EHR implementation. Hospital adoption exploded from less than a third in 2010 to near-universal penetration today. These systems trapped exquisitely detailed clinical narratives—progress notes, lab trends, imaging insights, and more—in incompatible digital fiefdoms. This data suddenly allowed the user to gain microscopic detail within institutions but lost macroscopic visibility across them.

Data is collected at several interfaces in this complex healthcare transaction model

Figure 9.1 illustrates the complex data flow in the US healthcare system, where information is collected at multiple points across the pharmaceutical and care delivery chain. The key stakeholders, such as manufacturers, wholesalers, pharmacies, hospitals, physicians, payers, pharmacy benefit managers, and patients, generate and exchange various data types, that is, EHR data, claims, prescriptions, employee activity, and audits. These data flows enable critical functions like reimbursement, clinical decision-making, marketing analysis, and operational optimization. The patient sits at the center of this ecosystem, with data converging from providers, pharmacies, and payers to inform better healthcare delivery and business decisions.

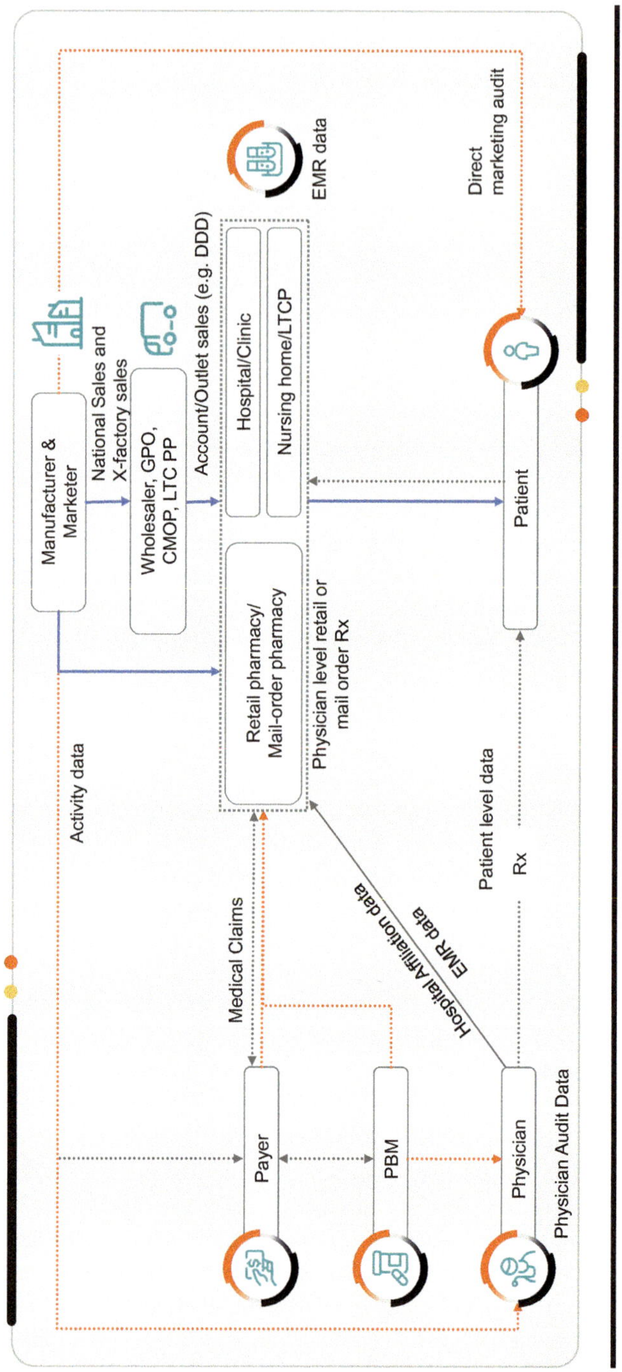

Figure 9.1 Data flow across pharmaceutical and care delivery points

Today, healthcare data is also expanding across new frontiers, which promise even greater insights in the future:

- **Remote monitoring:** Home-based sensors and connected devices are transforming chronic disease management, capturing blood pressure, glucose, and more, and enabling proactive, data-driven interventions.
- **Wearables:** Nearly half of adults now generate a ceaseless stream of heartbeats, steps, and sleep cycles recorded by a device like a smart watch, fueling a real-time feedback loop between users' daily routine and health management. Yet, very few clinicians integrate this data into care plans, creating a gap between patient-generated insights and clinical action.
- **Genomics:** Genetic testing has gone mainstream, with sequencing costs plummeting from more than $1 billion per genome the first time it was sequenced to less than $1,000 today. Yet EHRs remain ill-equipped to handle polygenic risk scores, limiting practical clinical utility to a fraction of its potential.

These new data streams are not just adding volume; they are transforming the very nature of healthcare, turning every individual into a living, breathing data source and pushing the boundaries of what's possible in prevention, diagnosis, and care.

Unfinished data transformation

Despite this data abundance, healthcare's digital revolution remains incomplete. Multiple barriers continue to plague the realization of value—the lack of cross-industry economic incentives to make the data generally available, and improving the experience for patients, remain the primary ones. Lack of clarity on required data security and policy-driven data privacy concerns complicates information sharing within the ecosystem. The data itself continues to be a mix of structured data and messy, unstructured data, defying easy analysis. The transformation of workflows also remains incomplete with a chaotic mix of cutting-edge technology and outdated paper processes. This dichotomy between data wealth and fragmentation creates a healthcare ecosystem in which information is plentiful, but insights are still scarce. This gap prevents healthcare resources from being directed at the areas where they could have the most impact. Figure 9.2 highlights the large gap between what matters (impact on health) and what US healthcare systems currently invest in each area (the US spends).

However, as we discuss throughout the remainder of this chapter, the promise of affordable and accessible technology has already shown us the way forward. While digital transformation still lacks industry-wide economic incentives and clear overarching policy guidance, it is well underway—propelled by some major policies, including the HITECH Act, the Health Insurance Portability and

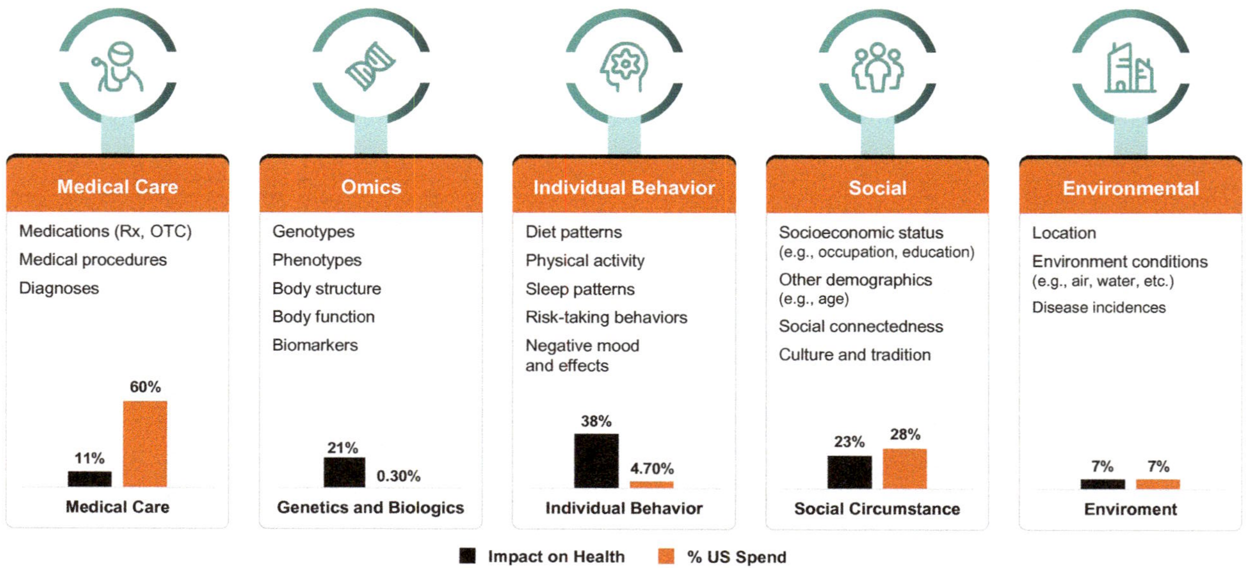

Figure 9.2 Misalignment between the US healthcare spending and impact on health outcomes

Accountability Act (HIPAA), the Affordable Care Act marketplace, the Centers for Medicare & Medicaid Services (CMS) Blue Button, Real-World Data (RWD), and Real-World Evidence (RWE). This technology revolution is further supported by significant investments across health systems, insurers, health services, and pharmaceutical manufacturers.

From chaos to clarity: Shaping the landscape of healthcare data

Today's healthcare data is a fragmented mess. Patient information is scattered across hospitals, insurers, pharmacies, and wearables, each operating in silos with incompatible systems. This chaos is compounded by several key challenges:

- **Multiple data sources:** Data lives in isolated systems such as EHRs (hospitals), claims (insurers), and prescriptions (pharmacies), making integration nearly impossible.
- **Inconsistent formats:** Even within the same data type (e.g., lab results), formats vary widely, complicating interoperability.
- **No universal patient ID:** Without a unique identifier, linking records relies on error-prone methods like matching names or birthdates.
- **Interoperability failures:** Proprietary systems and inconsistent adoption of standards (e.g., Health Level Seven Fast Healthcare Interoperability Resources for electronic data exchange) block seamless data sharing.
- **Privacy barriers:** Regulations such as HIPAA protect privacy but also create hurdles for data aggregation and practical application.

While fragmentation remains a persistent challenge, three major trends are inadvertently driving data aggregation: the rise of startup companies aggregating disparate datasets, industry mergers unifying siloed information, and regulations fostering transparency and interoperability.

The rise of data aggregators: Startups such as HealthVerity and Nebula Genomics are breaking down silos by aggregating disparate datasets through licensing deals, AI-driven linkage, and partnerships. While their motives may be profit-driven, they're laying the groundwork for advancements in precision medicine, population health analytics, and RWE generation.

Mergers that merge data: While consolidations often aim to achieve operational efficiencies or market dominance, they also inadvertently result in the unification of previously siloed datasets. For example, the merger of Aetna and CVS brought together Aetna's medical claims data with CVS' pharmacy/retail data, enabling comprehensive patient profiles that would have previously been impossible.

Regulatory drivers: Similarly, while many government regulations (e.g., CMS interoperability rules and 21st-century Cures Act) aim to improve transparency and accountability in healthcare, their side effect has been the creation of richer datasets that drive innovation in care delivery and population health management.

Together, these trends are aggregating fragmented data and unlocking new doors to innovation and efficiency. The critical questions remain: Who will ultimately capture the value of this transformation, and will it ultimately lead to innovation that benefits patients?

Mining the data mess: AI is organizing healthcare's unstructured data

Healthcare data is not just fragmented—it is overwhelmingly unstructured and messy. Unstructured data refers to information that does not fit neatly into rows and columns of a database. Approximately 80% of healthcare data falls into this category, encompassing such formats as clinical notes, medical images, audio recordings, and even patient-generated data from wearables. These sources are inherently heterogeneous, prioritizing detail over standardized formats. Traditionally, this has made them very difficult to analyze.

Efforts to address the challenges of unstructured healthcare data are being driven by advancements in technology and strategic frameworks. Key drivers of change include advancements in AI and generative AI (GenAI) and Natural Language Processing, as well as the development of standardized frameworks such as the Observational Medical Outcomes Partnership Common Data Model. For instance, GenAI now transforms doctor–patient conversations into structured clinical notes in real time, significantly reducing clinicians' administrative workload while enhancing operational efficiency. The driving force behind many of these innovations often lies in the economic incentives of private AI companies, which seek to monetize healthcare data or refine their algorithms to maintain a competitive edge in the market.

This raises a critical question: Who ultimately realizes the value created when unstructured data is transformed into structured insights? While AI companies gain economic benefits by developing proprietary tools and models, the structured data they produce can also create downstream value for other stakeholders. However, who will benefit, and whether this value will meaningfully reach the bedside to improve patient care or remain confined to boardrooms serving corporate interests, remains to be seen.

Cyber threats ignite a wave of security measures and innovation

Healthcare data is under constant threat from privacy breaches, security vulnerabilities, and cyberattacks. Healthcare data breaches have become a lucrative business for cybercriminals, with stolen patient records fetching prices far higher than financial data on the dark web.[1,2] Unlike credit card numbers, which can be easily canceled or replaced, medical records hold permanent and sensitive information such as Social Security numbers, birth dates, medical histories, and insurance details. These records are immensely valuable on the dark web, often selling for as much as $1,000 each—50 times the price of stolen credit card data—making them a prime target for hackers.

The challenges surrounding health data privacy and security are vast, but the response from governments and the private sector has been vigorous.

Government response: the stick and carrot approach

Governments have adopted a two-pronged strategy:

- Regulatory mandates: Updates to HIPAA now require measures such as encryption, multifactor authentication, and continuous monitoring to protect sensitive health information. Additionally, states (including New York) have implemented cybersecurity mandates specifically for healthcare institutions.
- Incentives and penalties**:** Federal grants are available to help smaller healthcare providers manage the high costs of compliance, while organizations that fail to meet these standards face steep financial penalties.

Private sector response: privacy and compliance become big business

At the same time, the private sector has stepped up with cutting-edge solutions to address these risks:

- Privacy-enhancing technologies (PETs): Innovations such as homomorphic encryption and tokenization enable secure data analysis without exposing raw patient data.
- AI-powered security tools: Artificial intelligence is being used to detect potential breaches in real time, stopping threats before they escalate.
- Data governance solutions: Frameworks for anonymization and risk management help maintain patient confidentiality while still enabling effective data use.

Significant advancements have been made to address the issues of fragmentation, unstructured formats, privacy, and security. The rise of data aggregators, the application of AI and GenAI, and the implementation of PETs have collectively transformed the landscape, creating a patient data ecosystem with immense potential for value generation. However, the critical question now shifts to how this value is realized and distributed. Ensuring this value reaches patients requires deliberate efforts from all stakeholders in the healthcare ecosystem. By aligning innovation with patient-centric goals, the industry can achieve a future where technological progress drives equitable and meaningful benefits for all.

Looking to the future: Technologies to enable systemic change

The US healthcare is being reshaped by ambitious digital reforms—including CMS's recent "Kill the Clipboard" campaign as part of its broader Health Tech Ecosystem initiative, and new rules around mandated interoperability. These efforts go beyond EHR digitization, driving industry-wide collaboration to eliminate paperwork, streamline manual processes, and give patients real-time access to their health data.

Kill the clipboard

The HITECH Act, the 21st-Century Cures Act and CMS' interoperability rules have prioritized the conversion of clinical data into digital format and accelerating the data exchange of these digital datasets. However, the efforts have been generally limited to EHR systems and ignored the usage of reams of paper and many manual processes that exist in the healthcare ecosystem such as patient intake at a clinic or hospital, how prescription flows through approval to fulfillment, care workflows, and the various trust and approval processes (consent, validation, data use, Business Associate Agreements, etc.).

There is a significant opportunity to eliminate administrative burden by digitizing data outside the EHR ecosystem, reducing provider and patient process burden, expanding digital identity services, and making the digital data exchange network more efficient. Building on this momentum, new platforms like BlinkRx and AmalgamRx now seamlessly connect with healthcare IT infrastructure—including EHRs, pharmacy systems, and clinical decision support tools—to replace paper transactions for prescriptions, lab orders, and administrative workflows with fully digital processes.

If implemented strategically, this ecosystem-wide digitization can address some of healthcare's most persistent blind spots, such as the critical gap between when a prescription is written and when it's actually presented to a pharmacy or transfer delays between various entities (lab routing, prescription fulfillment, clinical workflow execution). Improving processes in these areas offers the possibility of improving patient experience and eliminating barriers to medication adherence.

Recognizing the above, CMS has launched the "Kill the Clipboard"[3] initiative[4] as part of its broader Health Tech Ecosystem framework. This effort explicitly targets the manual, paper-based processes that persist outside EHR systems by encouraging healthcare providers and technology companies to adopt standardized digital alternatives for everything from patient intake forms to prescription workflows that can seamlessly integrate with existing infrastructure.

TEFCA mandated interoperability

TEFCA (Trusted Exchange Framework and Common Agreement) is a government-backed standard designed to connect all health IT systems nationwide for seamless data sharing. While CMS is driving adoption through regulatory pressure, there are no direct mandates or penalties yet. A big breakthrough came in Q2 2025 when Epic allowed patients to view their complete medical records across different providers, which had previously been impossible. With over 1,000 hospitals and 22,000 clinics now connected through Epic's TEFCA network alone, adoption is accelerating[5].

Epic and other EHR systems already share patient records between organizations (like Epic Care Everywhere), but TEFCA expands this beyond single-vendor networks to include insurance companies, public health agencies, and benefits programs.

However, participation and use, not just technical connectivity, must expand into payment, operations, and public health to deliver ROI. Cross-network trust, consent models, and data quality remain uneven, and aligning Standard Operating Procedure across networks is an ongoing governance challenge. Further, issues related to TEFCA favoring payors (with limited release of data) and fees associated with public and private partnering in data exchange still need to be resolved.

Together, these reforms are bringing healthcare closer to a future that's fast, connected, and truly focused on patient needs.

Embracing the revolution: A call to action

There are many opportunities across healthcare to improve patient outcomes, and almost all involve leveraging patient data in some way (see Figure 9.3). The greatest potential is in creating a connected ecosystem that leverages data as an underlying currency that's easily accessible, consistently interpreted, and responsibly used to deliver the best possible care. Yet, healthcare data does require significant expertise to understand and interpret for decision-making. At one end of the spectrum, such technologies as AI and advanced data analytics enable faster, more effective use of information, generating contextual, timely, and personalized insights. At the other end, advancement in digital technologies can bring the much-needed human-centered design to how patients interact with providers, payers, and other health service providers—ensuring the right balance of human and digital touchpoints. These innovations also build a care team around each patient, recognizing no one should navigate their health journey alone.

Data, when combined with innovations in technology, is transforming healthcare entities in meaningful ways. While evidence of this transformation so far is limited to a few organizations, these examples offer a glimpse into the opportunities we see becoming mainstream in the future. The biggest opportunities today are:

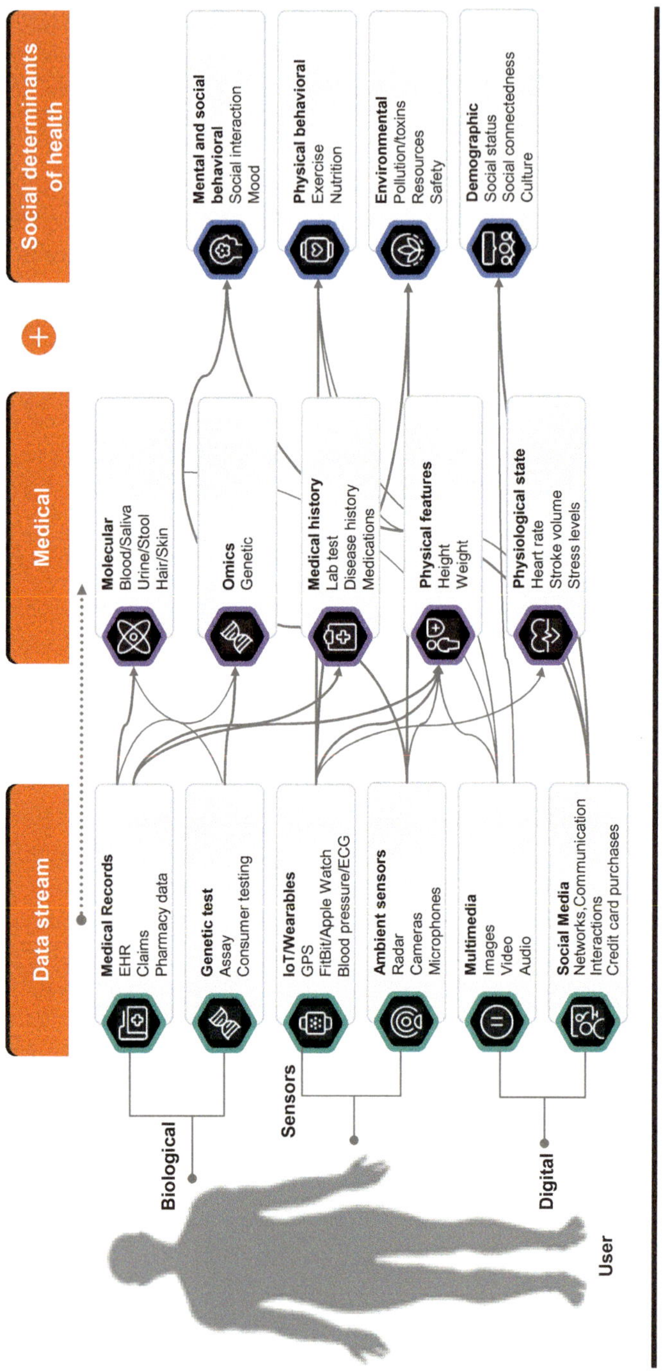

Figure 9.3 Patient data ecosystem

1. Personalized and precision care

Healthcare providers must move beyond simply delivering care to individuals to design institutional treatment pathways that are both standardized and tailored to individual patient needs. They should leverage data and analytics to develop and refine personalized interventions. For example:

- The Mayo Clinic's individualized medicine approach[6] uses genomics and proteomics to create treatment plans based on each patient's unique biological profile.
- Patient companion platforms (e.g., LillyDirect or MySugr) help patients manage every aspect of therapy, from nutrition and exercise to lab visits and medication adjustments, reducing friction and improving outcomes.

2. RWE, RWD, and research

New clinical evidence has historically been a major force behind improvements in healthcare, but the generation of this evidence has usually involved costly and time-consuming clinical trials. The data that healthcare providers generate every day, once analyzed, offers the opportunity to accelerate the identification and promulgation of best practices that lead to both improved patient outcomes and cost savings. For example:

- Integrating RWE into clinical decision-making bridges the gap between controlled trials and real-world care. Tools such as Clinical Decision Support Systems use patient-specific data to improve diagnoses and treatments.
- Organizations are leveraging RWD to generate additional or corroborating evidence to shape the standard of care and to cover patients who may benefit from such therapy (e.g., Pfizer's Ibrance approval for male breast cancer[7]).
- Patients can also contribute anonymized data for research, ensuring innovation is grounded in real-world needs and experiences.

3. Data-driven collaboration and innovation

Healthcare providers should embrace partnerships that amplify the impact of their data. For example:

- Platforms such as Mayo Clinic Platform Connect foster global partnerships, enabling secure data sharing and unlocking insights without compromising privacy.
- Digital solutions, such as the Cleveland Clinic Virtual Second Opinion service, make it easier to assess risk and get second opinions—ensuring a patient's condition is diagnosed correctly and the best possible treatment is recommended.

4. Patient empowerment and engagement

When patients are empowered as active participants in healthcare innovation, the benefits ripple across the system: outcomes improve, costs are reduced, research advances faster, and care becomes more personalized. The time to act is now—putting patients at the center of healthcare's data-driven future is not just a goal, it's a necessity. Tangible steps that can be taken include:

- Patients should take ownership of their health data by actively managing, curating, and sharing it. Tools like personal health records allow patients to update their medical histories, track symptoms, and even integrate wearable device data into their records. By taking charge of their data, patients become critical contributors to clinical decision-making and personalized care.
- For patients to succeed in these roles, healthcare providers, policymakers, technology developers, and researchers must work together to create an ecosystem that prioritizes patient empowerment. This includes providing tools, education, and systems that make data access and management seamless while fostering trust and transparency.

5. Regulatory agility and policy innovation

Regulators have often been seen as obstacles to progress, imposing strict rules that hinder innovation. However, recent events show they can act as accelerators of change. During the COVID-19 pandemic, agencies like CMS temporarily lifted restrictions on telehealth services. This allowed rapid adoption and ensured payment parity with in-person care, accelerating telehealth's integration into mainstream healthcare and demonstrating how regulatory agility can drive innovation. This experience emphasizes the need for proactive foresight—policymakers must anticipate future disruptions and establish frameworks that enable swift responses when crises arise.

The healthcare ecosystem stands at a pivotal and defining moment, driven by the transformative potential of health data and technology. Providers, regulators, patients, payers, and manufacturers must come together—not just as participants, but as architects of a data-driven revolution. The question is no longer whether we should act, but instead, how to act most effectively so we can harness data and technology to innovate healthcare.

Notes

1 Winder, D. (2025). Hackers Score $1,000 Per Healthcare Data Breach Vs. $5 Per Credit Card Theft. *Forbes*.

2 Green, D. (2025). *Data Breach Outlook: Healthcare Most Breached Industry in 2024*. Kroll.

3 CMS. (2025). *Patient Facing Apps—Kill the Clipboard, 2025*.

4 CMS. (2025). White House, Tech Leaders Commit to Create Patient-Centric Healthcare Ecosystem. Press Release.
5 Epic. (2025). Over 1,000 Hospitals Connect to TEFCA with Epic Nexus. Press Release.
6 Murphy, S. (2024). *Mayo Clinic's data-driven quest to advance individualized medicine*. Mayo Clinic.
7 Pagliarulo, N. (2019). *Pfizer wins expanded Ibrance approval using real world data.* BioPharma Dive.

Chapter 10

The Costs and Challenges of Reform

Anush Khandelwal and Joe Stevens

In the preceding chapters, we discussed the most important players in the US healthcare ecosystem. The scale and scope of this ecosystem are unlike those of other manufacturers or service providers—it is by itself one of the dominant economic forces in the country. Healthcare is one of the largest contributors to GDP, and it shapes the financial dynamics of both public and private sectors. Everyone will also eventually get sick and likely be personally impacted by the healthcare system's effectiveness or ineffectiveness, so it's of vital interest to everyone that this system works well. However, no single group we described in this book can deliver effective healthcare alone. Multiple groups must work together, each in their specialized roles, to deliver effective care to the patient. Individually, each group must also succeed as a business, which often puts them in conflict with other groups. This simultaneous need to both cooperate and compete has led to many of the unintended consequences of previous healthcare reforms and the failure of many otherwise promising innovations.

In this chapter, we:

- Discuss how big the healthcare business is and how resources are divided within it
- Analyze how money flows through the system between stakeholders and how this impacts decisions

 DOI: 10.4324/9781003603597-10

- Examine some well-meaning ideas that led to unintended consequences to illustrate the business dynamics as multiple groups interact
- Identify a few areas where reform is currently being discussed, and how they are likely to impact the system

How much does the US spend on healthcare?

The volume of resources involved in healthcare is enormous. Its scale and spending have deep ripple effects on national productivity, employment, and policymaking. Here is a closer look at healthcare's footprint as of 2023:[1]

- **Healthcare spending reached $4.9 trillion in 2023, making up 17.6% of the US GDP**
  This level of spending underscores healthcare's outsized role in the economy—larger than many industrial sectors combined. It signals the system's complexity, the excessive cost of services, and increasing demand for care, especially in an aging population.
- **Per capita healthcare spending climbed to $14,570, which is more than one-third of the median income**[2]
  For individuals, this creates a growing financial burden in the form of premiums, out-of-pocket expenses, and taxes that fund public programs.
- **Overall healthcare spending growth accelerated to 7.5% in 2023, up from 4.6% in 2022**[3]
  Much of this growth was driven by a rebound in healthcare use post-COVID, combined with rising prices—especially in private health insurance and Medicare services. This sharp jump has implications for public budgets and employer-sponsored coverage. Increases have been consistent across the various patient populations in the United States. Private health insurance spending saw the sharpest increase, rising by 11.5%—a reflection of escalating premiums, administrative overhead, and high-cost provider contracts common in employer-sponsored plans. Medicare expenditure grew by 8.1%, driven by an aging population entering retirement and requiring more frequent, intensive care services. Meanwhile, Medicaid spending rose by 7.9%, although its growth rate decelerated following the end of pandemic-related continuous enrollment provisions.
- **Almost everyone engages with the healthcare system in some way, with 92.5% of the US population insured in 2023**[4]
  Insurance gains, particularly through Medicaid and employer-based plans, indicate some progress toward universal coverage, but gaps in access and disparities in care quality persist. Additionally, at the time this book was written, the future of federal subsidies for healthcare is uncertain, and without subsidies, improvements in coverage may reverse.

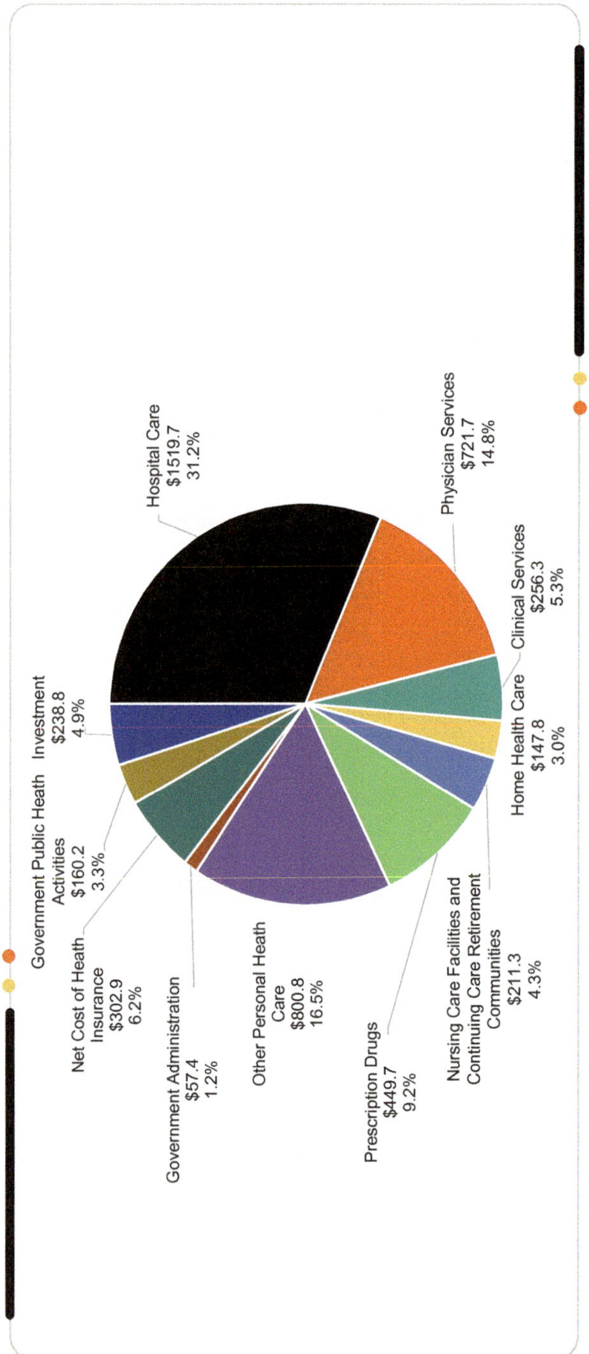

Figure 10.1 Healthcare spending across segments

Source: **National Healthcare Expenditure Data (NHEA), 2023, Centers for Medicare & Medicaid Services (CMS)**

Where all that money goes

How healthcare spending is distributed across the system can reveal insights into the operations of the complex ecosystem. Hospital care remained the single largest category, accounting for more than $1.5 trillion or 31.2% of the total spend. This includes inpatient services, surgeries, emergency care, and outpatient treatments—all of which continue to see rising costs due to infrastructure overhead, staffing, and technological investments (see Figure 10.1).[5]

Next in line were physician services, comprising $721.7 billion or 14.8% of total spending. These cover in-office consultations, diagnostic services, and specialist care. Alongside this, clinical services—which include lab tests, outpatient surgical centers, and imaging—made up 5.3%, reflecting both demand growth and the decentralization of diagnostic care beyond hospitals. Prescription drugs consumed $449.7 billion, about 9.2% of total spending, which remains one of the most controversial areas in healthcare, given the steep prices of innovative drugs and the high patient out-of-pocket costs often required. The net cost of health insurance—which includes administrative costs, profits, and taxes retained by insurers—stood at $302.9 billion (6.2%), highlighting the financial weight of the insurance infrastructure itself.[6]

A sizable portion, $800.8 billion or 16.5%, also went into other personal healthcare, which is a broad category that includes dental services, durable medical equipment, and other miscellaneous services not classified elsewhere. Long-term care services, including nursing home care ($211.3 billion) and home healthcare ($147.8 billion), together represent 7.3% of the total spend. These segments are increasingly vital as the US population ages and chronic conditions drive up the need for extended care.[7] The rest of the expenditure was spread across investment in structures and equipment ($238.8 billion), public health activities ($160.2 billion), and government administration ($57.4 billion), showcasing the essential, if less visible, components that support the healthcare system's functionality and resilience.[8]

United States vs. the world

It is also worth noting that US expenditures on healthcare are well above those in other countries—so much so, it's awkward to even plot them on the same graph (see Figure 10.2). For all this money, US health outcomes, as measured by things such as life expectancy, do not seem to be an outlier, as they fall at or below those of other developed countries. There are certainly problems with this simple analysis. What the US categorizes as healthcare spending isn't exactly the same as other countries; other non-healthcare goods and services are often also expensive in the United States, and as previous chapters have discussed, many factors other than healthcare contribute to health outcomes. Methodological criticism aside, it is clear that the United States expends an amazing amount of resources

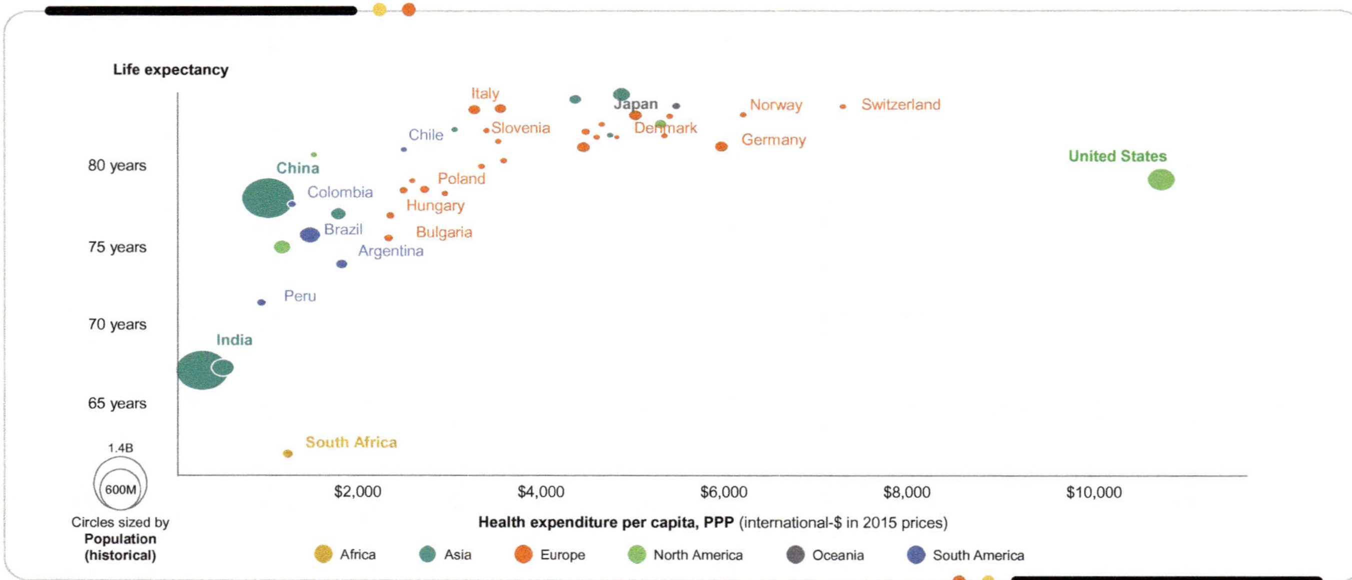

Figure 10.2 US versus the rest of the world, life expectancy, and health expenditure data

***Note*: Health expenditure is expressed in international-$ at 2015 prices**

Source: UN, World Population Prospects (2024); OECD Health Expenditure and Financing Database (2024)

on healthcare and doesn't seem to be getting an equally amazing return on its investment. Many people have proposed reforms or brought new ideas to try to make US healthcare more efficient, but costs seem to continue to increase. Why is reform so difficult?

Good ideas with unintended consequences

At first glance, the flow of money in healthcare appears straightforward and similar to a typical insurance market: Individuals pay premiums and out-of-pocket expenses, insurers reimburse providers, and providers deliver care. However, beneath this surface lies a highly fragmented and indirect financial ecosystem shaped by incentives, policies, and market dynamics that are often hidden from view. The financial flow in healthcare brings together multiple stakeholders, each operating with distinct roles, goals, and constraints. The reason any kind of reform of the US healthcare system becomes so difficult can only be understood as a function of this structure.

We examine two examples—negotiated rebates and the US government's 340B program—to illustrate how a policy that made sense from the perspective of some stakeholders can lead to suboptimal outcomes for either themselves or other parts of the ecosystem if the complex nature of financing and incentives isn't fully considered.

Controlling costs through negotiations

The largest US spending categories are hospital services, physician services, and prescription drugs. Payment for these involves a flow of money from payers who reimburse healthcare providers and pharmacies for the services they deliver to patients. This takes place usually after a claim is filed and negotiated rates are applied. As we discussed in previous chapters, these payments can take various forms, such as fee-for-service payments or value-based care arrangements that tie reimbursement to patient outcomes. Some costs are paid directly by the patient as well, but since most Americans have health insurance this is usually only a small portion of the total cost.

This simple description sounds logical but covers up many other stakeholders involved in the process. Depending on exactly which services or products are needed, players, including pharmaceutical manufacturers, pharmacy benefit managers (PBMs), wholesalers, and government price control programs, add complexity at every stage (as we discussed in the intermediaries chapter, this often makes the actual "price" of anything almost impossible to determine.).

For instance, a hospital may charge $3,000 for an MRI, but an insurer might negotiate that down to $900, and a patient with insurance might only pay $150 out of their own pocket, depending on their deductible or co-pay. Meanwhile, the actual cost to the hospital for running the MRI may only be $400, while another nearby hospital may charge a different price altogether for the same service. This disconnect between list price, negotiated rate, out-of-pocket cost, and clinical value creates a system in which patients, providers, or policymakers struggle to understand whether healthcare dollars are being spent effectively. Some of the greatest challenges caused by this system are in the pricing of prescription drugs.

"The rebate wall"

As we discussed in preceding chapters, PBMs act as intermediaries between insurers and drug companies. In exchange for placing a drug in a favorable tier on a health plan's formulary (the list of covered medications), PBMs receive rebates from manufacturers, which they then pass on to payers (after taking a fee), and payers then use that rebate to reduce costs for employers or other plan funders (after taking another fee). This system was originally intended to drive prices down. We shared an example in this chapter discussing intermediaries that demonstrated how as negotiated rebate increases, the cost to the payer decreases, while PBM fees go up and patient out-of-pocket costs remain the same. While this isn't a great result for the patient who must pay the out-of-pocket cost, one could argue the system is working as designed since reduced costs for the payer will eventually lead to lower premiums (and some insurance company profits). However, negotiating high rebates can also lead to unintended consequences. Consider the following situation:

- An effective new "Drug A" enters the market, generates high sales, and thus high costs for payers
- A payer negotiates a large rebate in exchange for being selected as the only "preferred" drug on its formulary for a particular usage (patient type, indication, etc.)
- In exchange for the pharma company signing the contract, the payer uses utilization management tools to encourage physicians to only use Drug A

At first glance, this appears to be a "win-win" for everybody. Patients get access to an expensive new drug. Payers have negotiated a price substantially below the list price for a product their patients need and physicians were planning to use anyway. The pharma company gets payer help in getting physicians to use Drug A instead of a competitor's drug. What could go wrong?

The challenges from this arrangement occur after a few years have passed and additional drugs enter the market. Maybe they are similar drugs and the manufacturer of new Drug B wants to offer a lower price than Drug A to the payer in exchange for a share. Alternatively, maybe the new drug is more efficacious or tolerable and physicians want to prescribe it more than Drug A. Let's consider the case where the payer wants to switch over to preferring Drug B:

- A payer negotiates a rebate with Drug B in exchange for being selected as a "preferred" drug on its formulary (either by itself or with others)
- As a result of this, the payer *loses* its contract with Drug A, which indicated it must be the *only* preferred drug for that usage
- After years of being preferred, many of the payer's patients are on Drug A and doing well—making switching these patients to a different drug almost impossible
- Without a contract, the payer will now have to pay full price for all Drug A patients since the price resets to full price

As this example implies, the payer is unlikely to ever contract to prefer Drug B in this case, even if it's cheaper or better. Paying full price for all its Drug A patients will create a huge cost for the payer. As drugs generally have few patients taking them in the beginning, new Drug B probably can't offer a large enough rebate to incentivize the payer to switch away from Drug A (i.e., the total spend on Drug B may be lower than the rebate received on Drug A).

This dynamic, where receiving high rebates creates a barrier to payers' adopting newer or cheaper treatments, is known as the "rebate wall." The payer made a rational decision to accept a high rebate in the beginning, but that decision hurt the company as the market landscape changed. An example, much like the above, happened years ago in pharmaceutical markets such as rheumatoid arthritis. Payers thankfully learned from those experiences, and today payers will usually avoid entering into a contract that specifies a drug to be the *only* preferred product for this reason. However, the dynamics of an existing rebate (or similar arrangement, such as protection from price increases), causing payers to prefer an old product that might not be selected today, still exist.

Controlling costs through government policy

The government, through programs such as Medicare and Medicaid, also reimburses healthcare providers for services provided to eligible populations, including the elderly and low-income individuals. These programs reimburse providers at rates generally lower than those negotiated by commercial insurers, which helps manage public spending but can pose challenges for hospitals and clinics operating on thin margins. Each program reflects an ongoing effort to balance cost control, access, and quality—goals that are not always easy to achieve simultaneously. The 340B drug pricing program provides a good example of why.

Paying for care for the poor

The 340B drug pricing program was created by Section 340B(a)(1) of the Public Health Service Act. The primary aims of creating the 340B program were twofold: to enable safety-net providers (defined as providers who served a disproportionate share of low-income patients) to stretch scarce federal resources, and to improve access to affordable medications for underserved populations.[9] Estimates peg the average 340B discount at around 55% of the list (wholesale acquisition cost) price,[10] although in some cases it leads to "penny pricing" where the calculated 340B price is zero and manufacturers charge a penny for the drug. The idea behind the program was to reduce the financial burden of prescription drugs and enhance the capacity of healthcare providers to deliver comprehensive, high-quality care to those in need by offering covered entities drugs at discounted prices.

How the program works

To receive the program's benefits, healthcare facilities (entities) are required to meet certain specific eligibility criteria. Some of the entities that can participate in the program include:

- **Federally qualified health centers** including Health Center Program Award recipients, Native Hawaiian Health Centers, and Health Center Program look-alikes
- **Hospitals** including children's hospitals, critical access hospitals, disproportionate share hospitals (DSHs), freestanding cancer hospitals, rural referral centers, and sole community hospitals
- **Specialized clinics** such as black lung clinics, comprehensive hemophilia diagnostic treatment centers, title X family planning clinics, sexually transmitted disease clinics, and tuberculosis clinics[11]

When enrolling in the 340B program, covered entities must choose whether they will use 340B drugs for their Medicaid fee-for-service patients (carve-in) or purchase drugs for these patients through other means (carve-out). The 340B drug program covers both branded and generic medicines to ensure a broad spectrum of drugs is accessible to those in need. Manufacturers can choose to opt out of the 340B program; however, this decision would mean the manufacturer cannot participate in the Medicaid program—so the incentive to remain in is strong for most manufacturers. Additionally, the choice to participate in the 340B program cannot be made on a drug-by-drug basis. The manufacturer needs to opt in or out for all its products—a requirement that virtually all drug manufacturers participate.

In the past two decades, the program has experienced exponential growth fueled by increased healthcare entities' participation. Between 2000 and 2020, the number of covered entity sites surged from just over 8,100–50,000, reflecting its expanding reach and significance in serving underserved communities.[12] The Affordable Care Act of 2010 marked a significant milestone for the 340B program, expanding eligibility to include freestanding cancer hospitals and critical access hospitals, regardless of their DSH status. The provisions of the Act also lowered the DSH threshold for rural referral centers and sole community hospitals, while permitting covered entities to use multiple contract pharmacies for medication access.[13]

Adverse incentives

Several problems arose from the creation of this program, most of which are due to the large financial incentives to maximize the program's use to the greatest extent possible.

The first challenge it created is the proliferation of mergers and contract pharmacies. 340B was sufficiently attractive as a program that substantial financial gains could be achieved if a larger 340B-eligible institution merged with a smaller non-eligible one, as long as the combined institution could successfully qualify as 340B eligible. Providers also created "contract pharmacies," which were not actually managed by 340B-eligible institutions but were authorized by that provider to buy and dispense 340B drugs at remote sites. Both these activities blurred the line of what is actually a 340B eligible entity and expanded the program outside the boundaries originally envisioned by the law.

As it expanded, so did bad behavior. Once drugs were purchased under the program, it became very difficult to determine where that drug was sent and what patient it was used on. This led to widespread accusations of drug diversion, particularly by the contract pharmacies. Additionally, drug diversion led to the problem of double dipping, where a drug purchased with the 340B discount is used on a commercially insured patient, whose insurer also received a rebate from the pharma companies that sell the drug (the double dipping is because only one of these rebates should apply). Since both rebates can be above 50%, at times this caused the pharma company to pay every time one of its products was used by having an effective discount rate at over 100%.

The final irony in this program is that in 2022, the US Supreme Court overturned the payment policy allowing the government to reimburse 340B drugs at a lower rate than regular drugs. As a result, the program no longer saves the government any money or makes care for the poor less expensive. It only creates a financial boon for providers and adverse incentives to conduct many activities that have no relation to improved patient care.

New ideas for old problems

Efforts to reduce the price of drugs did not end with negotiations and 340B. The most recent policy proposal is known as "Most Favored Nation" (MFN) pricing.

As of the writing of this book in 2025, the US federal government has been pushing this policy through an executive order[14] and letter-writing campaign[15] to pharmaceutical companies, demanding that drug manufacturers do not offer other developed countries lower prices than are available to patients in the United States. Indeed, today the price for many innovative drugs is much, much higher in the United States than in other developed countries. The executive order notes that "the United States has less than five percent of the world's population and yet funds around three quarters of global pharmaceutical profits" and sees this as "Foreign Nations Freeloading on American-Financed Innovation".

While many might see this as a laudable goal, for the reader who has made it this far in this book, it should also be obvious that *how* such a goal can be achieved is far from clear. The first challenge is how each country's prices will change to eliminate these cross-border differences across developed countries. This is complicated by the fact that outside the United States, pharma companies generally can't set the price at which they sell drugs in developed countries and instead rely on a price set by that country's government or insurance system. Pharma companies would certainly like to receive higher prices outside of the United States, and shortly prior to the executive order 30 European pharma companies had already sent a letter[16] to the president of the EU requesting a replacement of the pricing regime with a single Europe-wide price set closer to the US price. However, as this would obviously entail a very large cost to European government's health insurance systems, there appears to be little enthusiasm to grant their request.

Reducing the US price of these drugs to more closely match Europe will likely be equally challenging. Of course, the drug manufacturers are about as eager to accept less money for their drugs as EU governments are to pay more. However, the many stakeholders described in this book will create a myriad of additional challenges to the implementation of this type of policy. To begin with, it isn't even clear what "the price of prescription drugs" in the US even means. Is this the list price? The net price paid by insurers? The out-of-pocket cost for the patient? As we have described in Chapter 8, very few people actually pay the list price and even knowing the average net price beforehand is almost impossible since it is a function of the proportion of patients from each of many different insurance types, each receiving a different discount.

If it is possible to convince or coerce drug manufacturers into accepting a lower price, the impacts of this policy will also ripple through the entire healthcare system. As we discussed in Chapter 5, physician-administered drugs are an important part of the revenue of many provider organizations—particularly for the 340B institutions we discussed previously in this chapter. If the current "high list price coupled with high rebate" pricing model in the United States disappears, payers will also lose the ability to shift a larger portion of drug costs into patients' coinsurance as rebate rate increases, as we describe in Chapter 7. Finally, the business models of the many intermediaries such as PBMs and GPOs will also suffer, as many of their fees are based on a percentage of a drug's price.

The federal government recognizes these challenges, and the executive order adds reference to two policies designed to make MFN feasible. The first of these is the use of "trade policy" (assumably, tariffs on goods imported into the United States) to pressure foreign developed countries' governments to pay high drug prices. The second is to encourage manufacturers to "cut out the middlemen" and sell drugs directly to the patients and/or providers using the drug. This, presumably, is to allow pharma companies to keep a large share of what is paid for a product even as the US price declines.

While only time will reveal the impact of this policy, it is a great example of how making a small change to something in the healthcare ecosystem requires simultaneously modifying a number of things at the same time. Additionally, it creates a situation where for the reform to succeed, a large number of independent things must "go right" (e.g., pharma companies must lower prices in the United States, foreign governments must agree to pay more, a new distribution model must be created, and players in the old model such as PBMs must accept their destruction or reconfiguration). It is easy to imagine a future where some but not all of these reforms succeed, and we are left with another round of unintended consequences that create costs in unexpected places (i.e., what if prices rise without PBMs negotiating rebates?) or deny some patients access to needed medicines (i.e., what if a new and untested distribution system falters? What if some EU governments can't or won't pay, and no longer receive new drugs?, etc.).

Why reform is hard

In this chapter, we explored the scale and importance of the industry in the context of the overall US economy, and looked at how money flows through the system between stakeholders and how this impacts decisions. The fact is, healthcare spending continues to skyrocket, which has prompted various attempts at reform to get a handle on costs. Yet these efforts typically are stymied by the system's complexity, as we illustrated in the examples we discussed—where well-informed, professional decision-makers acted to reduce costs and increase efficiency, but ended up experiencing just the opposite outcomes. These examples are far from the only cases where this has happened. Why is that?

As we have described in this book, the healthcare ecosystem is made up of a multitude of specialized groups, each with its own expertise, constraints, and definition of success. Each group makes decisions to maximize that success from the group's own perspective, but the result of those decisions is determined by the interaction of all the stakeholders participating in patient care. In the case of the payers that ran into the rebate wall, they failed to consider that better or cheaper products would reach the market in a few years and also failed to realize the implications of a physician's unwillingness to switch patients who were doing well on a particular product. In the 340B example, the government failed to consider that the 340B program would incentivize providers to behave in ways that were orthogonal to the goal of efficient care for the poor. In both cases, the issues were knowable at the time each decision was made, but they were missed because all the problems happened in a different part of the ecosystem from the decision-maker. This is the major challenge of reforming the US healthcare system, and also one of the major reasons we decided to write this book.

Notes

1 Centers for Medicare & Medicaid Services. (n.d.). *National health expenditure data: Historical (NHE Infographic).* U.S. Department of Health and Human Services.
2 U.S. Census Bureau. (2025). *Real median personal income in the United States* (MEPAINUSA672N). FRED, Federal Reserve Bank of St. Louis.
3 Centers for Medicare & Medicaid Services. (n.d.). *National health expenditure data: Historical (NHE Infographic).* U.S. Department of Health and Human Services.
4 Centers for Medicare & Medicaid Services. (n.d.). *National health expenditure data: Historical (NHE Infographic).* U.S. Department of Health and Human Services.
5 Centers for Medicare & Medicaid Services. (n.d.). *National health expenditure data: Historical (NHE Tables).* U.S. Department of Health and Human Services.
6 Centers for Medicare & Medicaid Services. (n.d.). *National health expenditure data: Historical (NHE Tables).* U.S. Department of Health and Human Services.
7 Centers for Medicare & Medicaid Services. (n.d.). *National health expenditure data: Historical (NHE Tables).* U.S. Department of Health and Human Services.
8 Centers for Medicare & Medicaid Services. (n.d.). *National health expenditure data: Historical (NHE Tables).* U.S. Department of Health and Human Services.
9 Mulligan, K. (2021). *The 340B Drug Pricing Program: Background, ongoing challenges, and recent developments* (White Paper). USC Schaeffer Center for Health Policy & Economics.
10 Martin, R., Karne, H. (2023). *The 340B Drug Discount Program grew to $124B in 2023.* IQVIA.
11 U.S. Government Accountability Office. (2018). *Drug discount program: Federal oversight of compliance at 340B contract pharmacies needs improvement* (GAO-18-480).
12 Mulligan, K. (2021). *The 340B Drug Pricing Program: Background, ongoing challenges, and recent developments* (White Paper). USC Schaeffer Center for Health Policy & Economics.
13 Slafsky, T. (2022). *The 20 key moments in the 340B program's 30-year history.* Omnicell 340B Report. Omnicell.
14 Executive Orders. Delivering most-favored-nation prescription drug pricing to American patients. (2025). The White House.
15 Fact Sheet: President Donald J. Trump Announces Actions to Get Americans the Best Prices in the World for Prescription Drugs. (2025). The White House.
16 *European pharma companies push for higher drug prices in EU amid U.S. tariff threats.* (2025). Reuters.

Chapter 11

Reflections on the Road Ahead

Joe Stevens and Anush Khandelwal

This book aims to outline major players in the US healthcare ecosystem, trace their historical evolution over the years to understand their current roles, examine the incentives that drive their behavior, and explore how these incentives influence their decisions.

Trapped in a web of stakeholders

To understand how the healthcare system engages with patients, the best place to start is with payers who are typically the entry point for money flowing into the healthcare system. While payers are not inherently more important than the other stakeholders in the system, this book centers around the business of healthcare—and money plays a pivotal role in shaping incentives in other parts of the system. We discussed how the current system, which splits the population between private commercial insurance and government-run programs, is more of an accident of history than an intentional design. With this system, payers deploy various cost-containment strategies—such as utilization management, flat rate or diagnosis-related group, and value-based care (VBC) models. Each of these strategies emerged as a solution to a practical problem, but in turn, gave birth to new complexities and problems. We also examined how recently the biggest payers have turned to vertical integration with various intermediaries to align incentives

DOI: 10.4324/9781003603597-11

with other parts of the healthcare ecosystem and gain an advantage vis-à-vis other stakeholders.

We then examined the evolving provider landscape, noting how the conventional solo practitioner has largely been replaced by expansive health systems that consolidate nearly all care functions under a single management structure. Providers generally strive to balance three core priorities: clinical outcomes, patient experience, and financial success. However, with a large share of institutions today being financially distressed, economic or financial considerations often take precedence over clinical or experiential goals. As with payers, health systems have sought an advantage by getting larger and larger. While this consolidation has increased their bargaining power and streamlined some processes, the rise of this "industrial medicine" rarely benefits the patient as much as it benefits other parts of the ecosystem.

The shift in the organization of healthcare institutions has also driven a significant change in what it means to be a physician. A physician's role has shifted from one of independence and high autonomy to a situation in which the physician, often employed and evaluated by their institution, is part of a large, multifaceted care team that is enabled (or restricted) by sophisticated information and recordkeeping systems. A contemporary physician, in addition to directly caring for patients, spends a significant amount of time in recordkeeping, which feeds the calculation of a variety of metrics that are as important to their success as having happy patients (and in some cases, maybe even more so). Technological tools may one day streamline this activity, but haven't done so yet.

Supporting care delivery is a vast network of suppliers of pharmaceutical and medical devices. These markets—especially for drugs—are highly unique. No other industry faces such steep development costs, high risks, and long waits to reach the market, only to face a complicated and highly regulated customer environment. Despite having low marginal per-unit costs, successful products enjoy market exclusivity, limited competition, and high barriers to entry. This allows manufacturers to demand high prices, which in turn creates a variety of challenges for other stakeholders in the ecosystem.

Connecting the payers, providers, and pharmaceutical manufacturers involves a huge number of intermediaries. These intermediaries, in general, don't create anything that directly cares for the patient. Instead, they enable two or more stakeholders to engage and work together behind the scenes. The idea of intermediaries was conceived to solve a practical problem. For example, pharmacy benefit managers (PBMs) have a clear role in confirming a patient's insurance to the pharmacy, and group purchasing organizations have a straightforward way to consolidate purchasing. However, as these groups have scaled, they have gained more bargaining power, which is often used to extract value from one part of the healthcare system and deliver it to another—an activity that usually offers no benefit for the patient and creates significant barriers to any type of innovation or reform.

The interactions of all these ecosystem stakeholders have created a copious amount of data. Unfortunately, as of today, this data is siloed and underused. The newest healthcare ecosystem stakeholders are the many companies that seek to leverage this data to drive some change in the healthcare system's functioning. Although these companies' impact on day-to-day patient care is limited at present, when combined with advancements in AI and advanced analytics, the potential for transformative change becomes apparent, making this an area to watch in the future.

So, where does this all leave the patient? In the second chapter, we highlighted the growing frustration patients feel with their care experiences—and their increasing desire to take a more active role in their healthcare decisions and treatment journeys to improve them. This dissatisfaction is extremely disappointing, particularly due to the vast resources the US spends on healthcare and the remarkable scientific progress made in recent years. Yet, as the chapters that followed illustrated, the complexity and lack of transparency in the healthcare ecosystem make meaningful patient engagement a daunting challenge. We believe the most promising business opportunities in the future of healthcare will center on improving the patient experience. With that in mind, we would like to conclude this book with a few reflections on how that might be achieved.

Succeeding in a complex ecosystem

In writing this book, our goal was to explain the US healthcare ecosystem in a way that professionals across any of the key industry stakeholder groups could understand, to provide some insights on how these groups operate and can work together more effectively. The healthcare landscape includes an incredibly diverse range of businesses, each functioning in their own way—making it difficult to generalize about what the best future business might look like. That said, we believe there are four principles that will hold true in most, if not all, cases.

Today's biggest opportunities exist around customization rather than scale

A common theme presented in this book across multiple chapters has been how some participants of the ecosystem would gain sufficient scale and use that as a lever to succeed—for instance, health systems merging to standardize care delivery and negotiate better rates, payers vertically integrating, and PBMs covering more volume and generating more fees. Indeed, scale has made many existing healthcare businesses very successful.

We believe, however, that scale as a key success factor has largely run its course for two reasons. First, the biggest players in each of these categories are already so big that any new business will unlikely achieve sufficient scale to benefit from it for a very long time—and more likely, it will find itself as a small player negotiating with at least one, if not more, of the healthcare behemoths. Second, where scale has been achieved, it has largely been seen as not particularly beneficial to patients and to society, even if it was beneficial to the businesses themselves.

In the early days of modern healthcare, personal attention was provided automatically due to the patient–physician relationship and the primacy of the individual physician. However, the world has evolved to a different model of care delivery, and in doing so, that element of personalization has disappeared in the pursuit of quality and efficiency. The lack of personalization is a major cause for patient frustration, and solving that issue represents a big opportunity to improve the patient experience. Likewise, physicians, nurses, pharmacists, and many other individuals who work in healthcare feel frustrated with the system and would benefit from individual, personal engagement. We believe the opportunities of the future will be found in the *opposite* of scale—in customizing the delivery of healthcare to a smaller, more specific group, or even to the level of the individual.

The industry must make far better use of data, a huge store of untapped potential

If you accept our first point—that future opportunities exist around customization—the next question is, "How can this be achieved?" One of the most significant areas of untapped value, in our opinion, is the reams of data that are now being generated every day about every facet of the ecosystem. As we described in the healthcare data chapter, this data was historically siloed and unavailable. Today, however, it is organized and easily accessible. With the advent of generative AI, much of it is now machine-readable, which opens up countless new opportunities.

Data also can have a huge impact on healthcare providers' goals (clinical outcomes, patient experience, financial success, and sometimes employee satisfaction and/or health equity), which well-intentioned providers fail to meet in many small ways. We finally have the infrastructure to detect and deploy interventions on a large scale. We have data on what is happening, we have robust electronic health records systems that can drive activity at the time of patient interaction, and sophisticated analytics and AI-driven decision support systems. Where we lag is the absence of successful applications of these technologies to solve real-world problems. While there have been some successes, there have also been many failures—some because they didn't create value, and others because, despite creating value, they were too complex or burdensome for providers to leverage. Leveraging the massive amount of healthcare data to meaningfully improve the efficiency and effectiveness of patient care delivery is an area of huge untapped potential.

Businesses should focus on creating value for patients instead of just extracting it

Many of the stakeholders we described earlier in this book were partially or entirely focused not on caring for the patient, but on extracting value from somewhere in the healthcare system. Since healthcare takes up such a large share of GDP, there is certainly plenty of value to be extracted. However, this is fundamentally a zero-sum game—the value extracted comes from somewhere. If your business strategy is extraction, at least one of your counterparties (the one being extracted from) isn't likely to want to work with you if they have a choice. Additionally, with the huge number of intermediaries present in the US healthcare ecosystem already each skimming something off the top, it's hard to imagine that large opportunities exist in this area.

Instead, businesses should look to create something tangible, preferably unique value for the patient. As antagonistic as many of the ecosystem stakeholders are with each other, healthcare companies are almost always united by their desire to improve patients' lives. In the authors' experience, this is true culturally and increasingly true financially. From the cultural side, most executives we have met choose healthcare over some other industry due to a desire to make people healthy. Financially, while there are still some exceptions, in most cases, payment reforms and the shift to VBC mean it can be profitable to make people well and not just treat them when they are sick. If your innovation is creating tangible benefits for the patient, it will almost always create financial value for somebody who will then be willing to split it with you.

Consider the incentives of the ecosystem

Finally, as this book has outlined, each of the stakeholders in the ecosystem needs to succeed as a business. As such, the best idea in the world will unlikely be adopted if we don't sufficiently consider the incentives of each of the groups we must work with. In the costs and reform chapter, we discussed how well-intentioned policies like 340B ended up creating significant unintended consequences. The same trap awaits innovations—even potentially beneficial ones—if they do not consider the impact their introduction will have on the existing ecosystem. Indeed, the authors have seen many good ideas fail for this reason.

Engagement with other ecosystem stakeholders can take many forms. It could be something complex, such as an academic study or primary market research. It can also be simple, such as attending a conference and discussing your new idea with attendees. In our experience, healthcare executives generally have been very open with their praise or criticism of new ideas—we don't expect getting feedback will be particularly hard. We have been surprised at how willing our colleagues in the industry have been to engage in discussions on even controversial topics (at least, as long as it's "off the record"). With the complexity of the ecosystem, however, it can be difficult to formulate the right questions. Who is going to be impacted by this innovation? What should we ask them about?

We hope this book will help some future healthcare innovator ask the right questions and get reasonable answers, and in doing so contribute to improved patient care and the continuing evolution of healthcare in the United States.

Glossary

Terms	Definitions
340B (Section 340B of the Public Health Service Act)	A federal program that lets eligible hospitals and clinics buy outpatient drugs at reduced prices.
Academic Health Systems (AHSs)	Organizations combining hospitals, medical schools, and research institutions.
Academic Medical Centers (AMCs)	Hospitals affiliated with medical schools, offering advanced care, education, and research.
Affordable Care Act (ACA)	2010 law that expanded insurance access and aimed to improve healthcare affordability and quality.
Average Manufacturer's Price (AMP)	The average price wholesalers pay to drug manufacturers.
Average Sales Price (ASP)	The average price providers actually pay for drugs, factoring in discounts.
Average Wholesale Price (AWP)	A benchmark price for drugs, generally higher than actual sale prices.
Blue Button	A tool that allows Medicare users to download and manage their health records.
Children's Health Insurance Program (CHIP)	Offers low-cost health insurance to children in families who earn too much for Medicaid.
Clinically Integrated Networks (CINs)	Groups of healthcare providers who work together to improve care and reduce costs.
Compound Annual Growth Rate (CAGR)	The average yearly growth rate of an investment over a period.

Terms	Definitions
Diagnosis-Related Group (DRG)	A system that determines how much Medicare pays hospitals for a patient's stay, based on diagnosis.
Disproportionate Share Hospital (DSH)	Hospitals that receive extra funds for treating large numbers of low-income or uninsured patients.
EHR (Electronic Health Record)	A digital version of a patient's medical chart.
Federally Qualified Health Centers (FQHCs)	Community-based clinics provide primary care to underserved populations.
Food and Drug Administration (FDA)	The federal agency that ensures the safety and effectiveness of drugs, food, and medical products.
Group Purchasing Organizations (GPOs)	Organizations that help healthcare providers buy supplies in bulk at lower prices.
Health Information Technology for Economic and Clinical Health (HITECH) Act	A law that promotes the use of electronic health records and health IT.
Health Insurance Portability and Accountability Act of 1996 (HIPAA)	A law that protects patient privacy and secures health data.
Health Level 7 Fast Healthcare Interoperability Resources (HL7 FHIR)	A technical standard that enables easy and secure exchange of healthcare data electronically.
Healthcare Resource Utilization (HRU)	The use of healthcare services, such as visits, tests, or hospital stays, is often analyzed for efficiency and cost.
Hospital Consumer Assessment of Healthcare Providers & Systems (HCAHPS)	A survey that measures patients' experiences with hospital care.
Indian Health Service (IHS)	A federal health program for American Indians and Alaska Natives.
Inflation Reduction Act (IRA)	US law with provisions to lower prescription drug prices and cap Medicare drug costs.

Terms	Definitions
Integrated Delivery Networks (IDNs)	Health systems that combine hospitals, clinics, and providers under one organization.
Large Dialysis Organizations (LDOs)	Companies providing dialysis treatment at scale across the United States.
Medicaid	A state and federal program offering health coverage to low-income individuals and families.
Medicare	A federal health insurance program for people 65+ and younger people with certain disabilities.
Medicare Access and CHIP Reauthorization Act (MACRA)	A law that changed how Medicare pays doctors, rewarding quality and efficiency.
Medicare Part A	Covers inpatient hospital stays, skilled nursing, hospice, and limited home healthcare.
Medicare Part B	Covers outpatient care, doctor visits, preventive services, and medical equipment.
Medicare Part C (Medicare Advantage)	Private plans that include Parts A and B, often with extra benefits.
Medicare Part D	Covers prescription drugs through private plans approved by Medicare.
Medicare Shared Savings Program (MSSP)	A program that encourages providers to lower costs while maintaining care quality.
Natural Language Processing (NLP)	AI that helps computers understand and interpret human language, often used to process medical records.
New Technology Add-On Payment (NTAP)	Extra Medicare payments to hospitals for using new and costly technologies.
Observational Medical Outcomes Partnership (OMOP)	A common data model used for large-scale health data analysis.
Orphan Drug Act	US law that encourages development of drugs for rare diseases.

Terms	Definitions
Pharmacy Benefit Managers (PBMs)	Intermediaries who manage drug plans for insurers and negotiate drug prices.
Pharmacy Services Administrative Organizations (PSAOs)	Help independent pharmacies with contracts and negotiations.
Physician Buying Groups (PBGs)	Groups that help doctors buy drugs and supplies at reduced rates.
Real-World Data (RWD)	Health data collected outside of clinical trials, such as from EHRs or insurance claims.
Real-World Evidence (RWE)	Insights gained from analyzing real-world data to understand treatment outcomes.
Third-Party Administrator (TPA)	Companies that manage health insurance plans on behalf of employers or insurers.
TRICARE	Health insurance program for US military personnel, retirees, and their families.
Utilization Management	A process that evaluates the need and efficiency of healthcare services before or during care.
Value-Based Care	A model that pays healthcare providers based on patient outcomes, not service volume.
Wholesale Acquisition Cost (WAC)	The manufacturer's list price for a drug before any discounts.

Index